Praise for *Think Again*

"In a world of aggressive certitude, Adam Grant's latest book is a refreshing mandate for humble open-mindedness. *Think Again* offers a particularly powerful case for rethinking what we already know . . . that is not just a useful lesson; it could be a vital one."

—*Financial Times*

"Adam Grant's latest book pushes us to reconsider, rethink, reevaluate and reimagine our beliefs, thoughts, and identities and get to the core of why we believe what we do, why it is so important to us, and why we are steadfast to hold on to those ideas and beliefs. . . . It teaches us to stop digging our heels and doubling down and consider other people's points of view so that we may grow our own. Once again, Adam Grant succeeded in turning our very way of thinking upside down as he pushes us to examine the obvious."

—*Forbes*

"[A] fast-paced account by a leading authority on the psychology of thinking."

—*Library Journal* (starred review)

"Adam Grant makes a captivating argument that if we have the humility and curiosity to reconsider our beliefs, we can always reinvent ourselves. *Think Again* helped me learn about how great thinkers and achievers don't let expertise or experience stand in the way of being perpetual students."

—M. Night Shyamalan, director of *The Sixth Sense* and *Split*

"Rule number one: never miss a new Adam Grant book! I loved this one!"

—Malcolm Gladwell, #1 *New York Times* bestselling author of *Outliers* and host of *Revisionist History*

"*Think Again* is the perfect reminder of both the joy and the humility of finding fault in something you thought you knew. Adam Grant's work forces reflection and re-examination in a way that at first may seem intimidating, but quickly turns instead to an exhilarating experience of self-discovery. Regardless of where you are in your professional or personal path, we can all learn something from this book."

—Daniel Ek, cofounder and CEO of Spotify

"*Think Again* is a must-read for anyone who wants to create a culture of learning and exploration, whether at home, at work, or at school. With warmth and humor, Adam Grant distills complex research into a compelling case for why each of us should continually question old assumptions and embrace new ideas and perspectives. In an increasingly divided world, the lessons in this book are more important than ever."

—Bill and Melinda Gates

PENGUIN BOOKS

THINK AGAIN

Adam Grant is an organizational psychologist at The Wharton School, where he has been the top-rated professor for seven straight years. His books have sold millions of copies, his TED talks have been viewed more than thirty million times, and his podcast, *WorkLife with Adam Grant,* has topped the charts. His pioneering research has inspired people to rethink fundamental assumptions about motivation, generosity, and creativity. He has been recognized as one of the world's ten most influential management thinkers and as one of *Fortune*'s 40 Under 40, and he has received distinguished scientific achievement awards from the American Psychological Association and the National Science Foundation. Grant received his B.A. from Harvard University and his Ph.D. from the University of Michigan, and he is a former Junior Olympic springboard diver. He lives in Philadelphia with his wife and their three children.

ALSO BY ADAM GRANT

Give and Take

Originals

Option B (with Sheryl Sandberg)

Hidden Potential

THINK
Again

The Power of Knowing
What You Don't Know

ADAM GRANT

PENGUIN BOOKS

PENGUIN BOOKS
An imprint of Penguin Random House LLC
penguinrandomhouse.com

First published in the United States of America by Viking,
an imprint of Penguin Random House LLC, 2021
Published in Penguin Books 2023

Owing to limitations of space, image credits can be found on page 297.

Unless otherwise noted, charts illustrated by Matt Shirley.

ISBN 9781984878120 (paperback)

THE LIBRARY OF CONGRESS HAS CATALOGED THE HARDCOVER EDITION AS FOLLOWS:
Names: Grant, Adam M., author.
Title: Think again : the power of knowing what you don't know / Adam Grant.
Description: [New York, New York] : Viking, [2021] |
Includes bibliographical references and index.
Identifiers: LCCN 2020035237 (print) | LCCN 2020035238 (ebook) |
ISBN 9781984878106 (hardcover) | ISBN 9781984878113 (ebook) |
ISBN 9780593298749 (international edition)
Subjects: LCSH: Thought and thinking. | Questioning. |
Knowledge, Theory of. | Belief and doubt.
Classification: LCC BF441 .G693 2021 (print) | LCC BF441 (ebook) |
DDC 153.4/2—dc23
LC record available at https://lccn.loc.gov/2020035237
LC ebook record available at https://lccn.loc.gov/2020035238

Printed in the United States of America
5th Printing

Book design by Daniel Lagin

To Kaan, Jeremy, and Bill,
My three oldest friends—one thing I won't rethink

CONTENTS

Prologue | 1

PART I. Individual Rethinking
Updating Our Own Views

1. A Preacher, a Prosecutor, a Politician,
   and a Scientist Walk into Your Mind | 15

2. The Armchair Quarterback and the Impostor:
   Finding the Sweet Spot of Confidence | 33

3. The Joy of Being Wrong:
   The Thrill of Not Believing Everything You Think | 55

4. The Good Fight Club:
   The Psychology of Constructive Conflict | 77

PART II. Interpersonal Rethinking
Opening Other People's Minds

5. Dances with Foes: How to Win Debates
   and Influence People | 97

6. Bad Blood on the Diamond: Diminishing Prejudice
   by Destabilizing Stereotypes | 121

7. Vaccine Whisperers and Mild-Mannered Interrogators:
   How the Right Kind of Listening Motivates People to
   Change | 143

PART III. Collective Rethinking
Creating Communities of Lifelong Learners

8. **Charged Conversations:**
   Depolarizing Our Divided Discussions | 163

9. **Rewriting the Textbook:**
   Teaching Students to Question Knowledge | 185

10. **That's Not the Way We've Always Done It:**
    Building Cultures of Learning at Work | 205

PART IV. Conclusion

11. **Escaping Tunnel Vision: Reconsidering Our Best-Laid Career**
    and Life Plans | 225

Epilogue | 245

Actions for Impact | 253

Acknowledgments | 261

Notes | 267

Illustration Credits | 297

Index | 299

Prologue

□ □ □

After a bumpy flight, fifteen men dropped from the Montana sky. They weren't skydivers. They were smokejumpers: elite wildland firefighters parachuting in to extinguish a forest fire started by lightning the day before. In a matter of minutes, they would be racing for their lives.

The smokejumpers landed near the top of Mann Gulch late on a scorching August afternoon in 1949. With the fire visible across the gulch, they made their way down the slope toward the Missouri River. Their plan was to dig a line in the soil around the fire to contain it and direct it toward an area where there wasn't much to burn.

After hiking about a quarter mile, the foreman, Wagner Dodge, saw that the fire had leapt across the gulch and was heading straight at them. The flames stretched as high as 30 feet in the air. Soon the fire would be blazing fast enough to cross the length of two football fields in less than a minute.

By 5:45 p.m. it was clear that even containing the fire was off the table. Realizing it was time to shift gears from fight to flight, Dodge immediately turned the crew around to run back up the slope. The smokejumpers had to bolt up an extremely steep incline, through knee-high grass on rocky terrain. Over the next eight minutes they traveled nearly 500 yards, leaving the top of the ridge less than 200 yards away.

With safety in sight but the fire swiftly advancing, Dodge did something that baffled his crew. Instead of trying to outrun the fire, he stopped and bent over. He took out a matchbook, started lighting matches, and threw them into the grass. "We thought he must have gone nuts," one later recalled. "With the fire almost on our back, what the hell is the boss doing lighting another fire in front of us?" He thought to himself: *That bastard Dodge is trying to burn me to death.* It's no surprise that the crew didn't follow Dodge when he waved his arms toward his fire and yelled, "Up! Up this way!"

What the smokejumpers didn't realize was that Dodge had devised a survival strategy: he was building an escape fire. By burning the grass ahead of him, he cleared the area of fuel for the wildfire to feed on. He then poured water from his canteen onto his handkerchief, covered his mouth with it, and lay facedown in the charred area for the next fifteen minutes. As the wildfire raged directly above him, he survived in the oxygen close to the ground.

Tragically, twelve of the smokejumpers perished. A pocket watch belonging to one of the victims was later found with the hands melted at 5:56 p.m.

Why did only three of the smokejumpers survive? Physical fitness might have been a factor; the other two survivors managed to outrun the fire and reach the crest of the ridge. But Dodge prevailed because of his mental fitness.

□ □ □

WHEN PEOPLE REFLECT on what it takes to be mentally fit, the first idea that comes to mind is usually intelligence. The smarter you are, the more complex the problems you can solve—and the faster you can solve them. Intelligence is traditionally viewed as the ability to think and learn. Yet in a turbulent world, there's another set of cognitive skills that might matter more: the ability to rethink and unlearn.

Imagine that you've just finished taking a multiple-choice test, and you start to second-guess one of your answers. You have some extra time— should you stick with your first instinct or change it?

About three quarters of students are convinced that revising their answer will *hurt* their score. Kaplan, the big test-prep company, once warned students to "exercise great caution if you decide to change an answer. Experience indicates that many students who change answers change to the wrong answer."

With all due respect to the lessons of experience, I prefer the rigor of evidence. When a trio of psychologists conducted a comprehensive review of thirty-three studies, they found that in every one, the majority of answer revisions were from wrong to right. This phenomenon is known as the first-instinct fallacy.

In one demonstration, psychologists counted eraser marks on the exams of more than 1,500 students in Illinois. Only a quarter of the changes were from right to wrong, while half were from wrong to right. I've seen it in my own classroom year after year: my students' final exams have surprisingly few eraser marks, but those who do rethink their first answers rather than staying anchored to them end up improving their scores.

Of course, it's possible that second answers aren't inherently better; they're only better because students are generally so reluctant to switch that they only make changes when they're fairly confident. But recent studies point to a different explanation: it's not so much changing your answer that improves your score as considering whether you should change it.

We don't just hesitate to rethink our answers. We hesitate at the very idea of rethinking. Take an experiment where hundreds of college students were randomly assigned to learn about the first-instinct fallacy. The speaker taught them about the value of changing their minds and gave them advice about when it made sense to do so. On their next two tests, they still weren't any more likely to revise their answers.

Part of the problem is cognitive laziness. Some psychologists point out that we're mental misers: we often prefer the ease of hanging on to old views over the difficulty of grappling with new ones. Yet there are also deeper forces behind our resistance to rethinking. Questioning ourselves makes the world more unpredictable. It requires us to admit that the facts may have changed, that what was once right may now be wrong. Reconsidering something we believe deeply can threaten our identities, making it feel as if we're losing a part of ourselves.

Rethinking isn't a struggle in every part of our lives. When it comes to our possessions, we update with fervor. We refresh our wardrobes when they go out of style and renovate our kitchens when they're no longer in vogue. When it comes to our knowledge and opinions, though, we tend to stick to our guns. Psychologists call this seizing and freezing. We favor the comfort of conviction over the discomfort of doubt, and we let our beliefs get brittle long before our bones. We laugh at people who still use Windows 95, yet we still cling to opinions that we formed in 1995. We listen to views that make us feel good, instead of ideas that make us think hard.

At some point, you've probably heard that if you drop a frog in a pot of scalding hot water, it will immediately leap out. But if you drop the frog in lukewarm water and gradually raise the temperature, the frog will die. It lacks the ability to rethink the situation, and doesn't realize the threat until it's too late.

When I looked into the origins of this popular story, I discovered a wrinkle: it isn't true.

Tossed into the scalding pot, the frog will get burned badly and may or may not escape. The frog is actually better off in the slow-boiling pot: it will leap out as soon as the water starts to get uncomfortably warm.

It's not the frogs who fail to reevaluate. It's us. Once we hear the story and accept it as true, we rarely bother to question it.

□ □ □

AS THE MANN GULCH WILDFIRE raced toward them, the smokejumpers had a decision to make. In an ideal world, they would have had enough time to pause, analyze the situation, and evaluate their options. With the fire raging less than 100 yards behind, there was no chance to stop and think. "On a big fire there is no time and no tree under whose shade the boss and the crew can sit and have a Platonic dialogue about a blowup," scholar and former firefighter Norman Maclean wrote in *Young Men and Fire*, his award-winning chronicle of the disaster. "If Socrates had been foreman on the Mann Gulch fire, he and his crew would have been cremated while they were sitting there considering it."

Dodge didn't survive as a result of thinking slower. He made it out alive thanks to his ability to rethink the situation faster. Twelve smokejumpers paid the ultimate price because Dodge's behavior didn't make sense to them. They couldn't rethink their assumptions in time.

Under acute stress, people typically revert to their automatic, well-learned responses. That's evolutionarily adaptive—as long as you find yourself in the same kind of environment in which those reactions were necessary. If you're a smokejumper, your well-learned response is to put out a fire, not start another one. If you're fleeing for your life, your well-learned response is to run away from the fire, not toward it. In normal circumstances, those instincts might save your life. Dodge survived Mann Gulch because he swiftly overrode both of those responses.

No one had taught Dodge to build an escape fire. He hadn't even heard of the concept; it was pure improvisation. Later, the other two survivors testified under oath that nothing resembling an escape fire was covered in their training. Many experts had spent their entire careers studying wildfires without realizing it was possible to stay alive by burning a hole through the blaze.

When I tell people about Dodge's escape, they usually marvel at his resourcefulness under pressure. *That was genius!* Their astonishment quickly melts into dejection as they conclude that this kind of eureka moment is out of reach for mere mortals. *I got stumped by my fourth grader's math homework.* Yet most acts of rethinking don't require any special skill or ingenuity.

Moments earlier at Mann Gulch, the smokejumpers missed another opportunity to think again—and that one was right at their fingertips. Just before Dodge started tossing matches into the grass, he ordered his crew to drop their heavy equipment. They had spent the past eight minutes racing uphill while still carrying axes, saws, shovels, and 20-pound packs.

If you're running for your life, it might seem obvious that your first move would be to drop anything that might slow you down. For firefighters, though, tools are essential to doing their jobs. Carrying and taking care of equipment is deeply ingrained in their training and experience. It wasn't until Dodge gave his order that most of the smokejumpers set down their tools—and even then, one firefighter hung on to his shovel until a colleague took it out of his hands. If the crew had abandoned their tools sooner, would it have been enough to save them?

We'll never know for certain, but Mann Gulch wasn't an isolated incident. Between 1990 and 1995 alone, a total of twenty-three wildland firefighters perished trying to outrace fires uphill even though dropping their heavy equipment could have made the difference between life and death. In 1994, on Storm King Mountain in Colorado, high winds caused a fire to explode across a gulch. Running uphill on rocky ground with safety in view just 200 feet away, fourteen smokejumpers and wildland firefighters—four women, ten men—lost their lives.

Later, investigators calculated that without their tools and backpacks, the crew could have moved 15 to 20 percent faster. "Most would have lived had they simply dropped their gear and run for safety," one expert wrote. Had they "dropped their packs and tools," the U.S. Forest Service concurred, "the firefighters would have reached the top of the ridge before the fire."

It's reasonable to assume that at first the crew might have been running on autopilot, not even aware that they were still carrying their packs and tools. "About three hundred yards up the hill," one of the Colorado survivors testified, "I then realized I still had my saw over my shoulder!" Even after making the wise decision to ditch the 25-pound chainsaw, he wasted valuable time: "I irrationally started looking for a place to put it down where it wouldn't get burned. . . . I remember thinking, 'I can't believe I'm putting down my saw.'" One of the victims was found wearing his backpack, still clutching the handle of his chainsaw. Why would so many firefighters cling to a set of tools even though letting go might save their lives?

If you're a firefighter, dropping your tools doesn't just require you to unlearn habits and disregard instincts. Discarding your equipment means admitting failure and shedding part of your identity. You have to rethink your goal in your job—and your role in life. "Fires are not fought with bodies and bare hands, they are fought with tools that are often distinctive trademarks of firefighters," organizational psychologist Karl Weick explains: "They are the firefighter's reason for being deployed in the first place. . . . Dropping one's tools creates an existential crisis. Without my tools, who am I?"

Wildland fires are relatively rare. Most of our lives don't depend on split-second decisions that force us to reimagine our tools as a source of danger and a fire as a path to safety. Yet the challenge of rethinking assumptions is surprisingly common—maybe even common to all humans.

We all make the same kind of mistakes as smokejumpers and firefighters, but the consequences are less dire and therefore often go unnoticed. Our ways of thinking become habits that can weigh us down, and we don't bother to question them until it's too late. Expecting your squeaky brakes to keep working until they finally fail on the freeway. Believing the stock market will keep going up after analysts warn of an impending real estate bubble. Assuming your marriage is fine despite your partner's increasing emotional distance. Feeling secure in your job even though some of your colleagues have been laid off.

This book is about the value of rethinking. It's about adopting the kind of mental flexibility that saved Wagner Dodge's life. It's also about succeeding where he failed: encouraging that same agility in others.

You may not carry an ax or a shovel, but you do have some cognitive tools that you use regularly. They might be things you know, assumptions you make, or opinions you hold. Some of them aren't just part of your job—they're part of your sense of self.

TOOLS WE CLING TO

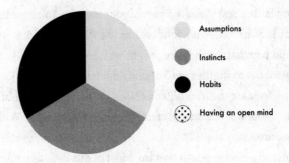

Consider a group of students who built what has been called Harvard's first online social network. Before they arrived at college, they had already connected more than an eighth of the entering freshman class in an "e-group." But once they got to Cambridge, they abandoned the network and shut it down. Five years later Mark Zuckerberg started Facebook on the same campus.

From time to time, the students who created the original e-group have felt some pangs of regret. I know, because I was one of the cofounders of that group.

Let's be clear: I never would have had the vision for what Facebook became. In hindsight, though, my friends and I clearly missed a series of chances for rethinking the potential of our platform. Our first instinct was to use the e-group to make new friends for ourselves; we didn't consider whether it would be of interest to students at other schools or in life beyond school. Our well-learned habit was to use online tools to connect with people far away; once we lived within walking distance on the same campus, we figured we no longer needed the e-group. Although one of the cofounders was studying computer science and another early member had already founded a successful tech startup, we made the flawed assumption that an online social network was a passing hobby, not a huge part of the future of the internet. Since I didn't know how to code, I didn't have the tools to build something more sophisticated. Launching a company wasn't part of my identity anyway: I saw myself as a college freshman, not a budding entrepreneur.

Since then, rethinking has become central to my sense of self. I'm a psychologist but I'm not a fan of Freud, I don't have a couch in my office, and I don't do therapy. As an organizational psychologist at Wharton, I've spent the past fifteen years researching and teaching evidence-based management. As an entrepreneur of data and ideas, I've been called by organizations like Google, Pixar, the NBA, and the Gates Foundation to help them reexamine how they design meaningful jobs, build creative teams, and shape collaborative cultures. My job is to think again about how we work, lead, and live—and enable others to do the same.

I can't think of a more vital time for rethinking. As the coronavirus pandemic unfolded, many leaders around the world were slow to rethink their assumptions—first that the virus wouldn't affect their countries, next that it would be no deadlier than the flu, and then that it could only be transmitted by people with visible symptoms. The cost in human life is still being tallied.

In the past few years we've all had to put our mental pliability to the test. We've been forced to question assumptions that we had long taken for granted: That it's safe to go to the hospital, eat in a restaurant, and hug our parents or grandparents. That live sports will always be on TV. That we can get toilet paper and hand sanitizer whenever we need them.

As schools closed, teachers had to reimagine their classrooms virtually. As offices shut down, leaders had to rethink their resistance to remote work. Once we got a taste of freedom, many of us decided we wanted more. During the Great Resignation, record numbers of people didn't just quit their jobs—they rethought their work and their lives. Some picked up and moved to different cities and countries. Others struck out on their own for the first time as entrepreneurs, freelancers, or creators.

In the midst of the pandemic, multiple acts of police brutality led many people to rethink their views on racial injustice and their roles in fighting it. The senseless deaths of three Black citizens—George Floyd, Breonna Taylor, and Ahmaud Arbery—left millions of white people realizing that just as sexism is not only a women's issue, racism is not only an issue for people of color. Many of those who had long been silent came to reckon with their responsibility to act against prejudice.

Despite these shared experiences, we live in an increasingly divisive time. Proponents of free speech are silencing conservative voices on college campuses. For some people a single mention of kneeling during the national anthem is enough to end a friendship. For others a single ballot at a voting booth is enough to end a marriage. Calcified ideologies are tearing American culture apart. Even our great governing document, the U.S. Constitution, allows for amendments. What if we were quicker to make amendments to our own mental constitutions?

My aim in this book is to explore how rethinking happens. I sought out the most compelling evidence and some of the world's most skilled rethinkers. The first section focuses on opening our own minds. You'll find out why a forward-thinking entrepreneur got trapped in the past, why a long-shot candidate for public office came to see impostor syndrome as an advantage, how a Nobel Prize–winning scientist embraces the joy of being wrong, how the world's best forecasters update their views, and how an Oscar-winning filmmaker has productive fights.

The second section examines how we can encourage other people to think again. You'll learn how an international debate champion wins arguments and a Black musician persuades white supremacists to abandon hate. You'll discover how a special kind of listening helped a doctor open parents' minds about vaccines, and helped a legislator convince a Ugandan warlord to join her in peace talks. And if you're a Yankees fan, I'm going to see if I can convince you to root for the Red Sox.

The third section is about how we can create communities of lifelong learners. In social life, a lab that specializes in difficult conversations will shed light on how we can communicate better about polarizing issues like abortion and climate change. In schools, you'll find out how educators teach kids to think again by treating classrooms like museums, approaching projects like carpenters, and rewriting time-honored textbooks. At work, you'll explore how to build learning cultures with the first Hispanic woman in space, who took the reins at NASA to prevent accidents after space shuttle *Columbia* disintegrated. I close by reflecting on the importance of reconsidering our best-laid plans.

It's a lesson that firefighters have learned the hard way. In the heat of the moment, Wagner Dodge's impulse to drop his heavy tools and take shelter in a fire of his own making made the difference between life and death. But his inventiveness wouldn't have even been necessary if not for a deeper, more systemic failure to think again. The greatest tragedy of Mann Gulch is that a dozen smokejumpers died fighting a fire that never needed to be fought.

As early as the 1880s, scientists had begun highlighting the important role that wildfires play in the life cycles of forests. Fires remove dead matter, send nutrients into the soil, and clear a path for sunlight. When fires are suppressed, forests are left too dense. The accumulation of brush, dry leaves, and twigs becomes fuel for more explosive wildfires.

Yet it wasn't until 1978 that the U.S. Forest Service put an end to its policy that every fire spotted should be extinguished by 10:00 a.m. the following day. The Mann Gulch wildfire took place in a remote area where human lives were not at risk. The smokejumpers were called in anyway because no one in their community, their organization, or their profession had done enough to question the assumption that wildfires should not be allowed to run their course.

This book is an invitation to let go of knowledge and opinions that are no longer serving you well, and to anchor your sense of self in flexibility rather than consistency. If you can master the art of rethinking, I believe you'll be better positioned for success at work and happiness in life. Thinking again can help you generate new solutions to old problems and revisit old solutions to new problems. It's a path to learning more from the people around you and living with fewer regrets. A hallmark of wisdom is knowing when it's time to abandon some of your most treasured tools—and some of the most cherished parts of your identity.

PART I

Individual Rethinking

Updating Our Own Views

CHAPTER 1

A Preacher, a Prosecutor, a Politician, and a Scientist Walk into Your Mind

□ □ □

> Progress is impossible without change; and those who
> cannot change their minds cannot change anything.
>
> —GEORGE BERNARD SHAW

You probably don't recognize his name, but Mike Lazaridis has had a defining impact on your life. From an early age, it was clear that Mike was something of an electronics wizard. By the time he turned four, he was building his own record player out of Legos and rubber bands. In high school, when his teachers had broken TVs, they called Mike to fix them. In his spare time, he built a computer and designed a better buzzer for high school quiz-bowl teams, which ended up paying for his first year of college. Just months before finishing his electrical engineering degree, Mike did what so many great entrepreneurs of his era would do: he dropped out of college. It was time for this son of immigrants to make his mark on the world.

Mike's first success came when he patented a device for reading the bar codes on movie film, which was so useful in Hollywood that it won an Emmy and an Oscar for technical achievement. That was small potatoes compared to his next big invention, which made his firm the fastest-growing company on the planet. Mike's flagship device quickly attracted a cult following, with loyal customers ranging from Bill Gates to Christina Aguilera. "It's literally changed my life," Oprah Winfrey gushed. "I cannot live without this." When he arrived at the White House, President Obama refused to relinquish his to the Secret Service.

Mike Lazaridis dreamed up the idea for the BlackBerry as a wireless communication device for sending and receiving emails. As of the summer of 2009, it accounted for nearly half of the U.S. smartphone market. By 2014, its market share had plummeted to less than 1 percent.

When a company takes a nosedive like that, we can never pinpoint a single cause of its downfall, so we tend to anthropomorphize it: *Black-Berry failed to adapt.* Yet adapting to a changing environment isn't something a company does—it's something *people* do in the multitude of decisions they make every day. As the cofounder, president, and co-CEO, Mike was in charge of all the technical and product decisions on the BlackBerry. Although his thinking may have been the spark that ignited the smartphone revolution, his struggles with rethinking ended up sucking the oxygen out of his company and virtually extinguishing his invention. Where did he go wrong?

Most of us take pride in our knowledge and expertise, and in staying true to our beliefs and opinions. That makes sense in a stable world, where we get rewarded for having conviction in our ideas. The problem is that we live in a rapidly changing world, where we need to spend as much time rethinking as we do thinking.

Rethinking is a skill set, but it's also a mindset. We already have many of the mental tools we need. We just have to remember to get them out of the shed and remove the rust.

SECOND THOUGHTS

With advances in access to information and technology, knowledge isn't just increasing. It's increasing at an increasing rate. In 2011, you consumed about five times as much information per day as you would have just a quarter century earlier. As of 1950, it took about fifty years for knowledge in medicine to double. By 1980, medical knowledge was doubling every seven years, and by 2010, it was doubling in half that time. The accelerating pace of change means that we need to question our beliefs more readily than ever before.

This is not an easy task. As we sit with our beliefs, they tend to become more extreme and more entrenched. *I'm still struggling to accept that Pluto may not be a planet.* In education, after revelations in history and revolutions in science, it often takes years for a curriculum to be updated and textbooks to be revised. Researchers have recently discovered that we need to rethink widely accepted assumptions about such subjects as Cleopatra's roots (her father was Greek, not Egyptian, and her mother's identity is unknown); the appearance of dinosaurs (paleontologists now think some tyrannosaurs had colorful feathers on their backs); and what's required for sight (blind people have actually trained themselves to "see"— sound waves can activate the visual cortex and create representations in the mind's eye, much like how echolocation helps bats navigate in the dark).* Vintage records, classic cars, and antique clocks might be valuable collectibles, but outdated facts are mental fossils that are best abandoned.

---

* For my part, I had assumed the phrase "blowing smoke up your arse" came from people gifting cigars to someone they wanted to impress, so you can imagine how intrigued I was when my wife told me its real origin: In the 1700s, it was common practice to revive drowning victims with tobacco enemas, literally blowing smoke up their behinds. Only later did they learn that it was toxic to the cardiac system.

We're swift to recognize when other people need to think again. We question the judgment of experts whenever we seek out a second opinion on a medical diagnosis. Unfortunately, when it comes to our own knowledge and opinions, we often favor *feeling* right over *being* right. In everyday life, we make many diagnoses of our own, ranging from whom we hire to whom we marry. We need to develop the habit of forming our own second opinions.

Imagine you have a family friend who's a financial adviser, and he recommends investing in a retirement fund that isn't in your employer's plan. You have another friend who's fairly knowledgeable about investing, and he tells you that this fund is risky. What would you do?

When a man named Stephen Greenspan found himself in that situation, he decided to weigh his skeptical friend's warning against the data available. His sister had been investing in the fund for several years, and she was pleased with the results. A number of her friends had been, too; although the returns weren't extraordinary, they were consistently in the double digits. The financial adviser was enough of a believer that he had invested his own money in the fund. Armed with that information, Greenspan decided to go forward. He made a bold move, investing nearly a third of his retirement savings in the fund. Before long, he learned that his portfolio had grown by 25 percent.

Then he lost it all overnight when the fund collapsed. It was the Ponzi scheme managed by Bernie Madoff.

Two decades ago my colleague Phil Tetlock discovered something peculiar. As we think and talk, we often slip into the mindsets of three different professions: preachers, prosecutors, and politicians. In each of these modes, we take on a particular identity and use a distinct set of tools. We go into preacher mode when our sacred beliefs are in jeopardy: we deliver sermons to protect and promote our ideals. We enter prosecutor mode when we recognize flaws in other people's reasoning: we marshal arguments to prove them wrong and win our case. We shift into politician mode when we're seeking to win over an audience: we campaign and lobby for the approval of our constituents. The risk is that we become so wrapped up in preaching that we're right, prosecuting others who are wrong, and politicking for support that we don't bother to rethink our own views.

When Stephen Greenspan and his sister made the choice to invest with Bernie Madoff, it wasn't because they relied on just one of those mental tools. All three modes together contributed to their ill-fated decision. When his sister told him about the money she and her friends had made, she was preaching about the merits of the fund. Her confidence led Greenspan to prosecute the friend who warned him against investing, deeming the friend guilty of "knee-jerk cynicism." Greenspan was in politician mode when he let his desire for approval sway him toward a yes—the financial adviser was a family friend whom he liked and wanted to please.

Any of us could have fallen into those traps. Greenspan says that he should've known better, though, because he happens to be an expert on gullibility. When he decided to go ahead with the investment, he had almost finished writing a book on why we get duped. Looking back, he wishes he had approached the decision with a different set of tools. He might have analyzed the fund's strategy more systematically instead of simply trusting in the results. He could have sought out more perspectives from credible sources. He would have experimented with investing smaller amounts over a longer period of time before gambling so much of his life's savings.

That would have put him in the mode of a scientist.

A DIFFERENT PAIR OF GOGGLES

If you're a scientist by trade, rethinking is fundamental to your profession. You're paid to be constantly aware of the limits of your understanding. You're expected to doubt what you know, be curious about what you don't know, and update your views based on new data. In the past century alone, the application of scientific principles has led to dramatic progress. Biological scientists discovered penicillin. Rocket scientists sent us to the moon. Computer scientists built the internet.

But being a scientist is not just a profession. It's a frame of mind—a mode of thinking that differs from preaching, prosecuting, and politicking. We move into scientist mode when we're searching for the truth: we run experiments to test hypotheses and discover knowledge. Scientific tools aren't reserved for people with white coats and beakers, and using them doesn't require toiling away for years with a microscope and a petri dish. Hypotheses have as much of a place in our lives as they do in the lab. Experiments can inform our daily decisions. That makes me wonder: is it possible to train people in other fields to think more like scientists, and if so, do they end up making smarter choices?

Recently, a quartet of European researchers decided to find out. They ran a bold experiment with more than a hundred founders of Italian startups in technology, retail, furniture, food, health care, leisure, and machinery. Most of the founders' businesses had yet to bring in any revenue, making it an ideal setting to investigate how teaching scientific thinking would influence the bottom line.

The entrepreneurs arrived in Milan for a training program in entrepreneurship. Over the course of four months, they learned to create a business strategy, interview customers, build a minimum viable product, and then refine a prototype. What they didn't know was that they'd been randomly assigned to either a "scientific thinking" group or a control group. The training for both groups was identical, except that one was encouraged to view startups through a scientist's goggles. From that perspective, their strategy is a theory, customer interviews help to develop hypotheses, and their minimum viable product and prototype are experiments to test those hypotheses. Their task is to rigorously measure the results and make decisions based on whether their hypotheses are supported or refuted.

Over the following year, the startups in the control group averaged under $300 in revenue. The startups in the scientific thinking group averaged over $12,000 in revenue. They brought in revenue more than twice as fast—and attracted customers sooner, too. Why? The entrepreneurs in the control group tended to stay wedded to their original strategies and products. It was too easy to preach the virtues of their past decisions, prosecute the vices of alternative options, and politick by catering to advisers who favored the existing direction. The entrepreneurs who had been taught to think like scientists, in contrast, pivoted more than twice as often. When their hypotheses weren't supported, they knew it was time to rethink their business models.

THE EFFECTS OF SCIENTIFIC THINKING ON STARTUP SUCCESS

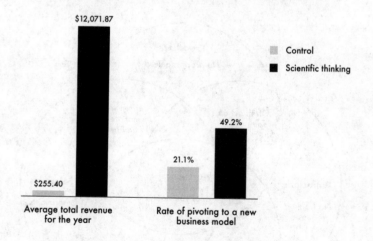

What's surprising about these results is that we typically celebrate great entrepreneurs and leaders for being strong-minded and clear-sighted. They're supposed to be paragons of conviction: decisive and certain. Yet evidence reveals that when business executives compete in tournaments to price products, the best strategists are actually slow and unsure. Like careful scientists, they take their time so they have the flexibility to change their minds. *I'm beginning to think decisiveness is overrated . . . but I reserve the right to change my mind.*

Just as you don't have to be a professional scientist to reason like one, being a professional scientist doesn't guarantee that someone will use the tools of their training. Scientists morph into preachers when they present their pet theories as gospel and treat thoughtful critiques as sacrilege. They veer into politician terrain when they allow their views to be swayed by popularity rather than accuracy. They enter prosecutor mode when they're hell-bent on debunking and discrediting rather than discovering. After upending physics with his theories of relativity, Einstein opposed the quantum revolution: "To punish me for my contempt of authority, Fate has made me an authority myself." Sometimes even great scientists need to think more like scientists.

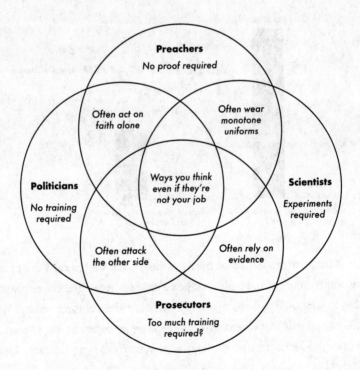

Decades before becoming a smartphone pioneer, Mike Lazaridis was recognized as a science prodigy. In middle school, he made the local news for building a solar panel at the science fair and won an award for reading every science book in the public library. If you open his eighth-grade yearbook, you'll see a cartoon showing Mike as a mad scientist, with bolts of lightning shooting out of his head.

When Mike created the BlackBerry, he was thinking like a scientist. Existing devices for wireless email featured a stylus that was too slow or a keyboard that was too small. People had to clunkily forward their work emails to their mobile device in-boxes, and they took forever to download. He started generating hypotheses and sent his team of engineers off to test them. What if people could hold the device in their hands and type with their thumbs rather than their fingers? What if there was a single mailbox synchronized across devices? What if messages could be relayed through a server and appear on the device only after they were decrypted?

As other companies followed BlackBerry's lead, Mike would take their smartphones apart and study them. Nothing really impressed him until the summer of 2007, when he was stunned by the computing power inside the first iPhone. "They've put a Mac in this thing," he said. What Mike did next might have been the beginning of the end for the Black-Berry. If the BlackBerry's rise was due in large part to his success in scientific thinking as an engineer, its demise was in many ways the result of his failure in rethinking as a CEO.

As the iPhone skyrocketed onto the scene, Mike maintained his belief in the features that had made the BlackBerry a sensation in the past. He was confident that people wanted a wireless device for work emails and calls, not an entire computer in their pocket with apps for home entertainment. As early as 1997, one of his top engineers wanted to add an internet browser, but Mike told him to focus only on email. A decade later, Mike was still certain that a powerful internet browser would drain the battery and strain the bandwidth of wireless networks. He didn't test the alternative hypotheses.

By 2008, the company's valuation exceeded $70 billion, but the BlackBerry remained the company's sole product, and it still lacked a reliable browser. In 2010, when his colleagues pitched a strategy to feature encrypted text messages, Mike was receptive but expressed concerns that allowing messages to be exchanged on competitors' devices would render the BlackBerry obsolete. As his reservations gained traction within the firm, the company abandoned instant messaging, missing an opportunity that WhatsApp later seized for upwards of $19 billion. As gifted as Mike was at rethinking the design of electronic devices, he wasn't willing to rethink the market for his baby. Intelligence was no cure—it might have been more of a curse.

THE SMARTER THEY ARE, THE HARDER THEY FAIL

Mental horsepower doesn't guarantee mental dexterity. No matter how much brainpower you have, if you lack the motivation to change your mind, you'll miss many occasions to think again. Research reveals that the higher you score on an IQ test, the more likely you are to fall for stereotypes, because you're faster at recognizing patterns. And recent experiments suggest that the smarter you are, the more you might struggle to update your beliefs.

One study investigated whether being a math whiz makes you better at analyzing data. The answer is yes—if you're told the data are about something bland, like a treatment for skin rashes. But what if the exact same data are labeled as focusing on an ideological issue that activates strong emotions—like gun laws in the United States?

Being a quant jock makes you more accurate in interpreting the results—as long as they support your beliefs. Yet if the empirical pattern clashes with your ideology, math prowess is no longer an asset; it actually becomes a liability. The better you are at crunching numbers, the more spectacularly you fail at analyzing patterns that contradict your views. If they were liberals, math geniuses did worse than their peers at evaluating evidence that gun bans failed. If they were conservatives, they did worse at assessing evidence that gun bans worked.

In psychology there are at least two biases that drive this pattern. One is confirmation bias: seeing what we expect to see. The other is desirability bias: seeing what we want to see. These biases don't just prevent us from applying our intelligence. They can actually contort our intelligence into a weapon against the truth. We find reasons to preach our faith more deeply, prosecute our case more passionately, and ride the tidal wave of our political party. The tragedy is that we're usually unaware of the resulting flaws in our thinking.

My favorite bias is the "I'm not biased" bias, in which people believe they're more objective than others. It turns out that smart people are more likely to fall into this trap. The brighter you are, the harder it can be to see your own limitations. Being good at thinking can make you worse at rethinking.

When we're in scientist mode, we refuse to let our ideas become ideologies. We don't start with answers or solutions; we lead with questions and puzzles. We don't preach from intuition; we teach from evidence. We don't just have healthy skepticism about other people's arguments; we dare to disagree with our own arguments.

Thinking like a scientist involves more than just reacting with an open mind. It means being *actively* open-minded. It requires searching for reasons why we might be wrong—not for reasons why we must be right—and revising our views based on what we learn.

That rarely happens in the other mental modes. In preacher mode, changing our minds is a mark of moral weakness; in scientist mode, it's a sign of intellectual integrity. In prosecutor mode, allowing ourselves to be persuaded is admitting defeat; in scientist mode, it's a step toward the truth. In politician mode, we flip-flop in response to carrots and sticks; in scientist mode, we shift in the face of sharper logic and stronger data.

I've done my best to write this book in scientist mode.* I'm a teacher, not a preacher. I can't stand politics, and I hope a decade as a tenured professor has cured me of whatever temptation I once felt to appease my audience. Although I've spent more than my share of time in prosecutor mode, I've decided that in a courtroom I'd rather be the judge. I don't expect you to agree with everything I think. My hope is that you'll be intrigued by *how* I think—and that the studies, stories, and ideas covered here will lead you to do some rethinking of your own. After all, the purpose of learning isn't to affirm our beliefs; it's to evolve our beliefs.

BELIEFS I STAND BY

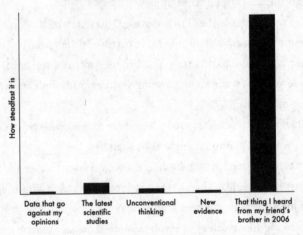

*I started not with answers but with questions about rethinking. Then I went looking for the best evidence available from randomized, controlled experiments and systematic field studies. Where the evidence didn't exist, I launched my own research projects. Only when I had reached a data-driven insight did I search for stories to illustrate and illuminate the studies. In an ideal world, every insight would come from a meta-analysis—a study of studies, where researchers cumulate the patterns across a whole body of evidence, adjusting for the quality of each data point. Where those aren't available, I've highlighted studies that I find rigorous, representative, or thought provoking. Sometimes I'll include details on the methods—not only so you can understand how the researchers formed their conclusions, but to offer a window into how scientists think. In many places, I'll summarize the results without going into depth on the studies themselves, under the assumption that you're reading to rethink like a scientist—not to become one. That said, if you felt a jolt of excitement at the mention of a meta-analysis, it might be time to (re)consider a career in social science.

One of my beliefs is that we shouldn't be open-minded in every circumstance. There are situations where it might make sense to preach, prosecute, and politick. That said, I think most of us would benefit from being more open more of the time, because it's in scientist mode that we gain mental agility.

When psychologist Mihaly Csikszentmihalyi studied eminent scientists like Linus Pauling and Jonas Salk, he concluded that what differentiated them from their peers was their cognitive flexibility, their willingness "to move from one extreme to the other as the occasion requires." The same pattern held for great artists, and in an independent study of highly creative architects.

We can even see it in the Oval Office. Experts assessed American presidents on a long list of personality traits and compared them to rankings by independent historians and political scientists. Only one trait consistently predicted presidential greatness after controlling for factors like years in office, wars, and scandals. It wasn't whether presidents were ambitious or forceful, friendly or Machiavellian; it wasn't whether they were attractive, witty, poised, or polished.

What set great presidents apart was their intellectual curiosity and openness. They read widely and were as eager to learn about developments in biology, philosophy, architecture, and music as in domestic and foreign affairs. They were interested in hearing new views and revising their old ones. They saw many of their policies as experiments to run, not points to score. Although they might have been politicians by profession, they often solved problems like scientists.

DON'T STOP UNBELIEVING

As I've studied the process of rethinking, I've found that it often unfolds in a cycle. It starts with intellectual humility—knowing what we don't know. We should all be able to make a long list of areas where we're ignorant. *Mine include art, financial markets, fashion, chemistry, food, why British accents turn American in songs, and why it's impossible to tickle yourself.* Recognizing our shortcomings opens the door to doubt. As we question our current understanding, we become curious about what information we're missing. That search leads us to new discoveries, which in turn maintain our humility by reinforcing how much we still have to learn. If knowledge is power, knowing what we don't know is wisdom.

THE RETHINKING CYCLE

THE OVERCONFIDENCE CYCLE

Humility → Doubt → Curiosity → Discovery → Humility

Pride → Conviction → Confirmation & Desirability Biases → Validation → Pride

Scientific thinking favors humility over pride, doubt over certainty, curiosity over closure. When we shift out of scientist mode, the rethinking cycle breaks down, giving way to an overconfidence cycle. If we're preaching, we can't see gaps in our knowledge: we believe we've already found the truth. Pride breeds conviction rather than doubt, which makes us prosecutors: we might be laser-focused on changing other people's minds, but ours is set in stone. That launches us into confirmation bias and desirability bias. We become politicians, ignoring or dismissing whatever doesn't win the favor of our constituents—our parents, our bosses, or the high school classmates we're still trying to impress. We become so busy putting on a show that the truth gets relegated to a backstage seat, and the resulting validation can make us arrogant. We fall victim to the fat-cat syndrome, resting on our laurels instead of pressure-testing our beliefs.

In the case of the BlackBerry, Mike Lazaridis was trapped in an overconfidence cycle. Taking pride in his successful invention gave him too much conviction. Nowhere was that clearer than in his preference for the keyboard over a touchscreen. It was a BlackBerry virtue he loved to preach—and an Apple vice he was quick to prosecute. As his company's stock fell, Mike got caught up in confirmation bias and desirability bias, and fell victim to validation from fans. "It's an iconic product," he said of the BlackBerry in 2011. "It's used by business, it's used by leaders, it's used by celebrities." By 2012, the iPhone had captured a quarter of the global smartphone market, but Mike was still resisting the idea of typing on glass. "I don't get this," he said at a board meeting, pointing at a phone with a touchscreen. "The keyboard is one of the reasons they buy Black-Berrys." Like a politician who campaigns only to his base, he focused on the keyboard taste of millions of existing users, neglecting the appeal of a touchscreen to billions of potential users. *For the record, I still miss the keyboard, and I'm excited that it's been licensed for an attempted comeback.*

When Mike finally started reimagining the screen and software, some of his engineers didn't want to abandon their past work. The failure to rethink was widespread. In 2011, an anonymous high-level employee inside the firm wrote an open letter to Mike and his co-CEO. "We laughed and said they are trying to put a computer on a phone, that it won't work," the letter read. "We are now 3–4 years too late."

Our convictions can lock us in prisons of our own making. The solution is not to decelerate our thinking—it's to accelerate our rethinking. That's what resurrected Apple from the brink of bankruptcy to become the world's most valuable company.

The legend of Apple's renaissance revolves around the lone genius of Steve Jobs. It was his conviction and clarity of vision, the story goes, that gave birth to the iPhone. The reality is that he was dead-set against the mobile phone category. His employees had the vision for it, and it was their ability to change his mind that really revived Apple. Although Jobs knew how to "think different," it was his team that did much of the rethinking.

THE MOST ANNOYING THINGS PEOPLE SAY INSTEAD OF RETHINKING

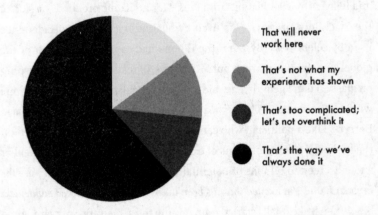

That will never work here

That's not what my experience has shown

That's too complicated; let's not overthink it

That's the way we've always done it

In 2004, a small group of engineers, designers, and marketers pitched Jobs on turning their hit product, the iPod, into a phone. "Why the f@*& would we want to do that?" Jobs snapped. "That is the dumbest idea I've ever heard." The team had recognized that mobile phones were starting to feature the ability to play music, but Jobs was worried about cannibalizing Apple's thriving iPod business. He hated cell-phone companies and didn't want to design products within the constraints that carriers imposed. When his calls dropped or the software crashed, he would sometimes smash his phone to pieces in frustration. In private meetings and on public stages, he swore over and over that he would never make a phone.

Yet some of Apple's engineers were already doing research in that area. They worked together to persuade Jobs that he didn't know what he didn't know and urged him to doubt his convictions. It might be possible, they argued, to build a smartphone that everyone would love using—and to get the carriers to do it Apple's way.

Research shows that when people are resistant to change, it helps to reinforce what will stay the same. Visions for change are more compelling when they include visions of continuity. Although our strategy might evolve, our identity will endure.

The engineers who worked closely with Jobs understood that this was one of the best ways to convince him. They assured him that they weren't trying to turn Apple into a phone company. It would remain a computer company—they were just taking their existing products and adding a phone on the side. Apple was already putting twenty thousand songs in your pocket, so why wouldn't they put everything else in your pocket, too? They needed to rethink their technology, but they would preserve their DNA. After six months of discussion, Jobs finally became curious enough to give the effort his blessing, and two different teams were off to the races in an experiment to test whether they should add calling capabilities to the iPod or turn the Mac into a miniature tablet that doubled as a phone. Just four years after it launched, the iPhone accounted for half of Apple's revenue.

The iPhone represented a dramatic leap in rethinking the smartphone. Since its inception, smartphone innovation has been much more incremental, with different sizes and shapes, better cameras, and longer battery life, but few fundamental changes to the purpose or user experience. Looking back, if Mike Lazaridis had been more open to rethinking his pet product, would BlackBerry and Apple have compelled each other to reimagine the smartphone multiple times by now?

The curse of knowledge is that it closes our minds to what we don't know. Good judgment depends on having the skill—and the will—to open our minds. I'm pretty confident that in life, rethinking is an increasingly important habit. Of course, I might be wrong. If I am, I'll be quick to think again.

MENTAL MODELS

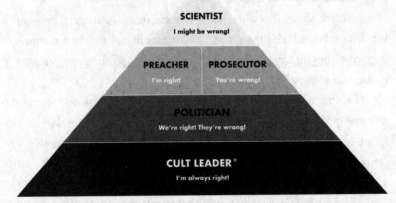

SCIENTIST
I might be wrong!

PREACHER
I'm right!

PROSECUTOR
You're wrong!

POLITICIAN
We're right! They're wrong!

CULT LEADER*
I'm always right!

*Does not apply to my wife, who is actually always right.

CHAPTER 2

The Armchair Quarterback and the Impostor

Finding the Sweet Spot of Confidence

□ □ □

Ignorance more frequently begets confidence
than does knowledge.

—CHARLES DARWIN

When Ursula Mercz was admitted to the clinic, she complained of headaches, back pain, and dizziness severe enough that she could no longer work. Over the following month her condition deteriorated. She struggled to locate the glass of water she put next to her bed. She couldn't find the door to her room. She walked directly into her bed frame.

Ursula was a seamstress in her midfifties, and she hadn't lost her dexterity: she was able to cut different shapes out of paper with scissors. She could easily point to her nose, mouth, arms, and legs, and had no difficulty describing her home and her pets. For an Austrian doctor named Gabriel Anton, she presented a curious case. When Anton put a red ribbon and scissors on the table in front of her, she couldn't name them, even though "she confirmed, calmly and faithfully, that she could see the presented objects."

She was clearly having problems with language production, which she acknowledged, and with spatial orientation. Yet something else was wrong: Ursula could no longer tell the difference between light and dark. When Anton held up an object and asked her to describe it, she didn't even try to look at it but instead reached out to touch it. Tests showed that her eyesight was severely impaired. Oddly, when Anton asked her about the deficit, she insisted she could see. Eventually, when she lost her vision altogether, she remained completely unaware of it. "It was now extremely astonishing," Anton wrote, "that the patient did not notice her massive and later complete loss of her ability to see . . . she was mentally blind to her blindness."

It was the late 1800s, and Ursula wasn't alone. A decade earlier a neuropathologist in Zurich had reported a case of a man who suffered an accident that left him blind but was unaware of it despite being "intellectually unimpaired." Although he didn't blink when a fist was placed in front of his face and couldn't see the food on his plate, "he thought he was in a dark humid hole or cellar."

Half a century later, a pair of doctors reported six cases of people who had gone blind but claimed otherwise. "One of the most striking features in the behavior of our patients was their inability to learn from their experiences," the doctors wrote:

> As they were not aware of their blindness when they walked about, they bumped into the furniture and walls but did not change their behavior. When confronted with their blindness in a rather pointed fashion, they would either deny any visual difficulty or remark: "It is so dark in the room; why don't they turn the light on?"; "I forgot my glasses," or "My vision is not too good, but I can see all right." The patients would not accept any demonstration or assurance which would prove their blindness.

This phenomenon was first described by the Roman philosopher Seneca, who wrote of a woman who was blind but complained that she was simply in a dark room. It's now accepted in the medical literature as Anton's syndrome—a deficit of self-awareness in which a person is oblivious to a physical disability but otherwise doing fairly well cognitively. It's known to be caused by damage to the occipital lobe of the brain. Yet I've come to believe that even when our brains are functioning normally, we're all vulnerable to a version of Anton's syndrome.

We all have blind spots in our knowledge and opinions. The bad news is that they can leave us blind to our blindness, which gives us false confidence in our judgment and prevents us from rethinking. The good news is that with the right kind of confidence, we can learn to see ourselves more clearly and update our views. In driver's training we were taught to identify our visual blind spots and eliminate them with the help of mirrors and sensors. In life, since our minds don't come equipped with those tools, we need to learn to recognize our cognitive blind spots and revise our thinking accordingly.

A TALE OF TWO SYNDROMES

On the first day of December 2015, Halla Tómasdóttir got a call she never expected. The roof of Halla's house had just given way to a thick layer of snow and ice. As she watched water pouring down one of the walls, the friend on the other end of the line asked if Halla had seen the Facebook posts about her. Someone had started a petition for Halla to run for the presidency of Iceland.

Halla's first thought was, *Who am I to be president?* She had helped start a university and then cofounded an investment firm in 2007. When the 2008 financial crisis rocked the world, Iceland was hit particularly hard; all three of its major private commercial banks defaulted and its currency collapsed. Relative to the size of its economy, the country faced the worst financial meltdown in human history, but Halla demonstrated her leadership skills by guiding her firm successfully through the crisis. Even with that accomplishment, she didn't feel prepared for the presidency. She had no political background; she had never served in government or in any kind of public-sector role.

It wasn't the first time Halla had felt like an impostor. At the age of eight, her piano teacher had placed her on a fast track and frequently asked her to play in concerts, but she never felt she was worthy of the honor—and so, before every concert, she felt sick. Although the stakes were much higher now, the self-doubt felt familiar. "I had a massive pit in my stomach, like the piano recital but much bigger," Halla told me. "It's the worst case of adult impostor syndrome I've ever had." For months, she struggled with the idea of becoming a candidate. As her friends and family encouraged her to recognize that she had some relevant skills, Halla was still convinced that she lacked the necessary experience and confidence. She tried to persuade other women to run—one of whom ended up ascending to a different office, as the prime minister of Iceland.

Yet the petition didn't go away, and Halla's friends, family, and colleagues didn't stop urging her on. Eventually, she found herself asking, *Who am I not to serve?* She ultimately decided to go for it, but the odds were heavily stacked against her. She was running as an unknown independent candidate in a field of more than twenty contenders. One of her competitors was particularly powerful—and particularly dangerous.

When an economist was asked to name the three people most responsible for Iceland's bankruptcy, she nominated Davíð Oddsson for all three spots. As Iceland's prime minister from 1991 to 2004, Oddsson put the country's banks in jeopardy by privatizing them. Then, as governor of Iceland's central bank from 2005 to 2009, he allowed the banks' balance sheets to balloon to more than ten times the national GDP. When the people protested his mismanagement, Oddsson refused to resign and had to be forced out by Parliament. *Time* magazine later identified him as one of the twenty-five people to blame for the financial crisis worldwide. Nevertheless, in 2016

Oddsson announced his candidacy for the presidency of Iceland: "My experience and knowledge, which is considerable, could go well with this office."

In theory, confidence and competence go hand in hand. In practice, they often diverge. You can see it when people rate their own leadership skills and are also evaluated by their colleagues, supervisors, or subordinates. In a meta-analysis of ninety-five studies involving over a hundred thousand people, women typically underestimated their leadership skills, while men overestimated their skills.

You've probably met some football fans who are convinced they know more than the coaches on the sidelines. That's the armchair quarterback syndrome, where confidence exceeds competence. Even after calling financial plays that destroyed an economy, Davíð Oddsson still refused to acknowledge that he wasn't qualified to coach—let alone quarterback. He was blind to his weaknesses.

"Let me interrupt your expertise with my confidence."

The opposite of armchair quarterback syndrome is impostor syndrome, where competence exceeds confidence. Think of the people you know who believe that they don't deserve their success. They're genuinely unaware of just how intelligent, creative, or charming they are, and no matter how hard you try, you can't get them to rethink their views. Even after an online petition proved that many others had confidence in her, Halla Tómasdóttir still wasn't convinced she was qualified to lead her country. She was blind to her strengths.

Although they had opposite blind spots, being on the extremes of confidence left both candidates reluctant to rethink their plans. The ideal level of confidence probably lies somewhere between being an armchair quarterback and an impostor. How do we find that sweet spot?

THE IGNORANCE OF ARROGANCE

One of my favorite accolades is a satirical award for research that's as entertaining as it is enlightening. It's called the Ig™ Nobel Prize, and it's handed out by actual Nobel laureates. One autumn in college, I raced to the campus theater to watch the ceremony along with over a thousand fellow nerds. The winners included a pair of physicists who created a magnetic field to levitate a live frog, a trio of chemists who discovered that the biochemistry of romantic love has something in common with obsessive-compulsive disorder, and a computer scientist who invented PawSense—software that detects cat paws on a keyboard and makes an annoying noise to deter them. *Unclear whether it also worked with dogs.*

Several of the awards made me laugh, but the honorees who made me think the most were two psychologists, David Dunning and Justin Kruger. They had just published a "modest report" on skill and confidence that would soon become famous. They found that in many situations, those who can't . . . don't know they can't. According to what's now known as the Dunning-Kruger effect, it's when we lack competence that we're most likely to be brimming with overconfidence.

In the original Dunning-Kruger studies, people who scored the lowest on tests of logical reasoning, grammar, and sense of humor had the most inflated opinions of their skills. On average, they believed they did better than 62 percent of their peers, but in reality outperformed only 12 percent of them. The less intelligent we are in a particular domain, the more we seem to overestimate our actual intelligence in that domain. In a group of football fans, the one who knows the least is most likely to be the armchair quarterback, prosecuting the coach for calling the wrong play and preaching about a better playbook.

This tendency matters because it compromises self-awareness, and it trips us up across all kinds of settings. Look what happened when economists evaluated the operations and management practices of thousands of companies across a wide range of industries and countries, and compared their assessments with managers' self-ratings:

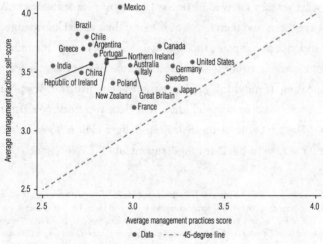

Managers Tend to Overrate Their Abilities
(Measured versus Self-Evaluated Management Practices Score)

Sources: World Management Survey; Bloom and Van Reenen 2007; and Maloney 2017b.

In this graph, if self-assessments of performance matched actual performance, every country would be on the dotted line. Overconfidence existed in every culture, and it was most rampant where management was the poorest.*

Of course, management skills can be hard to judge objectively. Knowledge should be easier—you were tested on yours throughout school. Compared to most people, how much do you think you know about each of the following topics—more, less, or the same?

- Why English became the official language of the United States
- Why women were burned at the stake in Salem
- What job Walt Disney had before he drew Mickey Mouse
- On which spaceflight humans first laid eyes on the Great Wall of China
- Why eating candy affects how kids behave

One of my biggest pet peeves is feigned knowledge, where people pretend to know things they don't. *It bothers me so much that at this very moment I'm writing an entire book about it.* In a series of studies, people rated whether they knew more or less than most people about a range of topics like these, and then took a quiz to test their actual knowledge. The more superior participants thought their knowledge was, the more they overestimated themselves—and the less interested they were in learning and updating. If you think you know more about history or science than most people, chances are you know less than you think. As Dunning quips, "The first rule of the Dunning-Kruger club is you don't know you're a member of the Dunning-Kruger club."†

---

*This looks like good news for countries like the United States, where self-assessments came fairly close to reality, but that doesn't hold across domains. In a recent study, English-speaking teenagers around the world were asked to rate their knowledge in sixteen different areas of math. Three of the subjects listed were entirely fake—declarative fractions, proper numbers, and subjunctive scaling—which made it possible to track who would claim knowledge about fictional topics. On average, the worst offenders were North American, male, and wealthy.

† My favorite example comes from Nina Strohminger, who once lamented: "My dad called this morning to tell me about the Dunning-Kruger effect, not realizing that his daughter with a Ph.D. in psychology would certainly know the Dunning-Kruger effect, thereby giving a tidy demonstration of the Dunning-Kruger effect."

On the questions above, if you felt you knew anything at all, think again. America has no official language, suspected witches were hanged in Salem but not burned, Walt Disney didn't draw Mickey Mouse (it was the work of an animator named Ub Iwerks), you can't actually see the Great Wall of China from space, and the average effect of sugar on children's behavior is zero.

Although the Dunning-Kruger effect is often amusing in everyday life, it was no laughing matter in Iceland. Despite serving as governor of the central bank, Davíð Oddsson had no training in finance or economics. Before entering politics, he had created a radio comedy show, written plays and short stories, gone to law school, and worked as a journalist. During his reign as Iceland's prime minister, Oddsson was so dismissive of experts that he disbanded the National Economic Institute. To force him out of his post at the central bank, Parliament had to pass an unconventional law: any governor would have to have at least a master's degree in economics. That didn't stop Oddsson from running for president a few years later. He seemed utterly blind to his blindness: he didn't know what he didn't know.

WHAT I KNOW

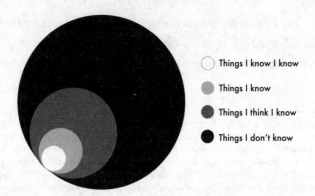

- Things I know I know
- Things I know
- Things I think I know
- Things I don't know

STRANDED AT THE SUMMIT OF MOUNT STUPID

The problem with armchair quarterback syndrome is that it stands in the way of rethinking. If we're certain that we know something, we have no reason to look for gaps and flaws in our knowledge—let alone fill or correct them. In one study, the people who scored the lowest on an emotional intelligence test weren't just the most likely to overestimate their skills. They were also the most likely to dismiss their scores as inaccurate or irrelevant—and the least likely to invest in coaching or self-improvement.

Yes, some of this comes down to our fragile egos. We're driven to deny our weaknesses when we want to see ourselves in a positive light or paint a glowing picture of ourselves to others. A classic case is the crooked politician who claims to crusade against corruption, but is actually motivated by willful blindness or social deception. Yet motivation is only part of the story.*

There's a less obvious force that clouds our vision of our abilities: a deficit in metacognitive skill, the ability to think about our thinking. Lacking competence can leave us blind to our own incompetence. If you're a tech entrepreneur and you're uninformed about education systems, you can feel certain that your master plan will fix them. If you're socially awkward and you're missing some insight on social graces, you can strut around believing you're James Bond. In high school, a friend told me I didn't have a sense of humor. What made her think that? "You don't

---

*There's an ongoing debate about the role of statistical measurement issues in the Dunning-Kruger effect, but the controversy is mostly around how strong the effect is and when it occurs—not whether it's real. Interestingly, even when people are motivated to accurately judge their knowledge, the least knowledgeable often struggle the most. After people take a logical reasoning test, when they're offered a $100 bill if they can correctly (and, therefore, humbly) guess how many questions they got right, they still end up being overconfident. On a twenty-question test, they think they got an average of 1.42 more questions right than they actually did—and the worst performers are the most overconfident.

laugh at all my jokes." *I'm hilarious . . . said no funny person ever. I'll leave it to you to decide who lacked the sense of humor.*

When we lack the knowledge and skills to achieve excellence, we sometimes lack the knowledge and skills to judge excellence. This insight should immediately put your favorite confident ignoramuses in their place. Before we poke fun at them, though, it's worth remembering that we all have moments when we *are* them.

We're all novices at many things, but we're not always blind to that fact. We tend to overestimate ourselves on desirable skills, like the ability to carry on a riveting conversation. We're also prone to overconfidence in situations where it's easy to confuse experience for expertise, like driving, typing, trivia, and managing emotions. Yet we *underestimate* ourselves when we can easily recognize that we lack experience—like painting, driving a race car, and rapidly reciting the alphabet backward. Absolute beginners rarely fall into the Dunning-Kruger trap. If you don't know a thing about football, you probably don't walk around believing you know more than the coach.

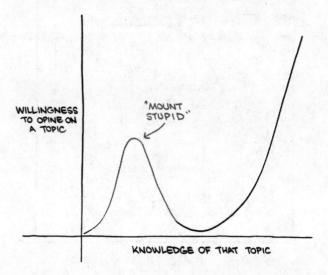

It's when we progress from novice to amateur that we become over-confident. A bit of knowledge can be a dangerous thing. In too many domains of our lives, we never gain enough expertise to question our opinions or discover what we don't know. We have just enough information to feel self-assured about making pronouncements and passing judgment, failing to realize that we've climbed to the top of Mount Stupid without making it over to the other side.

You can see this phenomenon in one of Dunning's experiments that involved people playing the role of doctors in a simulated zombie apocalypse. When they've seen only a handful of injured victims, their perceived and actual skills match. Unfortunately, as they gain experience,

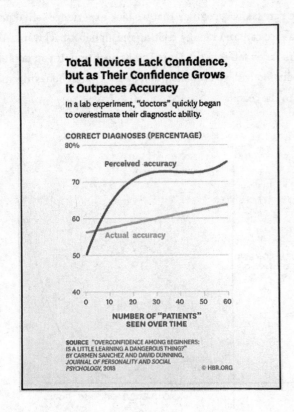

Total Novices Lack Confidence, but as Their Confidence Grows It Outpaces Accuracy

In a lab experiment, "doctors" quickly began to overestimate their diagnostic ability.

CORRECT DIAGNOSES (PERCENTAGE)

Perceived accuracy

Actual accuracy

NUMBER OF "PATIENTS" SEEN OVER TIME

SOURCE "OVERCONFIDENCE AMONG BEGINNERS: IS A LITTLE LEARNING A DANGEROUS THING?" BY CARMEN SANCHEZ AND DAVID DUNNING, JOURNAL OF PERSONALITY AND SOCIAL PSYCHOLOGY, 2018   © HBR.ORG

their confidence climbs faster than their competence, and confidence remains higher than competence from that point on.

This might be one of the reasons that patient mortality rates in hospitals seem to spike in July, when new residents take over. It's not their lack of skill alone that proves hazardous; it's their overestimation of that skill.

Advancing from novice to amateur can break the rethinking cycle. As we gain experience, we lose some of our humility. We take pride in making rapid progress, which promotes a false sense of mastery. That jump-starts an overconfidence cycle, preventing us from doubting what we know and being curious about what we don't. We get trapped in a beginner's bubble of flawed assumptions, where we're ignorant of our own ignorance.

That's what happened in Iceland to Davíð Oddsson, whose arrogance was reinforced by cronies and unchecked by critics. He was known to surround himself with "fiercely loyal henchmen" from school and bridge matches, and to keep a checklist of friends and enemies. Months before the meltdown, Oddsson refused help from England's central bank. Then, at the height of the crisis, he brashly declared in public that he had no intention of covering the debts of Iceland's banks. Two years later an independent truth commission appointed by Parliament charged him with gross negligence. Oddsson's downfall, according to one journalist who chronicled Iceland's financial collapse, was "arrogance, his absolute conviction that he knew what was best for the island."

What he lacked is a crucial nutrient for the mind: humility. The antidote to getting stuck on Mount Stupid is taking a regular dose of it. "Arrogance is ignorance plus conviction," blogger Tim Urban explains. "While humility is a permeable filter that absorbs life experience and converts it into knowledge and wisdom, arrogance is a rubber shield that life experience simply bounces off of."

by Doug Savage

www.savagechickens.com

WHAT GOLDILOCKS GOT WRONG

Many people picture confidence as a seesaw. Gain too much confidence, and we tip toward arrogance. Lose too much confidence, and we become meek. This is our fear with humility: that we'll end up having a low opinion of ourselves. We want to keep the seesaw balanced, so we go into Goldilocks mode and look for the amount of confidence that's just right. Recently, though, I learned that this is the wrong approach.

Humility is often misunderstood. It's not a matter of having low self-confidence. One of the Latin roots of *humility* means "from the earth." It's about being grounded—recognizing that we're flawed and fallible.

Confidence is a measure of how much you believe in yourself. Evidence shows that's distinct from how much you believe in your methods. You can be confident in your ability to achieve a goal in the future while maintaining the humility to question whether you have the right tools in the present. That's the sweet spot of confidence.

We become blinded by arrogance when we're utterly convinced of our strengths and our strategies. We get paralyzed by doubt when we lack conviction in both. We can be consumed by an inferiority complex when we know the right method but feel uncertain about our ability to execute it. What we want to attain is confident humility: having faith in our capability while appreciating that we may not have the right solution or even be addressing the right problem. That gives us enough doubt to reexamine our old knowledge and enough confidence to pursue new insights.

THE CONFIDENCE SWEET SPOT

Belief in Your Tools

	CERTAIN	UNCERTAIN
INSECURE	Obsessive Inferiority	Debilitating Doubt
SECURE	Blind Arrogance	Confident Humility

Belief in Yourself

When Spanx founder Sara Blakely had the idea for footless panty-hose, she believed in her ability to make the idea a reality, but she was full of doubt about her current tools. Her day job was selling fax machines door-to-door, and she was aware that she didn't know anything about fashion, retail, or manufacturing. When she was designing the prototype, she spent a week driving around to hosiery mills to ask them for help. When she couldn't afford a law firm to apply for a patent, she read a book on the topic and filled out the application herself. Her doubt wasn't debilitating—she was confident she could overcome the challenges in front of her. Her confidence wasn't in her existing knowledge—it was in her capacity to learn.

Confident humility can be taught. In one experiment, when students read a short article about the benefits of admitting what we don't know rather than being certain about it, their odds of seeking extra help in an area of weakness spiked from 65 to 85 percent. They were also more likely to explore opposing political views to try to learn from the other side.

Confident humility doesn't just open our minds to rethinking—it improves the quality of our rethinking. In college and graduate school, students who are willing to revise their beliefs get higher grades than their peers. In high school, students who admit when they don't know something are rated by teachers as learning more effectively and by peers as contributing more to their teams. At the end of the academic year, they have significantly higher math grades than their more self-assured peers. Instead of just assuming they've mastered the material, they quiz themselves to test their understanding.

When adults have the confidence to acknowledge what they don't know, they pay more attention to how strong evidence is and spend more time reading material that contradicts their opinions. In rigorous studies of leadership effectiveness across the United States and China, the most productive and innovative teams aren't run by leaders who are confident or humble. The most effective leaders score high in both confidence *and* humility. Although they have faith in their strengths, they're also keenly aware of their weaknesses. They know they need to recognize and transcend their limits if they want to push the limits of greatness.

If we care about accuracy, we can't afford to have blind spots. To get an accurate picture of our knowledge and skills, it can help to assess ourselves like scientists looking through a microscope. But one of my newly formed beliefs is that we're sometimes better off underestimating ourselves.

CONFIDENCE vs. COMPETENCE

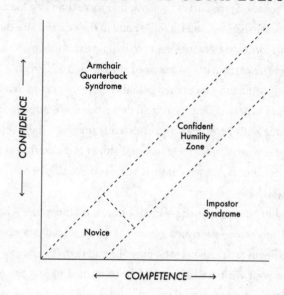

THE BENEFITS OF DOUBT

Just a month and a half before Iceland's presidential election, Halla Tó-masdóttir was polling at only 1 percent support. To focus on the most promising candidates, the network airing the first televised debate announced that they wouldn't feature anyone with less than 2.5 percent of the vote. On the day of the debate, Halla ended up barely squeaking through. Over the following month her popularity skyrocketed. She wasn't just a viable candidate; she was in the final four.

A few years later, when I invited her to speak to my class, Halla mentioned that the psychological fuel that propelled her meteoric rise was none other than impostor syndrome. Feeling like an impostor is typically viewed as a bad thing, and for good reason—a chronic sense of being unworthy can breed misery, crush motivation, and hold us back from pursuing our ambitions.

From time to time, though, a less crippling sense of doubt waltzes into many of our minds. Some surveys suggest that more than half the people you know have felt like impostors at some point in their careers. It's thought to be especially common among women and marginalized groups. Strangely, it also seems to be particularly pronounced among high achievers.

I've taught students who earned patents before they could drink and became chess masters before they could drive, but these same individuals still wrestle with insecurity and constantly question their abilities. The standard explanation for their accomplishments is that they succeed in spite of their doubts, but what if their success is actually driven in part *by* those doubts?

To find out, Basima Tewfik—then a doctoral student at Wharton, now an MIT professor—recruited a group of medical students who were preparing to begin their clinical rotations. She had them interact for more than half an hour with actors who had been trained to play the role of patients presenting symptoms of various diseases. Basima observed how the medical students treated the patients—and also tracked whether they made the right diagnoses.

A week earlier the students had answered a survey about how often they entertained impostor thoughts like *I am not as qualified as others think I am* and *People important to me think I am more capable than I think I am.* Those who self-identified as impostors didn't do any worse in their diagnoses, and they did significantly better when it came to bedside manner—they were rated as more empathetic, respectful, and professional, as well as more effective in asking questions and sharing information. In another study, Basima found a similar pattern with investment professionals: the more often they felt like impostors, the higher their performance reviews from their supervisors four months later.

This evidence is new, and we still have a lot to learn about when impostor syndrome is beneficial versus when it's detrimental. Still, it leaves me wondering if we've been misjudging impostor syndrome by seeing it solely as a disorder.

ARMCHAIR QUARTERBACK SYNDROME vs. IMPOSTOR SYNDROME

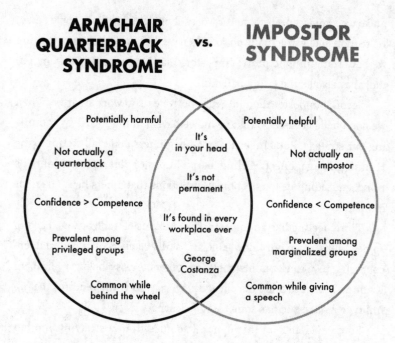

Potentially harmful

Not actually a quarterback

Confidence > Competence

Prevalent among privileged groups

Common while behind the wheel

It's in your head

It's not permanent

It's found in every workplace ever

George Costanza

Potentially helpful

Not actually an impostor

Confidence < Competence

Prevalent among marginalized groups

Common while giving a speech

When our impostor fears crop up, the usual advice is to ignore them—give ourselves the benefit of the doubt. Instead, we might be better off embracing those fears, because they can give us three benefits of doubt.

The first upside of feeling like an impostor is that it can motivate us to work harder. It's probably not helpful when we're deciding whether to start a race, but once we've stepped up to the starting line, it gives us the drive to keep running to the end so that we can earn our place among the finalists.* In some of my own research across call centers, military and government teams, and nonprofits, I've found that confidence can

---

*That reaction can vary based on gender. In Basima's study of investment professionals, impostor thoughts helped the task performance of both men and women, but were more likely to spur extra teamwork among men. Men were driven to compensate for their fear that they might fall short of expectations in their core tasks by doing extra collaborative work. Women were more dependent on confidence and more likely to feel debilitated by doubts.

make us complacent. If we never worry about letting other people down, we're more likely to actually do so. When we feel like impostors, we think we have something to prove. Impostors may be the last to jump in, but they may also be the last to bail out.

Second, impostor thoughts can motivate us to work smarter. When we don't believe we're going to win, we have nothing to lose by rethinking our strategy. Remember that total beginners don't fall victim to the Dunning-Kruger effect. Feeling like an impostor puts us in a beginner's mindset, leading us to question assumptions that others have taken for granted.

Third, feeling like an impostor can make us better learners. Having some doubts about our knowledge and skills takes us off a pedestal, encouraging us to seek out insights from others. As psychologist Elizabeth Krumrei Mancuso and her colleagues write, "Learning requires the humility to realize one has something to learn."

Some evidence on this dynamic comes from a study by another of our former doctoral students at Wharton, Danielle Tussing—now a professor at SUNY Buffalo. Danielle gathered her data in a hospital where the leadership role of charge nurse is rotated between shifts, which means that nurses end up at the helm even if they have doubts about their capabilities. Nurses who felt some hesitations about assuming the mantle were actually more effective leaders, in part because they were more likely to seek out second opinions from colleagues. They saw themselves on a level playing field, and they knew that much of what they lacked in experience and expertise they could make up by listening. There's no clearer case of that than Halla Tómasdóttir.

THE LEAGUE OF EXTRAORDINARY HUMILITY

When I sat down with Halla, she told me that in the past her doubts had been debilitating. She took them as a sign that she lacked the ability to succeed. Now she had reached a point of confident humility, and she interpreted doubts differently: they were a cue that she needed to improve her tools.

Plenty of evidence suggests that confidence is just as often the result of progress as the cause of it. We don't have to wait for our confidence to rise to achieve challenging goals. We can build it *through* achieving challenging goals. "I have come to welcome impostor syndrome as a good thing: it's fuel to do more, try more," Halla says. "I've learned to use it to my advantage. I actually thrive on the growth that comes from the self-doubt."

While other candidates were content to rely on the usual media coverage, Halla's uncertainty about her tools made her eager to rethink the way campaigns were run. She worked harder and smarter, staying up late to personally answer social media messages. She held Facebook Live sessions where voters could ask her anything, and learned to use Snapchat to reach young people. Deciding she had nothing to lose, she went where few presidential candidates had gone before: instead of prosecuting her opponents, she ran a positive campaign. *How much worse can it get?* she thought. It was part of why she resonated so strongly with voters: they were tired of watching candidates smear one another and delighted to see a candidate treat her competitors with respect.

Uncertainty primes us to ask questions and absorb new ideas. It protects us against the Dunning-Kruger effect. "Impostor syndrome always keeps me on my toes and growing because I never think I know it all," Halla reflects, sounding more like a scientist than a politician. "Maybe impostor syndrome is needed for change. Impostors rarely say, 'This is how we do things around here.' They don't say, 'This is the right way.' I was so eager to learn and grow that I asked everyone for advice on how I could do things differently." Although she doubted her tools, she had confidence in herself as a learner. She understood that knowledge is best sought from experts, but creativity and wisdom can come from anywhere.

Iceland's presidential election came down to Halla, Davíð Oddsson, and two other men. The three men all enjoyed more media coverage than Halla throughout the campaign, including front-page interviews, which she never received. They also had bigger campaign budgets. Yet on election day, Halla stunned her country—and herself—by winning more than a quarter of the vote.

She didn't land the presidency; she came in second. Her 28 percent fell shy of the victor's 39 percent. But Halla trounced Davíð Oddsson, who finished fourth, with less than 14 percent. Based on her trajectory and momentum, it's not crazy to imagine that with a few more weeks, she could have won.

Great thinkers don't harbor doubts because they're impostors. They maintain doubts because they know we're all partially blind and they're committed to improving their sight. They don't boast about how much they know; they marvel at how little they understand. They're aware that each answer raises new questions, and the quest for knowledge is never finished. A mark of lifelong learners is recognizing that they can learn something from everyone they meet.

Arrogance leaves us blind to our weaknesses. Humility is a reflective lens: it helps us see them clearly. Confident humility is a corrective lens: it enables us to overcome those weaknesses.

CHAPTER 3

The Joy of Being Wrong

The Thrill of Not Believing Everything You Think

□ □ □

I have a degree from Harvard. Whenever I'm wrong,
the world makes a little less sense.

—DR. FRASIER CRANE, PLAYED BY KELSEY GRAMMER

In the fall of 1959, a prominent psychologist welcomed new participants into a wildly unethical study. He had handpicked a group of
Harvard sophomores to join a series of experiments that would run
through the rest of their time in college. The students volunteered to
spend a couple of hours a week contributing to knowledge about how
personality develops and how psychological problems can be solved.
They had no idea that they were actually signing up to have their beliefs
attacked.

The researcher, Henry Murray, had originally trained as a physi-
cian and biochemist. After becoming a distinguished psychologist,
he was disillusioned that his field paid little attention to how people
navigate difficult interactions, so he decided to create them in his own
lab. He gave students a month to write out their personal philosophy of

life, including their core values and guiding principles. When they showed up to submit their work, they were paired with another student who had done the same exercise. They would have a day or two to read each other's philosophies, and then they would be filmed debating them. The experience would be much more intense than they anticipated.

Murray modeled the study on psychological assessments he had developed for spies in World War II. As a lieutenant colonel, Murray had been recruited to vet potential agents for the Office of Strategic Services, the precursor to the CIA. To gauge how candidates would handle pressure, he sent them down to a basement to be interrogated with a bright light shining in their faces. The examiner would wait for an inconsistency in their accounts to pop up and then scream, "You're a liar!" Some candidates quit on the spot; others were reduced to tears. Those who withstood the onslaught got the gig.

Now Murray was ready for a more systematic study of reactions to stress. He had carefully screened students to create a sample that included a wide range of personalities and mental health profiles. He gave them code names based on their character traits, including Drill, Quartz, Locust, Hinge, and Lawful—more on him later.

When students arrived for the debate, they discovered that their sparring partner was not a peer but a law student. What they didn't know was that the law student was in cahoots with the research team: his task was to spend eighteen minutes launching an aggressive assault on their worldviews. Murray called it a "stressful interpersonal disputation," having directed the law student to make the participants angry and anxious with a "mode of attack" that was "vehement, sweeping, and personally abusive." The poor students sweated and shouted as they struggled to defend their ideals.

The pain didn't stop there. In the weeks that followed, the students were invited back to the lab to discuss the films of their own interactions.

They watched themselves grimacing and stringing together incoherent sentences. All in all, they spent about eight hours reliving those humiliating eighteen minutes. A quarter century later, when the participants reflected on the experience, it was clear that many had found it agonizing. Drill described feeling "unabating rage." Locust recalled his bewilderment, anger, chagrin, and discomfort. "They have deceived me, telling me there was going to be a discussion, when in fact there was an attack," he wrote. "How could they have done this to me; what is the point of this?"

Other participants had a strikingly different response: they actually seemed to get a kick out of being forced to rethink their beliefs. "Some may have found the experience mildly discomforting, in that their cherished (and in my case, at least, sophomoric) philosophies were challenged in an aggressive manner," one participant remembers. "But it was hardly an experience that would blight one for a week, let alone a life." Another described the whole series of events as "highly agreeable." A third went so far as to call it "fun."

Ever since I first read about the participants who reacted enthusiastically, I've been fascinated by what made them tick. How did they manage to enjoy the experience of having their beliefs eviscerated—and how can the rest of us learn to do the same?

Since the records of the study are still sealed and the vast majority of the participants haven't revealed their identities, I did the next best thing: I went searching for people like them. I found a Nobel Prize–winning scientist and two of the world's top election forecasters. They aren't just comfortable being wrong; they actually seem to be thrilled by it. I think they can teach us something about how to be more graceful and accepting in moments when we discover that our beliefs might not be true. The goal is not to be wrong more often. It's to recognize that we're all wrong more often than we'd like to admit, and the more we deny it, the deeper the hole we dig for ourselves.

Savage Chickens by Doug Savage

www.savagechickens.com

THE DICTATOR POLICING YOUR THOUGHTS

When our son was five, he was excited to learn that his uncle was expecting a child. My wife and I both predicted a boy, and so did our son. A few weeks later, we found out the baby would be a girl. When we broke the news to our son, he burst into tears. "Why are you crying?" I asked. "Is it because you were hoping your new cousin would be a boy?"

"No!" he shouted, pounding his fists on the floor. "Because we were wrong!"

I explained that being wrong isn't always a bad thing. It can be a sign that we've learned something new—and that discovery itself can be a delight.

This realization didn't come naturally to me. Growing up, I was determined to be right. In second grade I corrected my teacher for misspelling the word *lightning* as *lightening*. When trading baseball cards I would rattle off statistics from recent games as proof that the price guide was valuing players inaccurately. My friends found this annoying and started calling me Mr. Facts. It got so bad that one day my best friend announced that he wouldn't talk to me until I admitted I was wrong. It was the beginning of my journey to become more accepting of my own fallibility.

In a classic paper, sociologist Murray Davis argued that when ideas survive, it's not because they're true—it's because they're interesting. What makes an idea interesting is that it challenges our weakly held opinions. Did you know that the moon might originally have formed inside a vaporous Earth out of magma rain? That a narwhal's tusk is actually a tooth? When an idea or assumption doesn't matter deeply to us, we're often excited to question it. The natural sequence of emotions is surprise ("Really?") followed by curiosity ("Tell me more!") and thrill ("Whoa!"). To paraphrase a line attributed to Isaac Asimov, great discoveries often begin not with "Eureka!" but with "That's funny . . ."

When a core belief is questioned, though, we tend to shut down rather than open up. It's as if there's a miniature dictator living inside our heads, controlling the flow of facts to our minds, much like Kim Jong-un controls the press in North Korea. The technical term for this in psychology is the totalitarian ego, and its job is to keep out threatening information.

It's easy to see how an inner dictator comes in handy when someone attacks our character or intelligence. Those kinds of personal affronts threaten to shatter aspects of our identities that are important to us and might be difficult to change. The totalitarian ego steps in like a bodyguard for our minds, protecting our self-image by feeding us comforting lies. *They're all just jealous. You're really, really, ridiculously good-looking. You're on the verge of inventing the next Pet Rock.* As physicist Richard Feynman quipped, "You must not fool yourself—and you are the easiest person to fool."

Our inner dictator also likes to take charge when our deeply held opinions are threatened. In the Harvard study of attacking students' worldviews, the participant who had the strongest negative reaction was code-named Lawful. He came from a blue-collar background and was unusually precocious, having started college at sixteen and joined the study at seventeen. One of his beliefs was that technology was harming civilization, and he became hostile when his views were questioned. Lawful went on to become an academic, and when he penned his magnum opus, it was clear that he hadn't changed his mind. His concerns about technology had only intensified:

> The Industrial Revolution and its consequences have been a disaster for the human race. They have greatly increased the life-expectancy of those of us who live in "advanced" countries, but they have destabilized society, have made life unfulfilling, have subjected human beings to indignities . . . to physical suffering as well . . . and have inflicted severe damage on the natural world.

That kind of conviction is a common response to threats. Neuroscientists find that when our core beliefs are challenged, it can trigger the amygdala, the primitive "lizard brain" that breezes right past cool rationality and activates a hot fight-or-flight response. The anger and fear are visceral: it feels as if we've been punched in the mind. The totalitarian ego comes to the rescue with mental armor. We become preachers or prosecutors striving to convert or condemn the unenlightened. "Presented with someone else's argument, we're quite adept at spotting the weaknesses," journalist Elizabeth Kolbert writes, but "the positions we're blind about are our own."

I find this odd, because we weren't born with our opinions. Unlike our height or raw intelligence, we have full control over what we believe is true. We choose our views, and we can choose to rethink them any time we want. This should be a familiar task, because we have a lifetime of evidence that we're wrong on a regular basis. *I was sure I'd finish a draft of this chapter by Friday. I was certain the cereal with the toucan on the box was Fruit Loops, but I just noticed the box says Froot Loops. I was sure I put the milk back in the fridge last night, but strangely it's sitting on the counter this morning.*

The inner dictator manages to prevail by activating an overconfidence cycle. First, our wrong opinions are shielded in filter bubbles, where we feel pride when we see only information that supports our convictions. Then our beliefs are sealed in echo chambers, where we hear only from people who intensify and validate them. Although the resulting fortress can appear impenetrable, there's a growing community of experts who are determined to break through.

ATTACHMENT ISSUES

Not long ago I gave a speech at a conference about my research on givers, takers, and matchers. I was studying whether generous, selfish, or fair people were more productive in jobs like sales and engineering. One of the attendees was Daniel Kahneman, the Nobel Prize–winning psychologist who has spent much of his career demonstrating how flawed our intuitions are. He told me afterward that he was surprised by my finding that givers had higher rates of failure than takers and matchers—but higher rates of success, too.

When you read a study that surprises you, how do you react? Many people would get defensive, searching for flaws in the study's design or the statistical analysis. Danny did the opposite. His eyes lit up, and a huge grin appeared on his face. "That was wonderful," he said. "I was wrong."

Later, I sat down with Danny for lunch and asked him about his reaction. It looked a lot to me like the joy of being wrong—his eyes twinkled as if he was having fun. He said that in his eighty-five years, no one had pointed that out before, but yes, he genuinely enjoys discovering that he was wrong, because it means he is now less wrong than before.

I knew the feeling. In college, what first attracted me to social science was reading studies that clashed with my expectations; I couldn't wait to tell my roommates about all the assumptions I'd been rethinking. In my first independent research project, I tested some predictions of my own, and more than a dozen of my hypotheses turned out to be false.* It was a major lesson in intellectual humility, but I wasn't devastated. I felt an immediate rush of excitement. Discovering I was wrong felt joyful because it meant I'd learned something. As Danny told me, "Being wrong is the only way I feel sure I've learned anything."

Danny isn't interested in preaching, prosecuting, or politicking. He's a scientist devoted to the truth. When I asked him how he stays in that mode, he said he refuses to let his beliefs become part of his identity. "I change my mind at a speed that drives my collaborators crazy," he explained. "My attachment to my ideas is provisional. There's no unconditional love for them."

Attachment. That's what keeps us from recognizing when our opinions are off the mark and rethinking them. To unlock the joy of being wrong, we need to detach. I've learned that two kinds of detachment are especially useful: detaching your present from your past and detaching your opinions from your identity.

Let's start with detaching your present from your past. In psychology, one way of measuring the similarity between the person you are right now and your former self is to ask: which pair of circles best describes how you see yourself?

---

*I was studying the factors that explain why some writers and editors performed better than others at a travel guide company where I was working. Performance wasn't related to their sense of autonomy, control, confidence, challenge, connection, collaboration, conflict, support, self-worth, stress, feedback, role clarity, or enjoyment. The best performers were the ones who started their jobs believing that their work would have a positive impact on others. That led me to predict that givers would be more successful than takers, because they would be energized by the difference their actions made in others' lives. I went on to test and support that hypothesis in a number of studies, but then I came across other studies in which generosity predicted lower productivity and higher burnout. Instead of trying to prove them wrong, I realized I was wrong—my understanding was incomplete. I set out to explore when givers succeed and when they fail, and that became my first book, *Give and Take*.

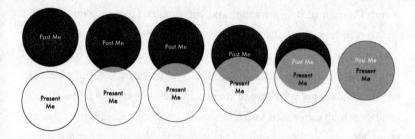

In the moment, separating your past self from your current self can be unsettling. Even positive changes can lead to negative emotions; evolving your identity can leave you feeling derailed and disconnected. Over time, though, rethinking who you are appears to become mentally healthy—as long as you can tell a coherent story about how you got from past to present you. In one study, when people felt detached from their past selves, they became less depressed over the course of the year. When you feel as if your life is changing direction, and you're in the process of shifting who you are, it's easier to walk away from foolish beliefs you once held.

My past self was Mr. Facts—I was too fixated on knowing. Now I'm more interested in finding out what I don't know. As Bridgewater founder Ray Dalio told me, "If you don't look back at yourself and think, 'Wow, how stupid I was a year ago,' then you must not have learned much in the last year."

The second kind of detachment is separating your opinions from your identity. I'm guessing you wouldn't want to see a doctor whose identity is Professional Lobotomist, send your kids to a teacher whose identity is Corporal Punisher, or live in a town where the police chief's identity is Stop-and-Frisker. Once upon a time, all of these practices were seen as reasonable and effective.

Most of us are accustomed to defining ourselves in terms of our beliefs, ideas, and ideologies. This can become a problem when it prevents us from changing our minds as the world changes and knowledge evolves. Our opinions can become so sacred that we grow hostile to the mere thought of being wrong, and the totalitarian ego leaps in to silence counterarguments, squash contrary evidence, and close the door on learning.

Who you are should be a question of what you value, not what you believe. Values are your core principles in life—they might be excellence and generosity, freedom and fairness, or security and integrity. Basing your identity on these kinds of principles enables you to remain open-minded about the best ways to advance them. You want the doctor whose identity is protecting health, the teacher whose identity is helping students learn, and the police chief whose identity is promoting safety and justice. When they define themselves by values rather than opinions, they buy themselves the flexibility to update their practices in light of new evidence.

BAD THINGS TO TIE YOUR IDENTITY TO

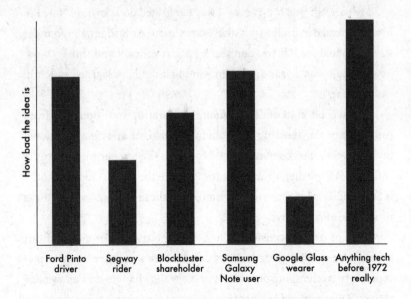

THE YODA EFFECT: "YOU MUST UNLEARN WHAT YOU HAVE LEARNED"

On my quest to find people who enjoy discovering they were wrong, a trusted colleague told me I had to meet Jean-Pierre Beugoms. He's in his late forties, and he's the sort of person who's honest to a fault; he tells the truth even if it hurts. When his son was a toddler, they were watching a space documentary together, and Jean-Pierre casually mentioned that the sun would one day turn into a red giant and engulf the Earth. His son was not amused. Between tears, he cried, "But I *love* this planet!" Jean-Pierre felt so terrible that he decided to bite his tongue instead of mentioning threats that could prevent the Earth from even lasting that long.

Back in the 1990s, Jean-Pierre had a hobby of collecting the predictions that pundits made on the news and scoring his own forecasts against them. Eventually he started competing in forecasting tournaments—international contests hosted by Good Judgment, where people try to predict the future. It's a daunting task; there's an old saying that historians can't even predict the past. A typical tournament draws thousands of entrants from around the world to anticipate big political, economic, and technological events. The questions are time-bound, with measurable, specific results. Will the current president of Iran still be in office in six months? Which soccer team will win the next World Cup? In the following year, will an individual or a company face criminal charges for an accident involving a self-driving vehicle?

Participants don't just answer yes or no; they have to give their odds. It's a systematic way of testing whether they know what they don't know. They get scored months later on accuracy and calibration—earning points not just for giving the right answer, but also for having the right level of conviction. The best forecasters have confidence in their predictions that come true and doubt in their predictions that prove false.

On November 18, 2015, Jean-Pierre registered a prediction that stunned his opponents. A day earlier, a new question had popped up in an open forecasting tournament: in July 2016, who would win the U.S. Republican presidential primary? The options were Jeb Bush, Ben Carson, Ted Cruz, Carly Fiorina, Marco Rubio, Donald Trump, and none of the above. With eight months to go before the Republican National Convention, Trump was largely seen as a joke. His odds of becoming the Republican nominee were only 6 percent according to Nate Silver, the celebrated statistician behind the website FiveThirtyEight. When Jean-Pierre peered into his crystal ball, though, he decided Trump had a 68 percent chance of winning.

Jean-Pierre didn't just excel in predicting the results of American events. His Brexit forecasts hovered in the 50 percent range when most of his competitors thought the referendum had little chance of passing. He successfully predicted that the incumbent would lose a presidential election in Senegal, even though the base rates of reelection were extremely high and other forecasters were expecting a decisive win. And he had, in fact, pegged Trump as the favorite long before pundits and pollsters even considered him a viable contender. "It's striking," Jean-Pierre wrote early on, back in 2015, that so many forecasters are "still in denial about his chances."

Based on his performance, Jean-Pierre might be the world's best election forecaster. His advantage: he thinks like a scientist. He's passionately dispassionate. At various points in his life, Jean-Pierre has changed his political ideologies and religious beliefs.* He doesn't come from a polling or statistics background; he's a military historian, which means he has no stake in the way things have always been done in forecasting. The statisticians were attached to their views about how to aggregate polls. Jean-Pierre paid more attention to factors that were hard to measure and overlooked.

---

* It's possible to change even your deep-seated beliefs while keeping your values intact. Psychologists recently compared people who walked away from their religions with those who were currently religious and never religious. Across Hong Kong, the Netherlands, New Zealand, and the United States, they found a religious residue effect: people who de-identified with religion were just as likely to keep volunteering, and gave more money to charity than those who were never religious.

For Trump, those included "Mastery at manipulating the media; Name recognition; and A winning issue (i.e., immigration and 'the wall')."

Even if forecasting isn't your hobby, there's a lot to be learned from studying how forecasters like Jean-Pierre form their opinions. My colleague Phil Tetlock finds that forecasting skill is less a matter of what we know than of how we think. When he and his collaborators studied a host of factors that predict excellence in forecasting, grit and ambition didn't rise to the top. Neither did intelligence, which came in second. There was another factor that had roughly triple the predictive power of brainpower.

The single most important driver of forecasters' success was how often they updated their beliefs. The best forecasters went through more rethinking cycles. They had the confident humility to doubt their judgments and the curiosity to discover new information that led them to revise their predictions.

In 2021, I teamed up with Good Judgment to run an open forecasting tournament. Thousands of people filled out a survey I designed about their tendencies to think like preachers, prosecutors, politicians, and scientists. Then they made over twenty thousand forecasts—from who would win Olympic events to who would win the commercial space race. The ones who thought like scientists updated their forecasts more often and achieved higher accuracy.

A key question here is how much rethinking is necessary. Although the sweet spot will always vary from one person and situation to the next, the averages can give us a clue. A few years into their tournaments, typical competitors updated their predictions about twice per question. The superforecasters updated their predictions more than four times per question.

Think about how manageable that is. Better judgment doesn't necessarily require hundreds or even dozens of updates. Just a few more efforts at rethinking can move the needle. It's also worth noting, though, how unusual that level of rethinking is. How many of us can even remember the last time we admitted being wrong and revised our opinions accordingly? As journalist Kathryn Schulz observes, "Although small amounts of evidence are sufficient to make us draw conclusions, they are seldom sufficient to make us revise them."

That's where the best forecasters excelled: they were eager to think again. They saw their opinions more as hunches than as truths—as possibilities to entertain rather than facts to embrace. They questioned ideas before accepting them, and they were willing to keep questioning them even after accepting them. They were constantly seeking new information and better evidence—especially disconfirming evidence.

On *Seinfeld*, George Costanza famously said, "It's not a lie if you believe it." I might add that it doesn't become the truth just because you believe it. It's a sign of wisdom to avoid believing every thought that enters your mind. It's a mark of emotional intelligence to avoid internalizing every feeling that enters your heart.

"And in this corner, still undefeated, Frank's long-held beliefs!"

Another of the world's top forecasters is Kjirste Morrell. She's obviously bright—she has a doctorate from MIT in mechanical engineering—but her academic and professional experience wasn't exactly relevant to predicting world events. Her background was in human hip joint mechanics, designing better shoes, and building robotic wheelchairs. When I asked Kjirste what made her so good at forecasting, she replied, "There's no benefit to me for being wrong for longer. It's much better if I change my beliefs sooner, and it's a good feeling to have that sense of a discovery, that surprise—I would think people would enjoy that."

Kjirste hasn't just figured out how to erase the pain of being wrong. She's transformed it into a source of pleasure. She landed there through a form of classical conditioning, like when Pavlov's dog learned to salivate at the sound of a bell. If being wrong repeatedly leads us to the right answer, the experience of being wrong itself can become joyful.

That doesn't mean we'll enjoy it every step of the way. One of Kjirste's biggest misses was her forecast for the 2016 U.S. presidential election, where she bet on Hillary Clinton to beat Donald Trump. Since she wasn't a Trump supporter, the prospect of being wrong was painful—it was too central to her identity. She knew a Trump presidency was possible, but she didn't want to think it was probable, so she couldn't bring herself to forecast it.

That was a common mistake in 2016. Countless experts, pollsters, and pundits underestimated Trump—and Brexit—because they were too emotionally invested in their past predictions and identities. If you want to be a better forecaster today, it helps to let go of your commitment to the opinions you held yesterday. *Just wake up in the morning, snap your fingers, and decide you don't care. It doesn't matter who's president or what happens to your country. The world is unjust and the expertise you spent decades developing is obsolete! It's a piece of cake, right? About as easy as willing yourself to fall out of love.* Somehow, Jean-Pierre Beugoms managed to pull it off.

When Donald Trump first declared his candidacy in the spring of 2015, Jean-Pierre gave him only a 2 percent chance of becoming the nominee. As Trump began rising in the August polls, Jean-Pierre was motivated to question himself. He detached his present from his past, acknowledging that his original prediction was understandable, given the information he had at the time.

Detaching his opinions from his identity was harder. Jean-Pierre didn't want Trump to win, so it would've been easy to fall into the trap of desirability bias. He overcame it by focusing on a different goal. "I wasn't so attached to my original forecast," he explained, because of "the desire to win, the desire to be the best forecaster." He still had a stake in the outcome he actually preferred, but he had an even bigger stake in not making a mistake. His values put truth above tribe: "If the evidence strongly suggests that my tribe is wrong on a particular issue, then so be it. I consider all of my opinions tentative. When the facts change, I change my opinions."

Research suggests that identifying even a single reason why we might be wrong can be enough to curb overconfidence. Jean-Pierre went further; he made a list of all the arguments that pundits were making about why Trump couldn't win and went looking for evidence that they (and he) were wrong. He found that evidence within the polls: in contrast with widespread claims that Trump was a factional candidate with narrow appeal, Jean-Pierre saw that Trump was popular across key Republican demographic groups. By mid-September, Jean-Pierre was an outlier, putting Trump's odds of becoming the nominee over 50 percent. "Accept the fact that you're going to be wrong," Jean-Pierre advises. "Try

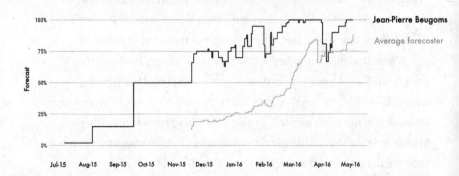

ODDS OF DONALD TRUMP WINNING THE REPUBLICAN PRIMARY

to disprove yourself. When you're wrong, it's not something to be depressed about. Say, 'Hey, I discovered something!'"

MISTAKES WERE MADE . . . MOST LIKELY BY ME

As prescient as Jean-Pierre's bet on Trump was, he still had trouble sticking to it in the face of his feelings. In the spring of 2016, he identified the media coverage of Hillary Clinton's emails as a red flag, and kept predicting a Trump victory for two months more. By the summer, though, as he contemplated the impending possibility of a Trump presidency, he found himself struggling to sleep at night. He changed his forecast to Clinton.

ODDS OF DONALD TRUMP WINNING THE PRESIDENTIAL ELECTION

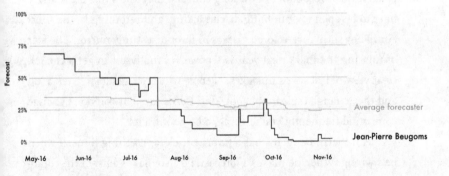

Looking back, Jean-Pierre isn't defensive about his decision. He freely admits that despite being an experienced forecaster, he made the rookie mistake of falling victim to desirability bias, allowing his preference to cloud his judgment. He focused on the forces that would enable him to predict a Clinton win because he desperately wanted a Trump loss. "That was just a way of me trying to deal with this unpleasant forecast I had issued," he says. Then he does something unexpected: he laughs at himself.

If we're insecure, we make fun of others. If we're comfortable being wrong, we're not afraid to poke fun at ourselves. Laughing at ourselves reminds us that although we might take our decisions seriously, we don't have to take *ourselves* too seriously. Research suggests that the more frequently we make fun of ourselves, the happier we tend to be.* Instead of beating ourselves up about our mistakes, we can turn some of our past misconceptions into sources of present amusement.

Being wrong won't always be joyful. The path to embracing mistakes is full of painful moments, and we handle those moments better when we remember they're essential for progress. But if we can't learn to find occasional glee in discovering we were wrong, it will be awfully hard to get anything right.

I've noticed a paradox in great scientists and superforecasters: the reason they're so comfortable being wrong is that they're terrified of being wrong. What sets them apart is the time horizon. They're determined to reach the correct answer in the long run, and they know that means they have to be open to stumbling, backtracking, and rerouting in the short run. They shun rose-colored glasses in favor of a sturdy mirror. The fear of missing the mark next year is a powerful motivator to get a crystal-clear view of last year's mistakes. "People who are right a lot listen a lot, and they change their mind a lot," Jeff Bezos says. "If you don't change your mind frequently, you're going to be wrong a lot."

Jean-Pierre Beugoms has a favorite trick for catching himself when he's wrong. When he makes a forecast, he also makes a list of the conditions in which it should hold true—as well as the conditions under which he would change his mind. He explains that this keeps him honest, preventing him from getting attached to a bad prediction.

---

*If you choose to make fun of yourself out loud, there's evidence that how people react depends on your gender. When men make self-deprecating jokes, they're seen as more capable leaders, but when women do it, they're judged as less capable. Apparently, many people have missed the memo that if a woman pokes fun at herself, it's not a reflection of incompetence or inadequacy. It's a symbol of confident humility and wit.

What forecasters do in tournaments is good practice in life. When you form an opinion, ask yourself what would have to happen to prove it false. Then keep track of your views so you can see when you were right, when you were wrong, and how your thinking has evolved. "I started out just wanting to prove myself," Jean-Pierre says. "Now I want to improve myself—to see how good I can get."

It's one thing to admit to ourselves that we've been wrong. It's another thing to confess that to other people. Even if we manage to overthrow our inner dictator, we run the risk of facing outer ridicule. In some cases we fear that if others find out we were wrong, it could destroy our reputations. How do people who accept being wrong cope with that?

In the early 1990s, the British physicist Andrew Lyne published a major discovery in the world's most prestigious science journal. He presented the first evidence that a planet could orbit a neutron star—a star that had exploded into a supernova. Several months later, while preparing to give a presentation at an astronomy conference, he noticed that he hadn't adjusted for the fact that the Earth moves in an elliptical orbit, not a circular one. He was embarrassingly, horribly wrong. The planet he had discovered didn't exist.

In front of hundreds of colleagues, Andrew walked onto the ballroom stage and admitted his mistake. When he finished his confession, the room exploded in a standing ovation. One astrophysicist called it "the most honorable thing I've ever seen."

Andrew Lyne is not alone. Psychologists find that admitting we were wrong doesn't make us look less competent. It's a display of honesty and a willingness to learn. Although scientists believe it will damage their reputation to admit that their studies failed to replicate, the reverse is true: they're judged more favorably if they acknowledge the new data rather than deny them. After all, it doesn't matter "whose fault it is that something is broken if it's your responsibility to fix it," actor Will Smith has said. "Taking responsibility is taking your power back."

LEARNING SOMETHING NEW TIMELINE

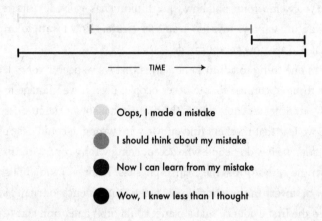

TIME ⟶

- Oops, I made a mistake
- I should think about my mistake
- Now I can learn from my mistake
- Wow, I knew less than I thought

When we find out we might be wrong, a standard defense is "I'm entitled to my opinion." I'd like to modify that: yes, we're entitled to hold opinions inside our own heads. If we choose to express them out loud, though, I think it's our responsibility to ground them in logic and facts, share our reasoning with others, and change our minds when better evidence emerges.

This philosophy takes us back to the Harvard students who had their worldviews attacked in that unethical study by Henry Murray. If I had to guess, I'd say the students who enjoyed the experience had a mindset similar to that of great scientists and superforecasters. They saw challenges to their opinions as an exciting opportunity to develop and evolve their thinking. The students who found it stressful didn't know how to detach. Their opinions were their identities. An assault on their worldviews was a threat to their very sense of self. Their inner dictator rushed in to protect them.

Take it from the student with the code name Lawful. He felt he had been damaged emotionally by the study. "Our adversary in the debate sub-jected us to various insults," Lawful reflected four decades later. "It was a highly unpleasant experience."

Today, Lawful has a different code name, one that's familiar to most Americans. He's known as the Unabomber.

Ted Kaczynski became a math professor turned anarchist and do-mestic terrorist. He mailed bombs that killed three people and injured twenty-three more. An eighteen-year-long FBI investigation culminated in his arrest after *The New York Times* and *The Washington Post* published his manifesto and his brother recognized his writing. He is now serving life in prison without parole.

The excerpt I quoted earlier was from Kaczynski's manifesto. If you read the entire document, you're unlikely to be unsettled by the content or the structure. What's disturbing is the level of conviction. Kaczynski displays little consideration of alternative views, barely a hint that he might be wrong. Consider just the opening:

> The Industrial Revolution and its consequences have been a disaster for the human race. . . . They have destabilized society, have made life unfulfilling. . . . The continued development of technology will worsen the situation. It will certainly subject human beings to greater indignities and inflict greater damage on the natural world. . . . If the system survives, the consequences will be inevitable: There is no way of reforming or modifying the system. . . .

Kaczynski's case leaves many questions about his mental health un-answered. Still, I can't help but wonder: If he had learned to question his opinions, would he still have been able to justify resorting to violence? If he had developed the capacity to discover that he was wrong, would he still have ended up doing something so wrong?

Every time you encounter new information, you have a choice. You can attach your opinions to your identity and stand your ground in the stubbornness of preaching and prosecuting. Or you can operate more like a scientist, defining yourself as a person committed to the pursuit of truth—even if it means proving yourself wrong. The faster you are to recognize when you're wrong, the faster you can move toward getting it right.

CHAPTER 4

The Good Fight Club

The Psychology of Constructive Conflict

□ □ □

Arguments are extremely vulgar, for everybody in good
society holds exactly the same opinions.

—OSCAR WILDE

As the two youngest boys in a big family, the bishop's sons did everything together. They launched a newspaper and built their own printing press together. They opened a bicycle shop and then started manufacturing their own bikes together. And after years of toiling away at a seemingly impossible problem, they invented the first successful airplane together.

Wilbur and Orville Wright first caught the flying bug when their father brought home a toy helicopter. After it broke, they built one of their own. As they advanced from playing together to working together to rethinking human flight together, there was no trace of sibling rivalry between them. Wilbur even said they "thought together." Even though it was Wilbur who launched the project, the brothers shared equal credit for their achievement. When it came time to decide who would pilot their historic flight at Kitty Hawk, they just flipped a coin.

New ways of thinking often spring from old bonds. The comedic chemistry of Tina Fey and Amy Poehler can be traced back to their early twenties, when they immediately hit it off in an improv class. The musical harmony of the Beatles started even earlier, when they were in high school. Just minutes after a mutual friend introduced them, Paul McCartney was teaching John Lennon how to tune a guitar. Ben & Jerry's Ice Cream grew out of a friendship between the two founders that began in seventh-grade gym class. It seems that to make progress together, we need to be in sync. But the truth, like all truths, is more complicated.

One of the world's leading experts on conflict is an organizational psychologist in Australia named Karen "Etty" Jehn. When you think about conflict, you're probably picturing what Etty calls relationship conflict—personal, emotional clashes that are filled not just with friction but also with animosity. *I hate your stinking guts. I'll use small words so that you'll be sure to understand, you warthog-faced buffoon. You bob for apples in the toilet . . . and you like it.*

But Etty has identified another flavor called task conflict—clashes about ideas and opinions. We have task conflict when we're debating whom to hire, which restaurant to pick for dinner, or whether to name our child Gertrude or Quasar. The question is whether the two types of conflict have different consequences.

A few years ago I surveyed hundreds of new teams in Silicon Valley on conflict several times during their first six months working together. Even if they argued constantly and agreed on nothing else, they agreed on what kind of conflict they were having. When their projects were finished, I asked their managers to evaluate each team's effectiveness.

The teams that performed poorly started with more relationship conflict than task conflict. They entered into personal feuds early on and were so busy disliking one another that they didn't feel comfortable challenging one another. It took months for many of the teams to make real headway on their relationship issues, and by the time they did manage to debate key decisions, it was often too late to rethink their directions.

LOW-PERFORMING GROUPS

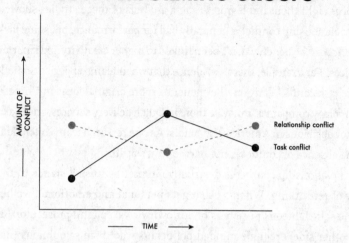

HIGH-PERFORMING GROUPS

What happened in the high-performing groups? As you might expect, they started with low relationship conflict and kept it low throughout their work together. That didn't stop them from having task conflict at the outset: they didn't hesitate to surface competing perspectives. As they resolved some of their differences of opinion, they were able to align on a direction and carry out their work until they ran into new issues to debate.

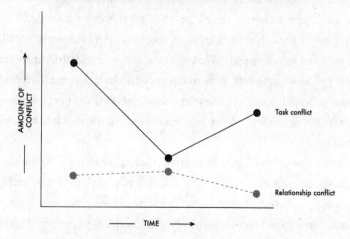

All in all, more than a hundred studies have examined conflict types in over eight thousand teams. A meta-analysis of those studies showed that relationship conflict is generally bad for performance, but some task conflict can be beneficial: it's been linked to higher creativity and smarter choices. For example, there's evidence that when teams experience moderate task conflict early on, they generate more original ideas in Chinese technology companies, innovate more in Dutch delivery services, and make better decisions in American hospitals. As one research team concluded, "The absence of conflict is not harmony, it's apathy."

Relationship conflict is destructive in part because it stands in the way of rethinking. When a clash gets personal and emotional, we become self-righteous preachers of our own views, spiteful prosecutors of the other side, or single-minded politicians who dismiss opinions that don't come from our side. Task conflict can be constructive when it brings diversity of thought, preventing us from getting trapped in overconfidence cycles. It can help us stay humble, surface doubts, and make us curious about what we might be missing. That can lead us to think again, moving us closer to the truth without damaging our relationships.

Although productive disagreement is a critical life skill, it's one that many of us never fully develop. The problem starts early: parents disagree behind closed doors, fearing that conflict will make children anxious or somehow damage their character. Yet research shows that how often parents argue has no bearing on their children's academic, social, or emotional development. What matters is how respectfully parents argue, not how frequently. Kids whose parents clash constructively feel more emotionally safe in elementary school, and over the next few years they actually demonstrate more helpfulness and compassion toward their classmates.

Being able to have a good fight doesn't just make us more civil; it also develops our creative muscles. In a classic study, highly creative architects were more likely than their technically competent but less original peers to come from homes with plenty of friction. They often grew up in households that were "tense but secure," as psychologist Robert Albert notes: "The creative person-to-be comes from a family that is anything but harmonious, one with a 'wobble.'" The parents weren't physically or verbally abusive, but they didn't shy away from conflict, either. Instead of telling their children to be seen but not heard, they encouraged them to stand up for themselves. The kids learned to dish it out—and take it. That's exactly what happened to Wilbur and Orville Wright.

When the Wright brothers said they thought together, what they really meant is that they fought together. Arguing was the family business. Although their father was a bishop in the local church, he included books by atheists in his library—and encouraged the children to read and debate them. They developed the courage to fight for their ideas and the resilience to lose a disagreement without losing their resolve. When they were solving problems, they had arguments that lasted not just for hours but for weeks and months at a time. They didn't have such incessant spats because they were angry. They kept quarreling because they enjoyed it and learned from the experience. "I like scrapping with Orv," Wilbur reflected. As you'll see, it was one of their most passionate and prolonged arguments that led them to rethink a critical assumption that had prevented humans from soaring through the skies.

The clearest sign of intellectual chemistry isn't agreeing with someone. It's enjoying your disagreements with them. Harmony is the pleasing arrangement of different tones, voices, or instruments, not the combination of identical sounds. Creative tension makes beautiful music.

THE PLIGHT OF THE PEOPLE PLEASER

As long as I can remember, I've been determined to keep the peace. Maybe it's because my group of friends dropped me in middle school. Maybe it's genetic. Maybe it's because my parents got divorced. Whatever the cause, in psychology there's a name for my affliction. It's called agreeableness, and it's one of the major personality traits around the world. Agreeable people tend to be nice. Friendly. Polite. Canadian.*

My first impulse is to avoid even the most trivial of conflicts. When I'm riding in an Uber and the air-conditioning is blasting, I struggle to bring myself to ask the driver to turn it down—I just sit there shivering in silence until my teeth start to chatter. When someone steps on my shoe, I've actually apologized for inconveniently leaving my foot in his path. When students fill out course evaluations, one of their most common complaints is that I'm "too supportive of stupid comments."

WHY I AVOID CONFLICT

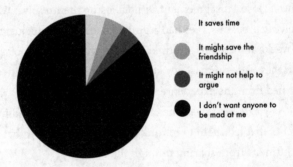

It saves time

It might save the friendship

It might not help to argue

I don't want anyone to be mad at me

Disagreeable people tend to be more critical, skeptical, and challenging—and they're more likely than their peers to become engineers and lawyers. They're not just comfortable with conflict; it energizes them. If you're highly disagreeable, you might be happier in an argument than in a friendly conversation. That quality often comes with a bad rap: disagreeable people get stereotyped as curmudgeons who complain about every idea, or Dementors who suck the joy out of every meeting. When I studied Pixar, though, I came away with a dramatically different view.

---

* In an analysis of over 40 million tweets, Americans were more likely than Canadians to use words like *sh*t*, *b*tch*, *hate*, and *damn*, while Canadians favored more agreeable words like *thanks*, *great*, *good*, and *sure*.

In 2000, Pixar was on fire. Their teams had used computers to rethink animation in their first blockbuster, *Toy Story*, and they were fresh off two more smash hits. Yet the company's founders weren't content to rest on their laurels. They recruited an outside director named Brad Bird to shake things up. Brad had just released his debut film, which was well reviewed but flopped at the box office, so he was itching to do something big and bold. When he pitched his vision, the technical leadership at Pixar said it was impossible: they would need a decade and $500 million to make it.

Brad wasn't ready to give up. He sought out the biggest misfits at Pixar for his project—people who were disagreeable, disgruntled, and dissatisfied. Some called them black sheep. Others called them pirates. When Brad rounded them up, he warned them that no one believed they could pull off the project. Just four years later, his team didn't only succeed in releasing Pixar's most complex film ever; they actually managed to lower the cost of production per minute. *The Incredibles* went on to gross upwards of $631 million worldwide and won the Oscar for Best Animated Feature.

Notice what Brad didn't do. He didn't stock his team with agreeable people. Agreeable people make for a great support network: they're excited to encourage us and cheerlead for us. Rethinking depends on a different kind of network: a challenge network, a group of people we trust to point out our blind spots and help us overcome our weaknesses. Their role is to activate rethinking cycles by pushing us to be humble about our expertise, doubt our knowledge, and be curious about new perspectives.

The ideal members of a challenge network are disagreeable, because they're fearless about questioning the way things have always been done and holding us accountable for thinking again. There's evidence that disagreeable people speak up more frequently—especially when leaders aren't receptive—and foster more task conflict. They're like the doctor in the show *House* or the boss in the film *The Devil Wears Prada*. They give the critical feedback we might not want to hear, but need to hear.

Harnessing disagreeable people isn't always easy. It helps if certain conditions are in place. Studies in oil drilling and tech companies suggest that dissatisfaction promotes creativity only when people feel committed and supported—and that cultural misfits are most likely to add value when they have strong bonds with their colleagues.*

Before Brad Bird arrived, Pixar already had a track record of encouraging talented people to push boundaries. But the studio's previous films had starred toys, bugs, and monsters, which were relatively simple to animate. Since making a whole film with lifelike human superheroes was beyond the capabilities of computer animation at the time, the technical teams balked at Brad's vision for *The Incredibles*. That's when he created his challenge network. He enlisted his band of pirates to foster task conflict and rethink the process.

Brad gathered the pirates in Pixar's theater and told them that although a bunch of bean counters and corporate suits might not believe in them, he did. After rallying them he went out of his way to seek out their ideas. "I want people who are disgruntled because they have a better way of doing things and they are having trouble finding an avenue," Brad told me. "Racing cars that are just spinning their wheels in a garage rather than racing. You open that garage door, and man, those people will take you somewhere." The pirates rose to the occasion, finding economical alternatives to expensive techniques and easy workarounds for hard problems. When it came time to animate the superhero family, they didn't toil over the intricate contours of interlocking muscles. Instead they figured out that sliding simple oval shapes against one another could become the building blocks of complex muscles.

When I asked Brad how he recognized the value of pirates, he told me it was because he *is* one. Growing up, when he went to dinner at

---

* In building a team, there are some dimensions where fit is important and others where misfit adds value. Research suggests that we want people with dissimilar traits and backgrounds but similar principles. Diversity of personality and experience brings fresh ideas for rethinking and complementary skills for new ways of doing. Shared values promote commitment and collaboration.

friends' houses, he was taken aback by the polite questions their parents asked about their day at school. Bird family dinners were more like a food fight, where they all vented, debated, and spoke their minds. Brad found the exchanges contentious but fun, and he brought that mentality into his first dream job at Disney. From an early age, he had been mentored and trained by a group of old Disney masters to put quality first, and he was frustrated that their replacements—who now supervised the new generation at the studio—weren't upholding the same standards. Within a few months of launching his animation career at Disney, Brad was criticizing senior leaders for taking on conventional projects and producing substandard work. They told him to be quiet and do his job. When he refused, they fired him.

I've watched too many leaders shield themselves from task conflict. As they gain power, they tune out boat-rockers and listen to bootlickers. They become politicians, surrounding themselves with agreeable yes-men and becoming more susceptible to seduction by sycophants. Research reveals that when their firms perform poorly, CEOs who indulge flattery and conformity become overconfident. They stick to their existing strategic plans instead of changing course—which sets them on a collision course with failure.

We learn more from people who challenge our thought process than those who affirm our conclusions. Strong leaders engage their critics and make themselves stronger. Weak leaders silence their critics and make themselves weaker. This reaction isn't limited to people in power. Although we might be on board with the principle, in practice we often miss out on the value of a challenge network.

In one experiment, when people were criticized rather than praised by a partner, they were over four times more likely to request a new partner. Across a range of workplaces, when employees received tough feedback from colleagues, their default response was to avoid those coworkers or drop them from their networks altogether—and their performance suffered over the following year.

Some organizations and occupations counter those tendencies by building challenge networks into their cultures. From time to time the Pentagon and the White House have used aptly named "murder boards" to stir up task conflict, enlisting tough-minded committees to shoot down plans and candidates. At X, Google's "moonshot factory," there's a rapid evaluation team that's charged with rethinking proposals: members conduct independent assessments and only advance the ones that emerge as both audacious and achievable. In science, a challenge network is often a cornerstone of the peer-review process. We submit articles anonymously, and they're reviewed blindly by independent experts. I'll never forget the rejection letter I once received in which one of the reviewers encouraged me to go back and read the work of Adam Grant. *Dude, I am Adam Grant.*

When I write a book, I like to enlist my own challenge network. I recruit a group of my most thoughtful critics and ask them to tear each chapter apart. I've learned that it's important to consider their values along with their personalities—I'm looking for disagreeable people who are givers, not takers. Disagreeable givers often make the best critics: their intent is to elevate the work, not feed their own egos. They don't criticize because they're insecure; they challenge because they care. They dish out tough love.*

Ernest Hemingway once said, "The most essential gift for a good writer is a built-in, shock-proof sh*t detector." My challenge network is my sh*t detector. I think of it as a good fight club. The first rule: avoiding an argument is bad manners. Silence disrespects the value of your views and our ability to have a civil disagreement.

Brad Bird lives by that rule. He has legendary arguments with his long-standing producer, John Walker. When making *The Incredibles*, they fought about every character detail, right down to their hair—from how receding the hairline should be on the superhero dad to whether the teenage daughter's hair should be long and flowing. At one point, Brad wanted the baby to morph into goo, taking on a jellylike shape, but John put his foot down. It would be too difficult to animate, and they were too far behind schedule. "I'm just trying to herd you toward the finish," John said, laughing. "I'm just trying to get us across the line, man." Pounding his fist, Brad shot back: "I'm trying to get us across the line in first place."

Eventually John talked Brad out of it, and the goo was gone. "I love working with John, because he'll give me the bad news straight to my face," Brad says. "It's good that we disagree. It's good that we fight it out. It makes the stuff stronger."

Those fights have helped Brad win two Oscars—and made him a better learner and a better leader. For John's part, he didn't flat-out refuse to animate a gooey baby. He just told Brad he would have to wait a little bit. Sure enough, when they got around to releasing a sequel to *The Incredibles* fourteen years later, the baby got into a fight with a raccoon and

---

* How well we take criticism can depend as much on our relationship with the messenger as it does on the message. In one experiment, people were at least 40 percent more receptive to criticism after they were told "I'm giving you these comments because I have very high expectations and I know that you can reach them." It's surprisingly easy to hear a hard truth when it comes from someone who believes in your potential and cares about your success.

transformed into goo. That scene might be the hardest I've ever seen my kids laugh.

If two people always have the same opinion, at least one of them isn't thinking critically—or speaking candidly. Intellectual friction isn't a relationship bug. It's a feature of learning.

DON'T AGREE TO DISAGREE

Hashing out competing views has potential downsides—risks that need to be managed. On the first *Incredibles* film, a rising star named Nicole Grindle had managed the simulation of the hair, watching John and Brad's interactions from a distance. When Nicole came in to produce the sequel with John, one of her concerns was that the volume of the arguments between the two highly accomplished leaders might drown out the voices of people who were less comfortable speaking up: newcomers, introverts, women, and minorities. It's common for people who lack power or status to shift into politician mode, suppressing their dissenting views in favor of conforming to the HIPPO—the HIghest Paid Person's Opinion. Sometimes they have no other choice if they want to survive.

To make sure their desire for approval didn't prevent them from introducing task conflict, Nicole encouraged new people to bring their divergent ideas to the table. Some voiced them directly to the group; others went to her for feedback and support. Although Nicole wasn't a pirate, as she found herself advocating for different perspectives she became more comfortable challenging Brad on characters and dialogue. "Brad is still the ornery guy who first came to Pixar, so you have to be ready for a spirited debate when you put forward a contrary point of view."

The notion of a spirited debate captures something important about how and why good fights happen. If you watch Brad argue with his colleagues—or the pirates fight with one another—you can quickly see that the tension is intellectual, not emotional. The tone is vigorous and feisty rather than combative or aggressive. They don't disagree just for the sake of it; they disagree because they care. "Whether you disagree loudly, or quietly yet persistently put forward a different perspective," Nicole explains, "we come together to support the common goal of excellence— of making great films."

After seeing their interactions up close, I finally understood what had long felt like a contradiction in my own personality: how I could be highly agreeable and still cherish a good argument. Agreeableness is about seeking social harmony, not cognitive consensus. It's possible to disagree without being disagreeable. Although I'm terrified of hurting other people's feelings, when it comes to challenging their thoughts, I have no fear. In fact, when I argue with someone, it's not a display of disrespect—it's a sign of respect. It means I value their views enough to contest them. If their opinions didn't matter to me, I wouldn't bother. I know I have chemistry with someone when we find it delightful to prove each other wrong.

Agreeable people don't always steer clear of conflict. They're highly attuned to the people around them and often adapt to the norms in the room. My favorite demonstration is an experiment by my colleagues Jennifer Chatman and Sigal Barsade. Agreeable people were significantly more accommodating than disagreeable ones—as long as they were in a cooperative team. When they were assigned to a competitive team, they acted just as disagreeably as their disagreeable teammates.

That's how working with Brad Bird influenced John Walker. John's natural tendency is to avoid conflict: at restaurants, if the waiter brings him the wrong dish, he just goes ahead and eats it anyway. "But when I'm involved in something bigger than myself," he observes, "I feel like I have an opportunity, a responsibility really, to speak up, speak out, debate. Fight like hell when the morning whistle blows, but go out for a beer after the one at five o'clock."

That adaptability was also visible in the Wright brothers' relationship. In Wilbur, Orville had a built-in challenge network. Wilbur was known to be highly disagreeable: he was unfazed by other people's opinions and had a habit of pouncing on anyone else's idea the moment it was raised. Orville was known as gentle, cheerful, and sensitive to criticism. Yet those qualities seemed to vanish in his partnership with his brother. "He's such a good scrapper," Wilbur said. One sleepless night Orville came up with an idea to build a rudder that was movable rather than fixed. The next morning at breakfast, as he got ready to pitch the idea to Wilbur, Orville winked at a colleague of theirs, expecting Wilbur to go into challenge mode and demolish it. Much to his surprise, Wilbur saw the potential in the idea immediately, and it became one of their major discoveries.

Disagreeable people don't just challenge us to think again. They also make agreeable people comfortable arguing, too. Instead of fleeing from friction, our grumpy colleagues engage it directly. By making it clear that they can handle a tussle, they create a norm for the rest of us to follow. If we're not careful, though, what starts as a scuffle can turn into a brawl. How can we avoid that slippery slope?

HOW TASK CONFLICT CAN TURN INTO RELATIONSHIP CONFLICT

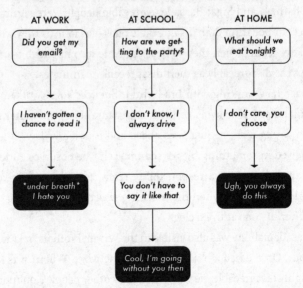

GETTING HOT WITHOUT GETTING MAD

A major problem with task conflict is that it often spills over into relationship conflict. One minute you're disagreeing about how much seasoning to put on the Thanksgiving turkey, and the next minute you find yourself yelling "You smell!"

Although the Wright brothers had a lifetime of experience discovering each other's hot buttons, that didn't mean they always kept their cool. Their last grand challenge before liftoff was their single hardest problem: designing a propeller. They knew their airplane couldn't take flight without one, but the right kind didn't exist. As they struggled with various approaches, they argued back and forth for hours at a time, often raising their voices. The feuding lasted for months as each took turns preaching the merits of his own solutions and prosecuting the other's points. Eventually their younger sister, Katharine, threatened to leave the house if they didn't stop fighting. They kept at it anyway, until one night it culminated in what might have been the loudest shouting match of their lives.

Strangely, the next morning, they came into the shop and acted as if nothing had happened. They picked up the argument about the propeller right where they had left off—only now without the yelling. Soon they were both rethinking their assumptions and stumbling onto what would become one of their biggest breakthroughs.

The Wright brothers were masters at having intense task conflict without relationship conflict. When they raised their voices, it reflected intensity rather than hostility. As their mechanic marveled, "I don't think they really got mad, but they sure got awfully hot."

Experiments show that simply framing a dispute as a debate rather than as a disagreement signals that you're receptive to considering dissenting opinions and changing your mind, which in turn motivates the other person to share more information with you. A disagreement feels personal and potentially hostile; we expect a debate to be about ideas, not emotions. Starting a disagreement by asking, "Can we debate?" sends a message that you want to think like a scientist, not a preacher or a prosecutor—and encourages the other person to think that way, too.

The Wright brothers had the benefit of growing up in a family where disagreements were seen as productive and enjoyable. When arguing with others, though, they often had to go out of their way to reframe their behavior. "Honest argument is merely a process of mutually picking the beams and motes out of each other's eyes so both can see clearly," Wilbur once wrote to a colleague whose ego was bruised after a fiery exchange about aeronautics. Wilbur stressed that it wasn't personal: he saw arguments as opportunities to test and refine their thinking. "I see that you are back at your old trick of giving up before you are half beaten in an argument. I feel pretty certain of my own ground but was anticipating the pleasure of a good scrap before the matter was settled. Discussion brings out new ways of looking at things."

When they argued about the propeller, the Wright brothers were making a common mistake. Each was preaching about *why* he was right and *why* the other was wrong. When we argue about why, we run the risk of becoming emotionally attached to our positions and dismissive of the other side's. We're more likely to have a good fight if we argue about *how*.

When social scientists asked people why they favor particular policies on taxes, health care, or nuclear sanctions, they often doubled down on their convictions. Asking people to explain how those policies would work in practice—or how they'd explain them to an expert—sometimes activated a rethinking cycle. They noticed gaps in their knowledge, doubted their conclusions, and in some cases became less extreme; they were now more curious about alternative options.

Psychologists find that many of us are vulnerable to an illusion of explanatory depth. Take everyday objects like a bicycle, a piano, or earbuds: how well do you understand them? People tend to be overconfident in their knowledge: they believe they know much more than they actually do about how these objects work. We can help them see the limits of their understanding by asking them to unpack the mechanisms. How do the gears on a bike work? How does a piano key make music? How do earbuds transmit sound from your phone to your ears? People are surprised by how much they struggle to answer those questions and quickly realize how little they actually know. That's what happened to the Wright brothers after their yelling match.

The next morning, the Wright brothers approached the propeller problem differently. Orville showed up at the shop first and told their mechanic that he had been wrong: they should design the propeller Wilbur's way. Then Wilbur arrived and started arguing against his own idea, suggesting that Orville might be right.

As they shifted into scientist mode, they focused less on why different solutions would succeed or fail, and more on how those solutions might work. Finally they identified problems with both of their approaches, and realized they were *both* wrong. "We worked out a theory of our own on the subject, and soon discovered," Orville wrote, "that all the propellers built heretofore are *all wrong*." He exclaimed that their new design was "*all right* (till we have a chance to test them down at Kitty Hawk and find out differently)."

Even after building a better solution, they were still open to rethinking it. At Kitty Hawk, they found that it was indeed the right one. The Wright brothers had figured out that their airplane didn't need a propeller. It needed *two* propellers, spinning in opposite directions, to function like a rotating wing.

That's the beauty of task conflict. In a great argument, our adversary is not a foil, but a propeller. With twin propellers spinning in divergent directions, our thinking doesn't get stuck on the ground; it takes flight.

PART II

Interpersonal Rethinking

Opening Other People's Minds

CHAPTER 5

Dances with Foes

How to Win Debates and Influence People

□ □ □

Exhausting someone in argument is not
the same as convincing him.

—TIM KREIDER

At thirty-one, Harish Natarajan has won three dozen international debate tournaments. He's been told it's a world record. But his opponent today presents a unique challenge.

Debra Jo Prectet is a prodigy hailing from Haifa, Israel. She's just eight years old, and although she made her first foray into public debating only last summer, she's been preparing for this moment for years. Debra has absorbed countless articles to accumulate knowledge, closely studied speechwriting to hone her clarity, and even practiced her delivery to incorporate humor. Now she's ready to challenge the champion himself. Her parents are hoping she'll make history.

Harish was a wunderkind too. By the time he was eight, he was outmaneuvering his own parents in dinner-table debates about the Indian caste system. He went on to become the European debate champion and a grand finalist in the world debate championship, and coached the

Filipino national school debate team at the world championship. I was introduced to Harish by an unusually bright former student who used to compete against him, and remembers having lost "many (likely all)" of their debates.

Harish and Debra are facing off in San Francisco in February 2019 in front of a large crowd. They've been kept in the dark about the debate topic. When they walk onstage, the moderator announces the subject: should preschools be subsidized by the government?

After just fifteen minutes of preparation, Debra will present her strongest arguments in favor of subsidies, and Harish will marshal his best case against them. Their goal is to win the audience over to their side on preschool subsidies, but their impact on me will be much broader: they'll end up changing my view of what it takes to win a debate.

Debra kicks off with a joke, drawing laughter from the crowd by telling Harish that although he may hold the world record in debate wins, he's never debated someone like her. Then she goes on to summarize an impressive number of studies—citing her sources—about the academic, social, and professional benefits of preschool programs. For good measure, she quotes a former prime minister's argument about preschool being a smart investment.

Harish acknowledges the facts that Debra presented, but then makes his case that subsidizing preschools is not the appropriate remedy for the damage caused by poverty. He suggests that the issue should be evaluated on two grounds: whether preschool is currently underprovided and underconsumed, and whether it helps those who are the least fortunate. He argues that in a world full of trade-offs, subsidizing preschool is not the best use of taxpayer money.

Going into the debate, 92 percent of the audience has already made up their minds. I'm one of them: it didn't take me long to figure out where I stood on preschool subsidies. In the United States, public education is free from kindergarten through high school. I'm familiar with evidence that early access to education in the first few years of children's lives may be even more critical to helping them escape poverty than anything they learn later. I believe education is a fundamental human right, like access to water, food, shelter, and health care. That puts me on Team Debra. As I watch the debate, her early arguments strike a chord. Here are some highlights:

> **Debra:** Research clearly shows that a good preschool can help kids overcome the disadvantages often associated with poverty.

Data for the win! Be still, my beating heart.

> **Debra:** You will possibly hear my opponent talk today about different priorities . . . he might say that subsidies are needed, but not for preschools. I would like to ask you, Mr. Natarajan . . . why don't we examine the evidence and the data and decide accordingly?

If Harish has an Achilles' heel, my former student has told me, it's that his brilliant arguments aren't always grounded in facts.

> **Harish:** Let me start by examining the main claim . . . that if we believe preschools are good in principle, surely it is worth giving money to subsidize those—but I don't think that is ever enough of a justification for subsidies.

Debra has clearly done her homework. She didn't just nail Harish on data—she anticipated his counterargument.

> **Debra:** The state budget is a big one, and there is room in it to subsidize preschools and invest in other fields. Therefore, the idea that there are more important things to spend on is irrelevant, because the different subsidies are not mutually exclusive.

Way to debunk Harish's case for trade-offs. Bravo.

> **Harish:** Maybe the state has the budget to do all the good things. Maybe the state has the budget to provide health care. Maybe it has the budget to provide welfare payments. Maybe it has the budget to provide running water as well as preschool. I would love to live in that world, but I don't think that *is* the world we live in. I think we live in a world where there are real constraints on what governments can spend money on—and even if those are not real, those are nonetheless political.

D'oh! Valid point. Even if a program has the potential to pay for itself, it takes a lot of political capital to make it happen—capital that could be invested elsewhere.

> **Debra:** Giving opportunities to the less fortunate should be a moral obligation of any human being, and it is a key role for the state. To be clear, we should find the funding for preschools and not rely on luck or market forces. This issue is too important to not have a safety net.

Yes! This is more than a political or an economic question. It's a moral question.

> **Harish:** I want to start by noting what [we] agree on. We agree that poverty is terrible. It is terrible when individuals do not have running water. It is terrible when . . . they are struggling to feed their family. It is terrible when they cannot get health care. . . . That is all terrible, and those are all things we need to address, and none of those are addressed just because you are going to subsidize preschool. Why is that the case?

Hmm. Can Debra argue otherwise?

> **Debra:** Universal full-day preschool creates significant economic savings in health care as well as decreased crime, welfare dependence, and child abuse.

> **Harish:** High-quality preschools will reduce crime. Maybe, but so would other measures in terms of crime prevention.

> **Debra:** High-quality preschool boosts high school graduation rates.

> **Harish:** High-quality preschools can lead to huge improvements in individuals' lives. Maybe, but I'm not sure if you massively increase the number of people going to preschool, they're all gonna be the ones going to the high-quality preschools.

Uh-oh. Harish is right: there's a risk that children from the poorest families will end up in the worst preschools. I'm starting to rethink my position.

> **Harish:** Even when you subsidize preschools, it doesn't mean that all individuals go. . . . The question is, who do you help? And the people you don't help are those individuals who are the poorest. You give unfair and exaggerated gains to those individuals who are in the middle class.

Point taken. Since preschool won't be free, the underprivileged still might not be able to afford it. Now I'm torn about where I stand.

You've seen arguments from both sides. Before I tell you who won, consider your own position: what was your opinion of preschool subsidies going into the debate, and how many times did you end up rethinking that opinion?

If you're like me, you reconsidered your views multiple times. Changing your mind doesn't make you a flip-flopper or a hypocrite. It means you were open to learning.

Looking back, I'm disappointed in myself for forming an opinion before the debate even started. Sure, I'd read some research on early child development, but I was clueless about the economics of subsidies and the alternative ways those funds could be invested. *Note to self: on my next trip to the top of Mount Stupid, remember to take a selfie.*

In the audience poll after the debate, the number of undecided people was the same, but the balance of opinion shifted away from Debra's position, toward Harish's. Support for preschool subsidies dropped from 79 to 62 percent, and opposition more than doubled from 13 to 30 percent. Debra not only had more data, better evidence, and more evocative imagery—she had the audience on her side going into the debate. Yet Harish convinced a number of us to rethink our positions. How did he do it, and what can we learn from him about the art of debate?

This section of the book is about convincing other people to rethink their opinions. When we're trying to persuade people, we frequently take an adversarial approach. Instead of opening their minds, we effectively shut them down or rile them up. They play defense by putting up a shield, play offense by preaching their perspectives and prosecuting ours, or play politics by telling us what we want to hear without changing what they actually think. I want to explore a more collaborative approach—one in which we show more humility and curiosity, and invite others to think more like scientists.

THE SCIENCE OF THE DEAL

A few years ago a former student named Jamie called me for advice on where to go to business school. Since she was already well on her way to building a successful career, I told her it was a waste of time and money.

I walked her through the lack of evidence that a graduate degree would make a tangible difference in her future, and the risk that she'd end up overqualified and underexperienced. When she insisted that her employer expected an MBA for promotions, I told her that I knew of exceptions and pointed out that she probably wouldn't spend her whole career at that firm anyway. Finally, she hit back: "You're a logic bully!"

A what?

"A logic bully," Jamie repeated. "You just overwhelmed me with rational arguments, and I don't agree with them, but I can't fight back."

At first I was delighted by the label. It felt like a solid description of one of my roles as a social scientist: to win debates with the best data. Then Jamie explained that my approach wasn't actually helpful. The more forcefully I argued, the more she dug in her heels. Suddenly I realized I had instigated that same kind of resistance many times before.

"Can I call you back? We're having our favorite argument."

Growing up, I was taught by my karate sensei never to start a fight unless I was prepared to be the only one standing at the end. That's how

I approached debates at work and with friends: I thought the key to victory was to go into battle armed with airtight logic and rigorous data. The harder I attacked, though, the harder my opponents fought back. I was laser-focused on convincing them to accept my views and rethink theirs, but I was coming across like a preacher and a prosecutor. Although those mindsets sometimes motivated me to persist in making my points, I often ended up alienating my audience. I was not winning.

For centuries, debating has been prized as an art form, but there's now a growing science of how to do it well. In a formal debate your goal is to change the mind of your audience. In an informal debate, you're trying to change the mind of your conversation partner. That's a kind of negotiation, where you're trying to reach an agreement about the truth. To build my knowledge and skills about how to win debates, I studied the psychology of negotiations and eventually used what I'd learned to teach bargaining skills to leaders across business and government. I came away convinced that my instincts—and what I'd learned in karate—were dead wrong.

A good debate is not a war. It's not even a tug-of-war, where you can drag your opponent to your side if you pull hard enough on the rope. It's more like a dance that hasn't been choreographed, negotiated with a partner who has a different set of steps in mind. If you try too hard to lead, your partner will resist. If you can adapt your moves to hers, and get her to do the same, you're more likely to end up in rhythm.

In a classic study, a team of researchers led by Neil Rackham examined what expert negotiators do differently. They recruited one group of average negotiators and another group of highly skilled ones, who had significant track records of success and had been rated as effective by their counterparts. To compare the participants' techniques, they recorded both groups doing labor and contract negotiations.

In a war, our goal is to gain ground rather than lose it, so we're often afraid to surrender a few battles. In a negotiation, agreeing with someone else's argument is disarming. The experts recognized that in their dance they couldn't stand still and expect the other person to make all the moves. To get in harmony, they needed to step back from time to time.

One difference was visible before anyone even arrived at the bargaining table. Prior to the negotiations, the researchers interviewed both groups about their plans. The average negotiators went in armed for battle, hardly taking note of any anticipated areas of agreement. The experts, in contrast, mapped out a series of dance steps they might be able to take with the other side, devoting more than a third of their planning comments to finding common ground.

As the negotiators started discussing options and making proposals, a second difference emerged. Most people think of arguments as being like a pair of scales: the more reasons we can pile up on our side, the more it will tip the balance in our favor. Yet the experts did the exact opposite: They actually presented fewer reasons to support their case. They didn't want to water down their best points. As Rackham put it, "A weak argument generally dilutes a strong one."

The more reasons we put on the table, the easier it is for people to discard the shakiest one. Once they reject one of our justifications, they can easily dismiss our entire case. That happened regularly to the average negotiators: they brought too many different weapons to battle. They lost ground not because of the strength of their most compelling point, but because of the weakness of their least compelling one.

These habits led to a third contrast: the average negotiators were more likely to enter into defend-attack spirals. They dismissively shot down their opponents' proposals and doubled down on their own positions, which prevented both sides from opening their minds. The skilled negotiators rarely went on offense or defense. Instead, they expressed curiosity with questions like "So you don't see any merit in this proposal at all?"

Questions were the fourth difference between the two groups. Of every five comments the experts made, at least one ended in a question

WHAT SKILLED NEGOTIATORS DO DIFFERENTLY

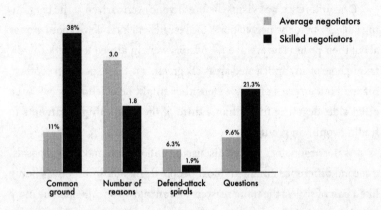

mark. They appeared less assertive, but much like in a dance, they led by letting their partners step forward.

Recent experiments show that having even one negotiator who brings a scientist's level of humility and curiosity improves outcomes for both parties, because she will search for more information and discover ways to make both sides better off. She isn't telling her counterparts what to think. She's asking them to dance. Which is exactly what Harish Natarajan does in a debate.

DANCING TO THE SAME BEAT

Since the audience started out favoring preschool subsidies, there was more room for change in Harish's direction—but he also had the more difficult task of advocating for the unpopular position. He opened the audience's mind by taking a page out of the playbook of expert negotiators.

Harish started by emphasizing common ground. When he took the stage for his rebuttal, he immediately drew attention to his and Debra's areas of agreement. "So," he began, "I think we disagree on far less than it may seem." He called out their alignment on the problem of poverty— and on the validity of some of the studies—before objecting to subsidies as a solution.

We won't have much luck changing other people's minds if we refuse to change ours. We can demonstrate openness by acknowledging where we agree with our critics and even what we've learned from them. Then, when we ask what views they might be willing to revise, we're not hypocrites.

Convincing other people to think again isn't just about making a good argument—it's about establishing that we have the right motives in doing so. When we concede that someone else has made a good point, we signal that we're not preachers, prosecutors, or politicians trying to advance an agenda. We're scientists trying to get to the truth. "Arguments are often far more combative and adversarial than they need to be," Harish told me. "You should be willing to listen to what someone else is saying and give them a lot of credit for it. It makes you sound like a reasonable person who is taking everything into account."

Being reasonable literally means that we can be reasoned with, that we're open to evolving our views in light of logic and data. So in the debate with Harish, why did Debra neglect to do that—why did she overlook common ground?

It's not because Debra is eight years old. It's because she isn't human.

Debra Jo Prectet is an anagram I invented. Her official name is Project Debater, and she's a machine. More specifically, an artificial intelligence developed by IBM to do for debate what Watson did for chess.

They first dreamed the idea up in 2011 and started working intensively on it in 2014. Just a few years later, Project Debater had developed the remarkable ability to conduct an intelligent debate in public, complete with facts, coherent sentences, and even counterarguments. Her knowledge corpus consists of 400 million articles, largely from credible newspapers and magazines, and her claim detection engine is designed to locate key arguments, identify their boundaries, and weigh the evidence. For any debate topic, she can instantaneously search her knowledge graph for relevant data points, mold them into a logical case, and deliver it clearly—even entertainingly—in a female voice within the time constraints. Her first words in the preschool subsidy debate were, "Greetings, Harish. I've heard you hold the world record in debate competition wins against humans, but I suspect you've never debated a machine. Welcome to the future."

Of course, it's possible that Harish won because the audience was biased against the computer and rooting for the human. It's worth noting, though, that Harish's approach in that debate is the same one that he's used to defeat countless humans on international stages. What amazes me is that the computer was able to master multiple complex capabilities while completely missing this crucial one.

After studying 10 billion sentences, a computer was able to say something funny—a skill that's normally thought to be confined to sentient beings with high levels of social and emotional intelligence. The computer had learned to make a logical argument and even anticipate the other side's counterargument. Yet it hadn't learned to agree with elements of the other side's argument, apparently because that behavior was all too rarely deployed across 400 million articles by humans. They were usually too busy preaching their arguments, prosecuting their enemies, or politicking for audience support to grant a valid point from the other side.

When I asked Harish how to improve at finding common ground, he offered a surprisingly practical tip. Most people immediately start with a straw man, poking holes in the weakest version of the other side's case. He does the reverse: he considers the strongest version of their case, which is known as the steel man. A politician might occasionally adopt that tactic to pander or persuade, but like a good scientist, Harish does it to learn. Instead of trying to dismantle the argument that preschool is good for kids, Harish accepted that the point was valid, which allowed him to relate to his opponent's perspective—and to the audience's. Then it was perfectly fair and balanced for him to express his concerns about whether a subsidy would give the most underprivileged kids access to preschool.

Drawing attention to common ground and avoiding defend-attack spirals weren't the only ways in which Harish resembled expert negotiators. He was also careful not to come on too strong.

DON'T STEP ON THEIR TOES

Harish's next advantage stemmed from one of his disadvantages. He would never have access to as many facts as the computer. When the audience was polled afterward about who taught them more, the overwhelming majority said they learned more from the computer than from Harish. But it was Harish who succeeded in swaying their opinions. Why?

The computer piled on study after study to support a long list of reasons in favor of preschool subsidies. Like a skilled negotiator, Harish focused on just two reasons against them. He knew that making too many points could come at the cost of developing, elaborating, and reinforcing his best ones. "If you have too many arguments, you'll dilute the power of each and every one," he told me. "They are going to be less well explained, and I don't know if any of them will land enough—I don't think the audience will believe them to be important enough. Most top debaters aren't citing a lot of information."

Is this always the best way to approach a debate? The answer is—like pretty much everything else in social science—it depends. The ideal number of reasons varies from one circumstance to another.

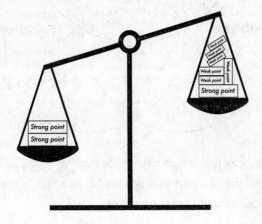

There are times when preaching and prosecuting can make us more persuasive. Research suggests that the effectiveness of these approaches hinges on three key factors: how much people care about the issue, how open they are to our particular argument, and how strong-willed they are in general. If they're not invested in the issue or they're receptive to our perspective, more reasons can help: people tend to see quantity as a sign of quality. The more the topic matters to them, the more the quality of reasons matters. It's when audiences are skeptical of our view, have a stake in the issue, and tend to be stubborn that piling on justifications is most likely to backfire. If they're resistant to rethinking, more reasons simply give them more ammunition to shoot our views down.

It's not just about the number of reasons, though. It's also how they fit together. A university once approached me to see if I could bring in donations from alumni who had never given a dime. My colleagues and I ran an experiment testing two different messages meant to convince thousands of resistant alumni to give. One message emphasized the opportunity to do good: donating would benefit students, faculty, and staff. The other emphasized the opportunity to feel good: donors would enjoy the warm glow of giving.

The two messages were equally effective: in both cases, 6.5 percent of the stingy alumni ended up donating. Then we combined them, because two reasons are better than one.

Except they weren't. When we put the two reasons together, the giving rate dropped below 3 percent. Each reason alone was more than twice as effective as the two combined.

The audience was already skeptical. When we gave them different kinds of reasons to donate, we triggered their awareness that someone was trying to persuade them—and they shielded themselves against it. A single line of argument feels like a conversation; multiple lines of argument can become an onslaught. The audience tuned out the preacher and summoned their best defense attorney to refute the prosecutor.

As important as the quantity and quality of reasons might be, the source matters, too. And the most convincing source is often the one closest to your audience.

A student in one of my classes, Rachel Breuhaus, noticed that although top college basketball teams have rabid fans, there are usually empty seats in their arenas. To study strategies for motivating more fans to show up, we launched an experiment in the week before an upcoming game targeting hundreds of season ticket holders. When left to their own devices, 77 percent of these supposedly die-hard fans actually made it to the game. We decided that the most persuasive message would come from the team itself, so we sent fans an email with quotes from players and coaches about how part of the home-court advantage stems from the energy of a packed house of cheering fans. It had no effect whatsoever: attendance in that group was 76 percent.

What did move the needle was an email with a different approach. We simply asked fans one question: are you planning to attend? Attendance climbed to 85 percent. The question gave fans the freedom to make their own case for going.

Psychologists have long found that the person most likely to persuade you to change your mind is *you*. You get to pick the reasons you find most compelling, and you come away with a real sense of ownership over them.

That's where Harish's final edge came in. In every round he posed more questions to contemplate. The computer spoke in declarative sentences, asking just a single question in the opening statement—and directing it at Harish, rather than at the audience. In his opening, Harish asked six different questions for the audience to ponder. Within the first minute, he asserted that just because preschools are good doesn't mean that they should be funded by the government, and then inquired, "Why is that the case?" He went on to ask whether preschools were under-provided, whether they did help the most disadvantaged—and then why they didn't, why they were so costly, and who they actually helped instead.

Taken together, these techniques increase the odds that during a disagreement, other people will abandon an overconfidence cycle and engage in a rethinking cycle. When we point out that there are areas where we agree and acknowledge that they have some valid points, we model confident humility and encourage them to follow suit. When we support our argument with a small number of cohesive, compelling reasons, we encourage them to start doubting their own opinion. And when we ask genuine questions, we leave them intrigued to learn more. We don't have to convince them that we're right—we just need to open their minds to the possibility that they might be wrong. Their natural curiosity might do the rest.

That said, these steps aren't always enough. No matter how nicely we ask, other people don't always want to dance. Sometimes they're so attached to their beliefs that the mere suggestion of getting in sync feels like an ambush. What do we do then?

DR. JEKYLL AND MR. HOSTILE

Some years ago, a Wall Street firm brought me in to consult on a project to attract and retain junior analysts and associates. After two months of research I submitted a report with twenty-six data-driven recommendations. In the middle of my presentation to the leadership team, one of the members interrupted and asked, "Why don't we just pay them more?"

I told him money alone probably wouldn't make a difference. Many studies across a range of industries have shown that once people are earning enough to meet their basic needs, paying them more doesn't stop them from leaving bad jobs and bad bosses. The executive started arguing with me: "That's not what I've found in *my* experience." I fired back in prosecutor mode: "Yes, that's why I brought you randomized, controlled experiments with longitudinal data: to learn rigorously from many people's experiences, not idiosyncratically from yours."

The executive pushed back, insisting that his company was different, so I rattled off some basic statistics from his own employees. In surveys and interviews, a grand total of zero had even mentioned compensation. They were already well paid (read: overpaid), and if that could have solved the problem, it already would have.* But the executive still refused to budge. Finally I became so exasperated that I did something out of character. I shot back, "I've never seen a group of smart people act so dumb."

In the hierarchy of disagreement created by computer scientist Paul Graham, the highest form of argument is refuting the central point, and the lowest is name-calling. In a matter of seconds I'd devolved from logic bully to playground bully.

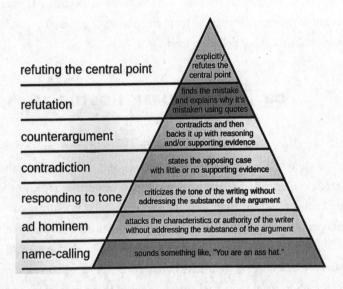

refuting the central point — explicitly refutes the central point

refutation — finds the mistake and explains why it's mistaken using quotes

counterargument — contradicts and then backs it up with reasoning and/or supporting evidence

contradiction — states the opposing case with little or no supporting evidence

responding to tone — criticizes the tone of the writing without addressing the substance of the argument

ad hominem — attacks the characteristics or authority of the writer without addressing the substance of the argument

name-calling — sounds something like, "You are an ass hat."

If I could do that session over, I'd start with common ground and fewer data points. Instead of attacking their beliefs with my research, I'd ask them what would open their minds to my data.

A few years later, I had a chance to test that approach. During a keynote speech on creativity, I cited evidence that Beethoven and Mozart didn't have higher hit rates than some of their peers; they generated a larger volume of work, which gave them more shots at greatness. A

---

* Pay isn't a carrot we need to dangle to motivate people—it's a symbol of how much we value them. Managers can motivate people by designing meaningful jobs in which people have freedom, mastery, belonging, and impact. They can show appreciation by paying people well.

member of the audience interrupted. "Bullsh*t!" he shouted. "You're disrespecting the great masters of music. You're totally ignorant—you don't know what you're talking about!"

Instead of reacting right then, I waited a few minutes until a scheduled break and then made my way to my heckler.

Me: You're welcome to disagree with the data, but I don't think that's a respectful way to express your opinion. It's not how I was trained to have an intellectual debate. Were you?

Music man: Well, no . . . I just think you're wrong.

Me: It's not my opinion—it's the independent finding of two different social scientists. What evidence would change your mind?

Music man: I don't believe you can quantify a musician's greatness, but I'd like to see the research.

When I sent him the study, he responded with an apology. I don't know if I succeeded in changing his mind, but I had done a better job of opening it.

When someone becomes hostile, if you respond by viewing the argument as a war, you can either attack or retreat. If instead you treat it as a dance, you have another option—you can sidestep. Having a conversation about the conversation shifts attention away from the substance of the disagreement and toward the process for having a dialogue. The more anger and hostility the other person expresses, the more curiosity and interest you show. When someone is losing control, your tranquility is a sign of strength. It takes the wind out of their emotional sails. It's pretty rare for someone to respond by screaming "SCREAMING IS MY PREFERRED MODE OF COMMUNICATION!"

This is a fifth move that expert negotiators made more often than average negotiators. They were more likely to comment on their feelings about the process and test their understanding of the other side's feelings: *I'm disappointed in the way this discussion has unfolded—are you frustrated with it? I was hoping you'd see this proposal as fair—do I understand correctly that you don't see any merit in this approach at all? Honestly, I'm a little confused by your reaction to my data—if you don't value the kind of work I do, why did you hire me?*

In a heated argument, you can always stop and ask, "What evidence would change your mind?" If the answer is "nothing," then there's no point in continuing the debate. You can lead a horse to water, but you can't make it think.

THE STRENGTH OF WEAK OPINIONS

When we hit a brick wall in a debate, we don't have to stop talking altogether. "Let's agree to disagree" shouldn't end a discussion. It should start a new conversation, with a focus on understanding and learning rather than arguing and persuading. That's what we'd do in scientist mode: take the long view and ask how we could have handled the debate more effectively. Doing so might land us in a better position to make the same case to a different person—or to make a different case to the same person on a different day.

When I asked one of the Wall Street executives for advice on how to approach debates differently in the future, he suggested expressing less conviction. I could easily have countered that I was uncertain about which of my twenty-six recommendations might be relevant. I could also have conceded that although money didn't usually solve the problem, I'd never seen anyone test the effect of million-dollar retention bonuses. *That would be a fun experiment to run, don't you think?*

A few years ago, I argued in my book *Originals* that if we want to fight groupthink, it helps to have "strong opinions, weakly held." Since then I've changed my mind—I now believe that's a mistake. If we hold an opinion weakly, expressing it strongly can backfire. You end up persuading yourself to hold it more strongly, and you come across as more extreme and entrenched. Communicating it with some uncertainty signals confident humility, invites curiosity, and leads to a more nuanced discussion. Expressing some doubts is an act of receptiveness. Research shows that in courtrooms, expert witnesses and deliberating jurors are more credible and more persuasive when they express moderate confidence, rather than high or low confidence.* And these principles aren't limited to debates—they apply in a wide range of situations where we're advocating for our beliefs or even for ourselves.

In 2014, a young woman named Michele Hansen came across a job opening for a product manager at an investment company. She was excited about the position but she wasn't qualified for it: she had no background in finance and lacked the required number of years of experience.

AN HONEST INTERVIEW

INTERVIEWER	INTERVIEWEE
Where do you see yourself in five years?	Taking your job and asking better interview questions
Describe yourself in a sentence	Concise
What's your biggest weakness?	Definitely my triceps
Why do you want to leave your current job?	I don't want to leave my current job; they want me to leave my current job
What's your biggest professional achievement?	I hold the office record for longest time without replying to a single email
Why do you want this job?	To earn money so I can buy food so I don't die
How do you handle pressure?	An even mix of angry outbursts and shutting down completely
What are your goals?	To earn money so I can buy food so I don't die
We will be in touch!	I am never hearing from you again, am I?

*In a meta-analysis of persuasion attempts, two-sided messages were more convincing than one-sided messages—as long as people refuted the main point of the other side. If they just presented both sides without taking a stance, they were less persuasive than if they preached only their side.

If you were in her shoes and you decided to go for it, what would you say in your cover letter?

The natural starting point would be to emphasize your strengths and downplay your weaknesses. As Michael Scott deadpanned on *The Office*, "I work too hard, I care too much, and sometimes I can be too invested in my job." But Michele Hansen did the opposite, taking a page out of the George Costanza playbook on *Seinfeld*: "My name is George. I'm unemployed and I live with my parents." Rather than trying to hide her shortcomings, Michele opened with them. "I'm probably not the candidate you've been envisioning," her cover letter began. "I don't have a decade of experience as a Product Manager nor am I a Certified Financial Planner." After establishing the drawbacks of her case, she emphasized a few reasons to hire her anyway:

> But what I do have are skills that can't be taught. I take ownership of projects far beyond my pay grade and what is in my defined scope of responsibilities. I don't wait for people to tell me what to do and go seek for myself what needs to be done. I invest myself deeply in my projects and it shows in everything I do, from my projects at work to my projects that I undertake on my own time at night. I'm entrepreneurial, I get things done, and I know I would make an excellent right hand for the co-founder leading this project. I love breaking new ground and starting with a blank slate. (And any of my previous bosses would be able to attest to these traits.)

A week later a recruiter contacted her for a phone screen, and then she had another phone screen with the team. On the calls, she asked about experiments they'd run recently that had surprised them. The question itself surprised the team—they ended up talking about times when they were sure they were right but were later proven wrong. Michele got the job, thrived, and was promoted to lead product development.

This success isn't unique to her: there's evidence that people are more interested in hiring candidates who acknowledge legitimate weaknesses as opposed to bragging or humblebragging.

Even after recognizing that she was fighting an uphill battle, Michele didn't go on defense or offense. She didn't preach her qualifications or prosecute the problems with the job description. By agreeing with the argument against her in her cover letter, she preempted knee-jerk rejection, demonstrating that she was self-aware enough to discern her shortcomings and secure enough to admit them.

An informed audience is going to spot the holes in our case anyway. We might as well get credit for having the humility to look for them, the foresight to spot them, and the integrity to acknowledge them. By emphasizing a small number of core strengths, Michele avoided argument dilution, focusing attention on her strongest points. And by showing curiosity about times the team had been wrong, she may have motivated them to rethink their criteria. They realized that they weren't looking for a set of skills and credentials—they were looking to hire a human being with the motivation and ability to learn. Michele knew what she didn't know and had the confidence to admit it, which sent a clear signal that she could learn what she needed to know.

By asking questions rather than thinking for the audience, we invite them to join us as a partner and think for themselves. If we approach an argument as a war, there will be winners and losers. If we see it more as a dance, we can begin to choreograph a way forward. By considering the strongest version of an opponent's perspective and limiting our responses to our few best steps, we have a better chance of finding a rhythm.

CHAPTER 6

Bad Blood on the Diamond

Diminishing Prejudice by Destabilizing Stereotypes

□ □ □

I hated the Yankees with all my heart, even to the point of
having to confess in my first holy confession that I wished
harm to others—namely that I wished various New York
Yankees would break arms, legs and ankles. . . .

—DORIS KEARNS GOODWIN

One afternoon in Maryland in 1983, Daryl Davis arrived at a lounge
to play the piano at a country music gig. It wasn't his first time
being the only Black man in the room. Before the night was out,
it would be his first time having a conversation with a white supremacist.

After the show, an older white man in the audience walked up to
Daryl and told him that he was astonished to see a Black musician play
like Jerry Lee Lewis. Daryl replied that he and Lewis were, in fact, friends,
and that Lewis himself had acknowledged that his style was influenced
by Black musicians. Although the man was skeptical, he invited Daryl to
sit down for a drink.

Soon the man was admitting that he'd never had a drink with a Black
person before. Eventually he explained to Daryl why. He was a member

of the Ku Klux Klan, the white supremacist hate group that had been murdering African Americans for over a century and had lynched a man just two years earlier.

If you found yourself sitting down with someone who hated you and all people who shared your skin color, your instinctive options might be fight, flight, or freeze—and rightfully so. Daryl had a different reaction: he burst out laughing. When the man pulled out his KKK membership card to show he wasn't joking, Daryl returned to a question that had been on his mind since he was ten years old. In the late 1960s, he was marching in a Cub Scout parade when white spectators started throwing cans, rocks, and bottles at him. It was the first time he remembers facing overt racism, and although he could justifiably have gotten angry, he was bewildered: "How can you hate me when you don't even know me?"

At the end of the conversation, the Klansman handed Daryl his phone number and asked if he would call him whenever he was playing locally. Daryl followed up, and the next month the man showed up with a bunch of his friends to see Daryl perform.

Over time a friendship grew, and the man ended up leaving the KKK. That was a turning point in Daryl's life, too. It wasn't long before Daryl was sitting down with Imperial Wizards and Grand Dragons—the Klan's highest officers—to ask his question. Since then, Daryl has convinced many white supremacists to leave the KKK and abandon their hatred.

I wanted to understand how that kind of change happens—how to break overconfidence cycles that are steeped in stereotypes and prejudice about entire groups of people. Strangely enough, my journey started at a baseball game.

HATE ME OUT AT THE BALLGAME

"Yankees suck! Yankees suck!" It was a summer night at Fenway Park, my first and only time at a Boston Red Sox baseball game. In the seventh inning, without warning, 37,000 people erupted into a chant. The entire stadium was dissing the New York Yankees in perfect harmony.

I knew the two teams had a century-long rivalry, widely viewed as the most heated in all of American professional sports. I took it for granted that the Boston fans would root against the Yankees. I just didn't expect it to happen that day, because the Yankees weren't even there.

The Red Sox were playing against the Oakland A's. The Boston fans were booing a team that was hundreds of miles away. It was as if Burger King fans were going head-to-head against Wendy's in a taste test and started chanting "McDonald's sucks!"

I started to wonder if Red Sox fans hate the Yankees more than they love their own team. Boston parents have been known to teach their kids to flip the bird at the Yankees and detest anything in pinstripes, and YANKEES SUCK is apparently among the most popular T-shirts in Boston history. When asked how much money it would take to get them to taunt their own team, Red Sox fans requested an average of $503. To root for the Yankees, they wanted even more: $560. The feelings run so deep that neuroscientists can watch them light up people's minds: when Red Sox fans see the Yankees fail, they show immediate activation in brain regions linked to reward and pleasure. Those feelings extend well beyond Boston: in a 2019 analysis of tweets, the Yankees were the most hated baseball team in twenty-eight of the fifty U.S. states, which may explain the popularity of this T-shirt:

MOMMY told me never to talk to strangers or Yankees fans.

Most "Hated" MLB Team in Every State
(Based on Geotagged Twitter Data during the 2019 Season)

I recently called a friend who's a die-hard Red Sox fan with a simple question: what would it take to get him to root for the Yankees? Without pausing, he said, "If they were playing Al Qaeda . . . maybe."

It's one thing to love your team. It's another to hate your rivals so much that you'd consider rooting for terrorists to crush them. If you despise a particular sports team—and its fans—you're harboring some strong opinions about a group of people. Those beliefs are stereotypes, and they often spill over into prejudice. The stronger your attitudes become, the less likely you are to rethink them.

Rivalries aren't unique to sports. A rivalry exists whenever we reserve special animosity for a group we see as competing with us for resources or threatening our identities. In business, the rivalry between footwear companies Puma and Adidas was so intense that for generations, families self-segregated based on their allegiance to the brands—they went to different bakeries, pubs, and shops, and even refused to date people who worked for the rival firm. In politics, you probably know some Democrats who view Republicans as being greedy, ignorant, heartless cretins, and some Republicans who regard Democrats as lazy, dishonest, hypersensitive snowflakes. As stereotypes stick and prejudice deepens, we don't just identify with our own group; we disidentify with our adversaries, coming to define who we are by what we're not. We don't just preach the virtues of our side; we find self-worth in prosecuting the vices of our rivals.

When people hold prejudice toward a rival group, they're often willing to do whatever it takes to elevate their own group and undermine their rivals—even if it means doing harm or doing wrong. We see people cross those lines regularly in sports rivalries.* Aggression extends well

---

*When Monica Seles was stabbed on a tennis court in 1993, I know at least one Steffi Graf fan who celebrated. In the 2019 NBA finals, when Kevin Durant went down with an injury, some Toronto Raptors fans started cheering, proving that even Canadians are capable of cruelty. One sports radio host argued, "There is not a single fan in professional sports who isn't happy when an opposing bigtime player gets injured and in theory will make your team's path to success easier." With all due respect, if you care more about whether your team wins a game than whether a human being is hurt in real life, you might be a sociopath.

beyond the playing field: from Barcelona to Brazil, fistfights frequently break out between soccer fans. Cheating scandals are rampant, too, and they aren't limited to athletes or coaches. When students at The Ohio State University were paid to participate in an experiment, they learned that if they were willing to lie to a student from a different school, their own pay would double and the other student's compensation would be cut in half. Their odds of lying quadrupled if the student attended the University of Michigan—their biggest rival—rather than Berkeley or Virginia.

Why do people form stereotypes about rival groups in the first place, and what does it take to get them to rethink them?

FITTING IN AND STANDING OUT

For decades psychologists have found that people can feel animosity toward other groups even when the boundaries between them are trivial. Take a seemingly innocuous question: is a hot dog a sandwich? When students answered this question, most felt strongly enough that they were willing to sacrifice a dollar to those who agreed with them to make sure those who disagreed got less.

THE HOT DOG SANDWICH SURVEY

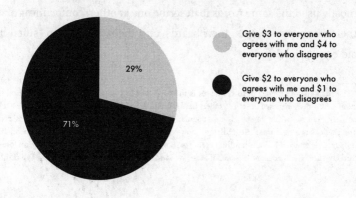

29%

71%

Give $3 to everyone who agrees with me and $4 to everyone who disagrees

Give $2 to everyone who agrees with me and $1 to everyone who disagrees

In every human society, people are motivated to seek belonging and status. Identifying with a group checks both boxes at the same time: we become part of a tribe, and we take pride when our tribe wins. In classic studies on college campuses, psychologists found that after their team won a football game, students were more likely to walk around wearing school swag. From Arizona State to Notre Dame to USC, students basked in the reflected glory of Saturday victories, donning team shirts and hats and jackets on Sunday. If their team lost, they shunned school apparel, and distanced themselves by saying "they lost" instead of "we lost." Some economists and finance experts have even found that the stock market rises if a country's soccer team wins World Cup matches and falls if they lose.*

Rivalries are most likely to develop between teams that are geographically close, compete regularly, and are evenly matched. The Yankees and Red Sox fit this pattern: they're both on the East Coast, they play each other eighteen or nineteen times a season, they both have histories of success, and as of 2019, they had competed over 2,200 times—with each team winning over 1,000 times. The two teams also have more fans than any other franchises in baseball.

I decided to test what it would take to get fans to rethink their beliefs about their bitter rivals. Working with a doctoral student, Tim Kundro, I ran a series of experiments with passionate Yankees and Red Sox supporters. To get a sense of their stereotypes, we asked over a thousand Red Sox and Yankees fans to list three negative things about their rivals. They mostly used the same words to describe one another, complaining about their respective accents, their beards, and their tendency to "smell like old corn chips."

*The stock market impact of soccer losses is the subject of extensive debate: although a number of studies have demonstrated the effect, others have failed to support it. My hunch is that it's more likely to occur in countries where the sport is most popular, the team is expected to win, the match is high stakes, and the loss is a near miss. Regardless of how sports influence markets, we know they can affect moods. One study of European military officers showed that when their favorite soccer team loses on Sunday, they're less engaged at work on Monday—and their performance might suffer as a result.

WHY RED SOX FANS HATE YANKEES FANS

WHY YANKEES FANS HATE RED SOX FANS

Once we've formed those kinds of stereotypes, for both mental and social reasons it's hard to undo them. Psychologist George Kelly observed that our beliefs are like pairs of reality goggles. We use them to make sense of the world and navigate our surroundings. A threat to our opinions cracks our goggles, leaving our vision blurred. It's only natural to put up our guard in response—and Kelly noticed that we become especially hostile when trying to defend opinions that we know, deep down, are false. Rather than trying on a different pair of goggles, we become mental contortionists, twisting and turning until we find an angle of vision that keeps our current views intact.

Socially, there's another reason stereotypes are so sticky. We tend to interact with people who share them, which makes them even more extreme. This phenomenon is called group polarization, and it's been demonstrated in hundreds of experiments. Juries with authoritarian beliefs recommend harsher punishments after deliberating together. Corporate boards are more likely to support paying outlandish premiums for companies after group discussions. Citizens who start out with a clear belief on affirmative action and gay marriage develop more extreme views on these issues after talking with a few others who share their stance. Their preaching and prosecuting move in the direction of their politics. Polarization is reinforced by conformity: peripheral members fit in and gain status by following the lead of the most prototypical member of the group, who often holds the most intense views.

Grow up in a family of Red Sox fans and you're bound to hear some unpleasant things about Yankees fans. Start making regular trips to a ballpark packed with people who share your loathing, and it's only a matter of time before your contempt intensifies and calcifies. Once that happens, you're motivated to see the best in your team and the worst in your opponent. Evidence shows that when teams try to downplay a rivalry by reminding fans that it's just a game, it backfires. Fans feel their identity is being devalued and actually become more aggressive. My first idea for disrupting this pattern came from outer space.

HYPOTHESIS 1:
NOT IN A LEAGUE OF THEIR OWN

If you ever leave the planet Earth, you'll probably end up rethinking some of your feelings about other human beings. A team of psychologists has studied the effects of outer space on inner space, assessing the changes in more than a hundred astronauts and cosmonauts through interviews, surveys, and analyses of autobiographies. Upon returning from space, astronauts are less focused on individual achievements and personal happiness, and more concerned about the collective good. "You develop an instant global consciousness . . . an intense dissatisfaction with the state of the world, and a compulsion to do something about it," Apollo 14 astronaut Edgar Mitchell reflected. "From out there on the moon, international politics looks so petty. You want to grab a politician by the scruff of the neck and drag him a quarter of a million miles out and say, 'Look at that, you son of a b*tch.'"

This reaction is known as the overview effect. The astronaut who described it most vividly to me is space shuttle commander Jeff Ashby.

He recalled that the first time he looked back at the Earth from outer space, it changed him forever:

On Earth, astronauts look to the stars—most of us are star fanatics—but in space, the stars look the same as they do on Earth. What is so different is the planet—the perspective that it gives you. My first glimpse of the Earth from space was about fifteen minutes into my first flight, when I looked up from my checklist and suddenly we were over the lit part of the Earth with our windows facing down. Below me was the continent of Africa, and it was moving by much as a city would move by from an airline seat. Circling the entire planet in ninety minutes, you see that thin blue arc of the atmosphere. Seeing how fragile the little layer is in which all of humankind exists, you can easily from space see the connection between someone on one side of the planet to someone on the other—and there are no borders evident. So it appears as just this one common layer that we all exist in.

When you get to see an overview of the Earth from outer space, you realize you share a common identity with all human beings. I wanted to create a version of the overview effect for baseball fans.

There's some evidence that common identity can build bridges between rivals. In one experiment, psychologists randomly assigned Manchester United soccer fans a short writing task. They then staged an emergency in which a passing runner slipped and fell, screaming in pain as he held his ankle. He was wearing the T-shirt of their biggest rival, and the question was whether they would stop to help him. If the soccer fans had just written about why they loved their team, only 30 percent helped. If they had written about what they had in common with other soccer fans, 70 percent helped.

When Tim and I tried to get Red Sox and Yankees fans to reflect on their common identity as baseball fans, it didn't work. They didn't end up with more positive views of one another or a greater willingness to help one another outside emergency situations. Shared identity doesn't stick in every circumstance. If a rival fan has just had an accident, thinking about a common identity might motivate us to help. If he's not in danger or dire need, though, it's too easy to dismiss him as just another jerk—or not our responsibility. "We both love baseball," one Red Sox supporter commented. "The Yankees fans just like the wrong team." Another stated that their shared love of baseball had no effect on his opinions: "The Yankees suck, and their fans are annoying."

HYPOTHESIS 2: FEELING FOR OUR FOES

I next turned to the psychology of peace. Years ago the pioneering psychologist and Holocaust survivor Herb Kelman set out to challenge some of the stereotypes behind the Israel-Palestine conflict by teaching the two sides to understand and empathize with one another. He designed interactive problem-solving workshops in which influential Israeli and Palestinian leaders talked off the record about paths to peace. For years, they came together to share their own experiences and perspectives, address one another's needs and fears, and explore novel solutions to the conflict. Over time, the workshops didn't just shatter stereotypes—some of the participants ended up forming lifelong friendships.

Humanizing the other side should be much easier in sports, because the stakes are lower and the playing field is more level. I started with another of the biggest rivalries in sports: UNC-Duke. I asked Shane Battier, who led Duke to an NCAA basketball championship in 2001, what it would take for him to root for UNC. His immediate reply: "If they were playing the Taliban." *I had no idea so many people fantasized about crushing terrorists in their favorite sport.* I wondered whether humanizing a Duke student would change UNC students' stereotypes of the group.

In an experiment with my colleagues Alison Fragale and Karren

Knowlton, we asked UNC students to help improve the job application of a peer. If we mentioned that he went to Duke rather than UNC, as long as he was facing significant financial need, participants spent extra time helping him. Once they felt empathy for his plight, they saw him as a unique individual deserving of assistance and liked him more. Yet when we measured their views of Duke students in general, the UNC students were just as likely to see them as their rivals, to say that it felt like a personal compliment if they heard someone criticize Duke, and to take it as a personal insult if they heard Duke praised. We had succeeded in changing their attitudes toward the student, but failed in changing their stereotypes of the group.

Something similar happened when Tim and I tried to humanize a Yankees fan. We had Red Sox fans read a story written by a baseball buff who had learned the game as a child with his grandfather and had fond memories of playing catch with his mom. At the very end of the piece he mentioned that he was a die-hard supporter of the Yankees. "I think this person is very authentic and is a rare Yankee fan," one Red Sox supporter commented. "This person gets it and is not your typical Yankee fan," a second observed. "Ugh, I really liked this text until I got to the part about them being a Yankees fan," a third fan lamented, but "I think this particular person I would have more in common with than the typical, stereotypical Yankees fan. This person is okay."

Herb Kelman ran into the same problem with Israelis and Palestinians. In the problem-solving workshops, they came to trust the individuals across the table, but they still held on to their stereotypes of the group.

In an ideal world, learning about individual group members will humanize the group, but often getting to know a person better just establishes her as different from the rest of her group. When we meet group members who defy a stereotype, our first instinct isn't to see them as exemplars and rethink the stereotype. It's to see them as exceptions and cling to our existing beliefs. So that attempt also failed. Back to the drawing board again.

HYPOTHESIS 3: BEASTS OF HABIT

My all-time favorite commercial starts with a close-up of a man and a woman kissing. As the camera zooms out, you see that he's wearing an Ohio State Buckeyes sweatshirt and she's wearing a Michigan Wolverines T-shirt. The caption: "Without sports, this wouldn't be disgusting."

As a lifelong Wolverine fan, I was raised to boo at Buckeye fans. My uncle filled his basement with Michigan paraphernalia, got up at 3:00 a.m. on Saturdays to start setting up for tailgates, and drove a van with the Michigan logo emblazoned on the side. When I went back home to Michigan for grad school and one of my college roommates started medical school at Ohio State, it was only natural for me to preach my school's superiority by phone and prosecute his intelligence by text.

A few years ago, I got to know an unusually kind woman in her seventies who works with Holocaust survivors. Last summer, when she mentioned that she had gone to Ohio State, my first response was "yuck." My next reaction was to be disgusted with myself. *Who cares where she went to school half a century ago? How did I get programmed this way?* Suddenly it seemed odd that anyone would hate a team at all.

In ancient Greece, Plutarch wrote of a wooden ship that Theseus sailed from Crete to Athens. To preserve the ship, as its old planks decayed, Athenians would replace them with new wood. Eventually all the planks had been replaced. It looked like the same ship, but none of its parts was the same. Was it still the same ship? Later, philosophers added a wrinkle: if you collected all the original planks and fashioned them into a ship, would *that* be the same ship?

The ship of Theseus has a lot in common with a sports franchise. If you hail from Boston, you might hate the 1920 Yankees for taking Babe Ruth or the 1978 Yankees for dashing your World Series hopes. Although the current team carries the same name, the pieces are different. The players are long gone. So are the managers and coaches. The stadium has been replaced. "You're actually rooting for the clothes," Jerry Seinfeld quipped. "Fans will be so in love with a player, but if he goes to a different team, they boo him. This is the same human being in a different shirt; they hate him now. Boo! Different shirt! Boo!"

I think it's a ritual. A fun but arbitrary ritual—a ceremony that we perform out of habit. We imprinted on it when we were young and impressionable, or were new to a city and looking for esprit de corps. Sure, there are moments where team loyalty does matter in our lives: it allows us to high-five acquaintances at bars and hug strangers at victory parades. It gives us a sense of solidarity. If you reflect on it, though, hating an opposing team is an accident of birth. If you had been born in New York instead of Boston, would you really hate the Yankees?

For our third approach, Tim and I recruited fans of the Red Sox and Yankees. To prove their allegiance, they had to correctly name one of their team's players from a photo—and the last year his team had won the World Series. Then we took some steps to open their minds. First, to help them recognize the complexity of their own beliefs, we asked them to list three positives and three negatives about fans of the opposing team. You saw the most common negatives earlier, but they were able to come up with some positives, too:

WHAT RED SOX FANS LIKE ABOUT YANKEES FANS

WHAT YANKEES FANS LIKE ABOUT RED SOX FANS

Then we randomly assigned half of them to go the extra step of reflecting on the arbitrariness of their animosity:

> Think and write about how Yankee fans and Red Sox fans dislike each other for reasons that are fairly arbitrary. For example, if you were born into a family of fans of the rival team, you would likely also be a fan of them today.

To gauge their animosity toward their opponents, we gave them a chance to decide how spicy the hot sauce sold in the rival team's stadium should be. The backstory was that consumer product researchers were planning to do taste tests of hot sauces in baseball stadiums. People who were randomly assigned to reflect on the arbitrariness of their stereotypes selected less fiery hot sauce for their rival's stadium. We also gave them a chance to sabotage a rival fan's performance on a timed, paid math test by assigning harder problems, and those who considered the arbitrariness of their stereotypes picked easier questions for the rival fan.

People weren't just more sympathetic toward a single fan—they changed their views toward their rival team as a whole. They were less likely to see their rival's failure as their success, their rival's success as a personal insult, and criticism of their rival as a personal compliment. And they were more likely to support their rival team in ways that would normally be unthinkable: wearing the rival team's jerseys, sitting in its dugout at games, voting for its players in the All-Star Game, and even endorsing the team on social media. For some fans, it was almost like breaking a religious code, but their comments made it clear that they were rethinking their stances:

> I think it is pretty dumb to hate someone just based on the sports teams they enjoy supporting. Thinking about that makes me want to reconsider how I feel about some supporters of teams that I dislike.

If someone hated me because of the team that I loved, it would feel unfair. Almost like a form of prejudice because they are judging me based on one thing about me and hating me for that reason. After feeling these thoughts, I may change the way I interact with Red Sox fans.

The team they support is not necessarily indicative of who they are. Even though they are wrong.

We'd finally made some progress. Our next step was to examine the key ingredients behind the shift in fans' views. We found that it was thinking about the arbitrariness of their animosity—not the positive qualities of their rival—that mattered. Regardless of whether they generated reasons to like their rivals, fans showed less hostility when they reflected on how silly the rivalry was. Knowing what it felt like to be disliked for

STEREOTYPE TIMELINE

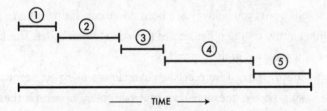

—— TIME ——→

(1) Having an experience: A kid with a mohawk stole my bike

(2) Forming a stereotype: Kids with mohawks are thieves

(3) Having a new experience: A kid with a mohawk was nice to me

(4) Questioning the stereotype: Maybe mohawk kids aren't so bad?

(5) Questioning stereotypes in general: You can't judge a kid by his cover

ridiculous reasons helped them see that this conflict had real implications, that hatred for opposing fans isn't all fun and games.

ENTERING A PARALLEL UNIVERSE

Outside the lab, dismantling stereotypes and decreasing prejudice rarely happen overnight. Even if people aren't on guard from the start, they're quick to put their defenses up when their attitudes are challenged. Getting through to them requires more than just telling them that their views are arbitrary. A key step is getting them to do some counterfactual thinking: helping them consider what they'd believe if they were living in an alternative reality.

In psychology, counterfactual thinking involves imagining how the circumstances of our lives could have unfolded differently. When we realize how easily we could have held different stereotypes, we might be more willing to update our views.* To activate counterfactual thinking, you might ask people questions like: How would your stereotypes be different if you'd been born Black, Hispanic, Asian, or Native American? What opinions would you hold if you'd been raised on a farm versus in a city, or in a culture on the other side of the world? What beliefs would you cling to if you lived in the 1700s?

You've already learned from debate champions and expert negotiators that asking people questions can motivate them to rethink their

---

*This isn't to say that stereotypes never have a basis in reality. Psychologists find that when comparing groups, many stereotypes match up with the average in a group, but that doesn't mean they're useful for understanding individual members of the group. Thousands of years ago, when it was rare to interact with different groups, beliefs about the tendencies of different tribes might have helped our ancestors protect their own tribe. Yet today, when intergroup interactions are so common, assumptions about a group no longer have the same utility: it's much more helpful to learn something about individuals. The same psychologists have shown that our stereotypes become consistently and increasingly inaccurate when we're in conflict with another group—and when we're judging the ideologies of groups that are very different from our own. When a stereotype spills over into prejudice, it's a clue that it might be time to think again.

conclusions. What's different about these kinds of counterfactual questions is that they invite people to explore the origins of their own beliefs—and reconsider their stances toward other groups.

People gain humility when they reflect on how different circumstances could have led them to different beliefs. They might conclude that some of their past convictions had been too simplistic and begin to question some of their negative views. That doubt could leave them more curious about groups they've stereotyped, and they might end up discovering some unexpected commonalities.

Recently, I stumbled onto an opportunity to encourage some counterfactual thinking. A startup founder asked me to join an all-hands meeting to share insights on how to better understand other people's personalities and our own. During our virtual fireside chat, she mentioned that she was an astrology fan and the company was full of them. I wondered if I could get some of them to see that they held inaccurate stereotypes about people based on the month in which they happened to be born. Here's an excerpt of what happened:

Me: You know we have no evidence whatsoever that horoscopes influence personality, right?

Founder: That's such a Capricorn thing to say.

Me: I think I'm a Leo. I'd love to find out what evidence would change your mind.

Founder: So my partner has been trying for as long as we've been dating. He's given up. There's nothing that can convince me otherwise.

Me: Then you're not thinking like a scientist. This is a religion for you.

Founder: Yeah, well, maybe a little.

Me: What if you'd been born in China instead of the U.S.? Some evidence just came out that if you're a Virgo in China, you get discriminated against in hiring and also in dating. These poor Virgos are stereotyped as being difficult and ornery.*

Founder: So in the West, Adam, that same discrimination happens to Scorpios.

Although the founder started out resistant to my argument, after considering how she might hold different stereotypes if she lived in China, she recognized a familiar pattern. She'd seen an entire group of people mistreated as a result of the positions of the sun and the moon on the day they happened to enter the world.

Realizing how unfair discrimination based on zodiac signs was, the founder ended up jumping in to help me build my case. As we wrapped up the conversation, I offered to do a follow-up discussion on the science of personality. More than a quarter of the company signed up to participate. Afterward, one of the participants wrote that "the biggest takeaway from this chat is the importance of 'unlearning' things to avoid being ignorant." Having grasped how arbitrary their stereotypes were, people were now more open to rethinking their views.

Psychologists find that many of our beliefs are cultural truisms: widely shared, but rarely questioned. If we take a closer look at them, we often discover that they rest on shaky foundations. Stereotypes don't have the structural integrity of a carefully built ship. They're more like a tower in the game of Jenga—teetering on a small number of blocks, with some key supports missing. To knock it over, sometimes all we need to do is

---

*Psychologists have actually studied this recently and found that the arbitrary names of zodiac signs can give rise to stereotypes and discrimination. Virgo was translated into Chinese as "virgin," which calls to mind prejudice against old virgins—spinsters—as critical, germophobic, fussy, and picky.

give it a poke. The hope is that people will rise to the occasion and build new beliefs on a stronger foundation.

Can this approach extend to bigger divisions among people? To find out, we recruited people on opposite sides of the abortion debate. When we asked them to write notes to each other, they preached the virtues of their own views and prosecuted their opponents for being "devil worshipers who sacrificed children" and "misogynists who pretend to care." But when we randomly assigned some of them to consider how they might hold different beliefs if they'd been born in a different household or a different decade, their hostility melted away: "Thank you for sharing your point of view. I respectfully disagree with your position" and "I understand where you are coming from and it is a valid opinion, though not one I necessarily agree with." They were even more willing to date someone from the other side—their openness climbed from under 60 percent to over 70 percent.

I don't believe for a minute that counterfactual thinking will solve the Israel-Palestine conflict or stop racism. I do think it's a step, though, toward something more fundamental than merely rethinking our stereotypes. We might question the underlying belief that it makes sense to hold opinions about groups at all.

If you get people to pause and reflect, they might decide that the very notion of applying group stereotypes to individuals is absurd. Research suggests that there are more similarities between groups than we recognize. And there's typically more variety within groups than between them.

Sometimes letting go of stereotypes means realizing that many members of a hated group aren't so terrible after all. And that's more likely to happen when we actually come face-to-face with them. For over half a century, social scientists have tested the effects of intergroup contact. In a meta-analysis of over five hundred studies with over 250,000 participants, interacting with members of another group reduced prejudice in 94 percent of the cases. Although intergroup communication isn't a panacea, that is a staggering statistic. The most effective way to help people pull the unsteady Jenga blocks out of their stereotype towers is to talk with them in person. Which is precisely what Daryl Davis did.

HOW A BLACK MUSICIAN CONFRONTS WHITE SUPREMACISTS

One day, Daryl was driving his car with the chief officer of a KKK chapter, whose official title was Exalted Cyclops. Before long, the Cyclops was sharing his stereotypes of Black people. They were an inferior species, he said—they had smaller brains, which made them unintelligent, and a genetic predisposition toward violence. When Daryl pointed out that he was Black but had never shot anyone or stolen a car, the Cyclops told him his criminal gene must be latent. It hadn't come out yet.

Daryl decided to beat the Cyclops at his own game. He challenged him to name three Black serial killers. When the Cyclops couldn't name any, Daryl rattled off a long list of well-known white serial killers and told the Cyclops that *he* must be one. When the Cyclops protested that he'd never killed anybody, Daryl turned his own argument against him and said that his serial-killer gene must be latent.

"Well, that's stupid," the flustered Cyclops replied. "Well, duh!" Daryl agreed. "You're right. What I said about you was stupid, but no more stupid than what you said about me." The Cyclops got very quiet and changed the subject. Several months later, he told Daryl that he was still thinking about that conversation. Daryl had planted a seed of doubt and made him curious about his own beliefs. The Cyclops ended up quitting the KKK and giving his hood and his robe to Daryl.

Daryl is obviously extraordinary—not only in his ability to wage a one-man war on prejudice, but also in his inclination to do so. As a general rule, it's those with greater power who need to do more of the rethinking, both because they're more likely to privilege their own perspectives and because their perspectives are more likely to go unquestioned. In most cases, the oppressed and marginalized have already done a great deal of contortion to fit in.

Having been the target of racism since childhood, Daryl had a lifetime of legitimate reasons to harbor animosity toward white people. He was still willing to approach white supremacists with an open mind and give them the opportunity to rethink their views. But it shouldn't have been Daryl's responsibility to challenge white supremacists and put himself at risk. In an ideal world, the Cyclops would have taken it upon himself to educate his peers. Some other former KKK members have stepped up, working independently and with Daryl to advocate for the oppressed and reform the structures that produce oppression in the first place.

As we work toward systemic change, Daryl urges us not to overlook the power of conversation. When we choose not to engage with people because of their stereotypes or prejudice, we give up on opening their minds. "We are living in space-age times, yet there are still so many of us thinking with stone-age minds," he reflects. "Our ideology needs to catch up to our technology." He estimates that he has helped upwards of two hundred white supremacists rethink their beliefs and leave the KKK and other neo-Nazi groups. Many of them have gone on to educate their families and friends. Daryl is quick to point out that he hasn't directly persuaded these men to change their minds. "I didn't convert anybody," he says. "I gave them reason to think about their direction in life, and they thought about it, and thought, 'I need a better path, and this is the way to go.'"

Daryl doesn't do this by preaching or prosecuting. When he begins a dialogue with white supremacists, many are initially surprised by his thoughtfulness. As they start to see him as an individual and spend more time with him, they often tap into a common identity around shared interests in topics like music. Over time, he helps them see that they joined these hate groups for reasons that weren't their own—it was a family tradition dating back multiple generations, or someone had told them their jobs were being taken by Black men. As they realize how little they truly know about other groups, and how shallow stereotypes are, they start to think again.

After getting to know Daryl, one Imperial Wizard didn't stop at leaving the KKK. He shut down the chapter. Years later, he asked Daryl to be his daughter's godfather.

CHAPTER 7

Vaccine Whisperers and Mild-Mannered Interrogators

How the Right Kind of Listening Motivates People to Change

□ □ □

> It's a rare person who wants to hear
> what he doesn't want to hear.
>
> —ATTRIBUTED TO DICK CAVETT

When Marie-Hélène Étienne-Rousseau went into labor, she broke down in tears. It was September 2018, and her baby wasn't due until December. Just before midnight, Tobie arrived, weighing just two pounds. His body was so tiny that his head could fit in the palm of her hand, and Marie-Hélène was terrified that he wouldn't survive. Tobie spent only a few seconds in her arms before he was rushed to the neonatal intensive care unit. He needed a mask to breathe and was soon taken to surgery for internal bleeding. It would be months before he was allowed to go home.

While Tobie was still in the hospital, Marie-Hélène was shopping for diapers when she saw a headline about measles spreading in her province of Quebec. She hadn't had Tobie vaccinated. It wasn't even a question—he seemed too fragile. She hadn't vaccinated her three other children, either; it wasn't the norm in her community. Her friends and neighbors took it for granted that vaccines were dangerous and passed around horror stories about their side effects. Still, the fact remained: Quebec had already had two serious measles outbreaks that decade.

Today in the developed world, measles is on the rise for the first time in at least half a century, and its mortality rate is around one in a thousand. In the developing world, it's closer to one in a hundred. Estimates suggest that from 2016 to 2018, measles deaths spiked worldwide by 58 percent, with over a hundred thousand casualties. These deaths could have been prevented by the vaccine, which has saved roughly 20 million lives in the past two decades. Although epidemiologists recommend two doses of the measles vaccine and a minimum immunization rate of 95 percent, around the globe only 85 percent of people get the first dose and just 67 percent continue to the second. Many of those who skip the shot simply do not believe in the science.

Government officials have tried to prosecute the problem, some warning that the unvaccinated could be fined up to a thousand dollars and sentenced to jail for up to six months. Many schools shut their doors to unvaccinated children, and one county even banned them from enclosed public places. When such measures failed to solve the problem, public officials turned to preaching. Since people held unfounded fears about vaccines, it was time to educate them with a dose of the truth.

The results were often disappointing. In a pair of experiments in Germany, introducing people to the research on vaccine safety backfired: they ended up seeing vaccines as riskier. Similarly, when Americans read accounts of the dangers of measles, saw pictures of children suffering from it, or learned of an infant who nearly died from it, their interest in vaccination didn't rise at all. And when they were informed that there was no evidence that the measles vaccine causes autism, those who already had concerns actually became less interested in vaccinating. It seemed that no logical argument or data-driven explanation could shake their conviction that vaccines were unsafe.

This is a common problem in persuasion: what doesn't sway us can make our beliefs stronger. Much like a vaccine inoculates our physical immune system against a virus, the act of resistance fortifies our psychological immune system. Refuting a point of view produces antibodies against future influence attempts. We become more certain of our opinions and less curious about alternative views. Counterarguments no longer surprise us or stump us—we have our rebuttals ready.

Marie-Hélène Étienne-Rousseau had been through that journey. Visits to the doctor with her older kids followed a familiar script. The doctor extolled the benefits of vaccines, warned her about the risks of refusing them, and stuck to generic messaging instead of engaging with her particular questions. The whole experience reeked of condescension. Marie-Hélène felt as if she were being attacked, "as if she were accusing me of wanting my kids to get sick. As if I were a bad mother."

When tiny Tobie was finally cleared to leave after five months in the hospital, he was still extremely vulnerable. The nurses knew it was their last chance to have him vaccinated, so they called in a vaccine whisperer—a local doctor with a radical approach for helping young parents rethink their resistance to immunizations. He didn't preach to parents or prosecute them. He didn't get political. He put on his scientist hat and interviewed them.

MOTIVATING THROUGH INTERVIEWING

In the early 1980s, a clinical psychologist named Bill Miller was troubled by his field's attitude toward people with addictions. It was common for therapists and counselors to accuse their substance-abusing clients of being pathological liars who were living in denial. That didn't track with what Miller was seeing up close in his own work treating people with alcohol problems, where preaching and prosecuting typically boomeranged. "People who drink too much are usually aware of it," Miller told me. "If you try to persuade them that they do drink too much or need to make a change, you evoke resistance, and they are less likely to change."

Instead of attacking or demeaning his clients, Miller started asking them questions and listening to their answers. Soon afterward, he published a paper on his philosophy, which found its way into the hands of Stephen Rollnick, a young nurse trainee working in addiction treatment. A few years later, the two happened to meet in Australia and realized that what they were exploring was much bigger than just a new approach to treatment. It was an entirely different way of helping people change.

Together, they developed the core principles of a practice called motivational interviewing. The central premise is that we can rarely motivate someone else to change. We're better off helping them find their own motivation to change.

Let's say you're a student at Hogwarts, and you're worried your uncle is a fan of Voldemort. A motivational interview might go like this:

You: I'd love to better understand your feelings about He Who Must Not Be Named.

Uncle: Well, he's the most powerful wizard alive. Also, his followers promised me a fancy title.

You: Interesting. Is there anything you dislike about him?

Uncle: Hmm. I'm not crazy about all the murdering.

You: Well, nobody's perfect.

Uncle: Yeah, but the killing is really bad.

You: Sounds like you have some reservations about Voldemort. What's stopped you from abandoning him?

Uncle: I'm afraid he might direct the murdering toward me.

You: That's a reasonable fear. I've felt it too. I'm curious: are there any principles that matter so deeply to you that you'd be willing to take that risk?

Motivational interviewing starts with an attitude of humility and curiosity. We don't know what might motivate someone else to change, but we're genuinely eager to find out. The goal isn't to tell people what to do; it's to help them break out of overconfidence cycles and see new possibilities. Our role is to hold up a mirror so they can see themselves more clearly, and then empower them to examine their beliefs and behaviors. That can activate a rethinking cycle, in which people approach their own views more scientifically. They develop more humility about their knowledge, doubt in their convictions, and curiosity about alternative points of view.

The process of motivational interviewing involves three key techniques:

- Asking open-ended questions
- Engaging in reflective listening
- Affirming the person's desire and ability to change

As Marie-Hélène was getting ready to take Tobie home, the vaccine whisperer the nurses called was a neonatologist and researcher named

Arnaud Gagneur. His specialty was applying the techniques of motivational interviewing to vaccination discussions. When Arnaud sat down with Marie-Hélène, he didn't judge her for not vaccinating her children, nor did he order her to change. He was like a scientist or "a less abrasive Socrates," as journalist Eric Boodman described him in reporting on their meeting.

Arnaud told Marie-Hélène he was afraid of what might happen if Tobie got the measles, but he accepted her decision and wanted to understand it better. For over an hour, he asked her open-ended questions about how she had reached the decision not to vaccinate. He listened carefully to her answers, acknowledging that the world is full of confusing information about vaccine safety. At the end of the discussion, Arnaud reminded Marie-Hélène that she was free to choose whether or not to immunize, and he trusted her ability and intentions.

Before Marie-Hélène left the hospital, she had Tobie vaccinated. A key turning point, she recalls, was when Arnaud "told me that whether I chose to vaccinate or not, he respected my decision as someone who wanted the best for my kids. Just that sentence—to me, it was worth all the gold in the world."

Marie-Hélène didn't just allow Tobie to be vaccinated—she had his older siblings vaccinated at home by a public health nurse. She even asked if Arnaud would speak with her sister-in-law about vaccinating her children. She said her decision was unusual enough in her antivaccination community that "it was like setting off a bomb."

Marie-Hélène Étienne-Rousseau is one of many parents who have undergone a conversion like this. Vaccine whisperers don't just help people change their beliefs; they help them change their behaviors, too. In Arnaud's first study, with mothers in the maternity ward after birth, 72 percent said they planned to vaccinate their children; after a motivational interviewing session with a vaccine counselor, 87 percent were onboard. In Arnaud's next experiment, if mothers attended a motivational interviewing session, children were 9 percent more likely to be fully vaccinated two years later. If this sounds like a small effect, remember that it was the result of only a single conversation in the maternity ward—and it was sufficient to change behavior as far out as twenty-four months later. Soon the government health ministry was investing millions of dollars in Arnaud's motivational interviewing program, with a plan to send vaccine whisperers into the maternity wards of every hospital in Quebec.

Today, motivational interviewing is used around the world by tens of thousands of practitioners—there are registered trainers throughout America and in many parts of Europe, and courses to build the necessary skills are offered as widely as Argentina, Malaysia, and South Africa. Motivational interviewing has been the subject of more than a thousand controlled trials; a bibliography that simply lists them runs sixty-seven pages. It's been used effectively by health professionals to help people stop smoking, abusing drugs and alcohol, gambling, and having unsafe sex, as well as to improve their diets and exercise habits, overcome eating disorders, and lose weight. It's also been applied successfully by coaches to build grit in professional soccer players, teachers to nudge students to get a full night's sleep, consultants to prepare teams for organizational change, public health workers to encourage people to disinfect water in Zambia, and environmental activists to help people do something about climate change. Similar techniques have opened the minds of prejudiced voters, and when conflict mediators help separated parents resolve disputes about their children, motivational interviewing is twice as likely to result in a full agreement as standard mediation.

Overall, motivational interviewing has a statistically and clinically meaningful effect on behavior change in roughly three out of four studies, and psychologists and physicians using it have a success rate of four in five. There aren't many practical theories in the behavioral sciences with a body of evidence this robust.

Motivational interviewing isn't limited to professional settings—it's relevant to everyday decisions and interactions. One day a friend called me for advice on whether she should get back together with her ex. I was a fan of the idea, but I didn't think it was my place to tell her what to do. Instead of offering my opinion, I asked her to walk through the pros and cons and tell me how they stacked up against what she wanted in a partner. She ended up talking herself into rekindling the relationship. The conversation felt like magic, because I hadn't tried to persuade her or even given any advice.*

When people ignore advice, it isn't always because they disagree with it. Sometimes they're resisting the sense of pressure and the feeling that someone else is controlling their decision. To protect their freedom, instead of giving commands or offering recommendations, a motivational interviewer might say something along the lines of "Here are a few things that have helped me—do you think any of them might work for you?"

BAD MOTIVATION
B I N G O

Scare tactics	Withholding love	Telling me it's for my own good	Trying to make it seem like it was my idea
Yelling	Demeaning	Withholding support	Lecturing
Manipulation	Not listening to what I have to say	Dismissing my feelings	Dismissing my ideas
Belittling me	Withholding respect	Passive-aggressiveness	Shaming

---

*It seems that humans have understood the magic of talking ourselves into change for thousands of years. I learned recently that the word *abracadabra* comes from a Hebrew phrase that means "I create as I speak."

You've seen how asking questions can help with self-persuasion. Motivational interviewing goes a step further, guiding others to self-discovery. You got a glimpse of it in action when Daryl Davis asked KKK members how they could hate him when they didn't even know him, and now I want to unpack the relevant techniques in depth. When we try to convince people to think again, our first instinct is usually to start talking. Yet the most effective way to help others open their minds is often to listen.

BEYOND THE CLINIC

Years ago I got a call asking for help from a biotechnology startup. The CEO, Jeff, was a scientist by training; he liked to have all the necessary data before making a decision. After more than a year and a half at the helm, he still hadn't rolled out a vision for the company, and it was in danger of failing. A trio of consultants tried to convince him to offer some direction, and he fired them all. Before the head of HR threw in the towel, she threw a Hail Mary pass and contacted an academic. It was the perfect time for a motivational interview: Jeff seemed reluctant to change, and I had no idea why. When we met, I decided to see if I could help him find his motivation to change. Here are the pivotal moments from our conversation:

Me: I really enjoy being the guy who gets hired after three consultants get fired. I'd love to hear how they screwed up.

Jeff: The first consultant gave me answers instead of asking questions. That was arrogant: how could he solve a problem before he'd even taken the time to understand it? The next two did a better job learning from me, but they still ended up trying to tell me how to do my job.

Me: So why did you bother to bring in another outsider?

Jeff: I'm looking for some fresh ideas on leadership.

Me: It's not my place to tell you how to lead. What does leadership mean to you?

Jeff: Making systemic decisions, having a well-thought-out strategy.

Me: Are there any leaders you admire for those qualities?

Jeff: Abraham Lincoln, Martin Luther King Jr., Steve Jobs.

That was a turning point. In motivational interviewing, there's a distinction between sustain talk and change talk. Sustain talk is commentary about maintaining the status quo. Change talk is referencing a desire, ability, need, or commitment to make adjustments. When contemplating a change, many people are ambivalent—they have some reasons to consider it but also some reasons to stay the course. Miller and Rollnick suggest asking about and listening for change talk, and then posing some questions about why and how they might change.

Say you have a friend who mentions a desire to stop smoking. You might respond by asking why she's considering quitting. If she says a doctor recommended it, you might follow up by inquiring about her own motivations: what does she think of the idea? If she offers a reason why she's determined to stop, you might ask what her first step toward quitting could be. "Change talk is a golden thread," clinical psychologist Theresa Moyers says. "What you need to do is you need to pick that thread up and pull it." So that's what I did with Jeff.

Me: What do you appreciate most about the leaders you named?

Jeff: They all had vivid visions. They inspired people to achieve extraordinary things.

Me: Interesting. If Steve Jobs were in your shoes right now, what do you think he'd do?

Jeff: He'd probably get his leadership team fired up about a bold idea and create a reality distortion field to make it seem possible. Maybe I should do that, too.

A few weeks later, Jeff stood up at an executive off-site to deliver his first-ever vision speech. When I heard about it, I was beaming with pride: I had conquered my inner logic bully and led him to find his own motivation.

Unfortunately, the board ended up shutting down the company anyway.

Jeff's speech had fallen flat. He stumbled through notes on a napkin and didn't stir up enthusiasm about the company's direction. I had overlooked a key step—helping him think about how to execute the change effectively.

There's a fourth technique of motivational interviewing, which is often recommended for the end of a conversation and for transition points: summarizing. The idea is to explain your understanding of other people's reasons for change, to check on whether you've missed or misrepresented anything, and to inquire about their plans and possible next steps.

The objective is not to be a leader or a follower, but a guide. Miller and Rollnick liken it to hiring a tour guide in a foreign country: we don't want her to order us around, but we don't want her to follow us around, either. I was so excited that Jeff had decided to share his vision that I didn't ask any questions about what it was—or how he would present it. I had worked with him to rethink whether and when to give a speech, but not what was in it.

If I could go back, I'd ask Jeff how he was considering conveying his message and how he thought his team would receive it. A good guide doesn't stop at helping people change their beliefs or behaviors. Our work isn't done until we've helped them accomplish their goals.

Part of the beauty of motivational interviewing is that it generates more openness in both directions. Listening can encourage others to reconsider their stance toward us, but it also gives us information that can lead us to question our own views about them. If we take the practices of motivational interviewing seriously, we might become the ones who think again.

It's not hard to grasp how motivational interviewing can be effective for consultants, doctors, therapists, teachers, and coaches. When people have sought out our assistance—or accepted that it's our job to help—we're in a position to earn their trust. Yet we all face situations in which we're tempted to steer people in the direction we prefer. Parents and mentors often believe they know what's best for their children and protégés.

WILL YOU CHANGE MY MIND?

Salespeople, fundraisers, and entrepreneurs have a vested interest in getting to yes.

Motivational interviewing pioneers Miller and Rollnick have long
warned that the technique shouldn't be used manipulatively. Psychologists
have found that when people detect an attempt at influence, they have
sophisticated defense mechanisms. The moment people feel that we're
trying to persuade them, our behavior takes on a different meaning. A
straightforward question is seen as a political tactic, a reflective listening
statement comes across as a prosecutor's maneuvering, an affirmation
of their ability to change sounds like a preacher's proselytizing.

Motivational interviewing requires a genuine desire to help people
reach their goals. Jeff and I both wanted his company to succeed. Marie-
Hélène and Arnaud both wanted Tobie to be healthy. If your goals don't
seem to be aligned, how do you help people change their own minds?

THE ART OF INFLUENTIAL LISTENING

Betty Bigombe had already hiked eight miles through the jungle, and
there was still no sign of life. She was no stranger to a long walk: growing
up in northern Uganda, she walked four miles each way to school. She
subsisted on one meal a day in a communal homestead where her uncle
had eight wives. Now she had made it all the way to the Ugandan Parliament, and she was undertaking a challenge that none of her colleagues
would brave: trying to make peace with a warlord.

Joseph Kony was the leader of the Lord's Resistance Army. He and
his rebel group would eventually be held responsible for murdering over
a hundred thousand people, abducting over thirty thousand children,
and displacing over two million Ugandans. In the early 1990s, Betty
convinced the Ugandan president to send her in to see if she could stop
the violence.

When Betty finally made contact with the rebels after months of effort, they were insulted at the prospect of negotiating with a woman. Yet Betty negotiated her way into getting permission to meet Kony himself. Soon he was referring to her as Mummy, and he even agreed to leave the jungle to start peace talks. Although the peace effort didn't succeed, opening Kony's mind to conversation was a remarkable accomplishment in itself.* For her efforts to end the violence, Betty was named Uganda's Woman of the Year. When I spoke to her recently, I asked how she had succeeded in getting through to Kony and his people. The key, she explained, was not persuading or even coaxing, but listening.

Listening well is more than a matter of talking less. It's a set of skills in asking and responding. It starts with showing more interest in other people's interests rather than trying to judge their status or prove our own. We can all get better at asking "truly curious questions that don't have the hidden agenda of fixing, saving, advising, convincing or correcting," journalist Kate Murphy writes, and helping to "facilitate the clear expression of another person's thoughts."†

When we're trying to get people to change, that can be a difficult task. Even if we have the best intentions, we can easily slip into the mode of a preacher perched on a pulpit, a prosecutor making a closing argument, or a politician giving a stump speech. We're all vulnerable to the "righting reflex," as Miller and Rollnick describe it—the desire to fix problems and offer answers. A skilled motivational interviewer resists the righting reflex—although people want a doctor to fix their broken bones, when it comes to the problems in their heads, they often want sympathy rather than solutions.

---

*The peace talks fell apart when the Ugandan president disregarded Betty's request to set the ground rules for the peace talks and instead publicly threatened Kony, who retaliated by massacring several hundred people in Atiak. Devastated, Betty left and went to work for the World Bank. A decade later, she initiated another round of peace talks with the rebels. She returned to Uganda as the chief mediator, spending her own money instead of accepting funds from the government so she could work independently. She was on the verge of success when Kony backed out at the last minute. Today, his rebel army has shrunk to a fraction of its original size and is no longer considered a major threat.

†Quaker retreats have "clearness committees" that serve this very purpose, posing questions to help people crystallize their thinking and resolve their dilemmas.

That's what Betty Bigombe set out to provide in Uganda. She started traveling through rural areas to visit camps for internally displaced people. She figured some might have relatives in Joseph Kony's army and might know something of his whereabouts. Although she hadn't been trained in motivational interviewing, she intuitively understood the philosophy. At each camp, she announced to people that she wasn't there to lecture them, but to listen to them.

Her curiosity and confident humility caught the Ugandans by surprise. Other peacemakers had come in ordering them to stop fighting. They had preached about their own plans for conflict resolution and prosecuted the past efforts that failed. Now Betty, a politician by profession, wasn't telling them what to do. She just sat patiently for hours in front of a bonfire, taking notes and chiming in from time to time to ask questions. "If you want to call me names, feel free to do so," she said. "If you want me to leave, I will."

To demonstrate her commitment to peace, Betty stayed in the camps even though they lacked sufficient food and proper sanitation. She invited people to air their grievances and suggest remedial measures to be taken. They told her that it was rare and refreshing for an outsider to give them the opportunity to share their views. She empowered them to generate their own solutions, which gave them a sense of ownership. They ended up calling her Megu, which translates literally to "mother" and is also a term of endearment for elders. Bestowing this honorific was particularly striking since Betty was representing the government—which was seen as the oppressor in many of the camps. It wasn't long before people were offering to introduce her to coordinators and commanders in Joseph Kony's guerrilla army. As Betty muses, "Even the devil appreciates being listened to."

In a series of experiments, interacting with an empathetic, nonjudgmental, attentive listener made people less anxious and defensive. They felt less pressure to avoid contradictions in their thinking, which encouraged them to explore their opinions more deeply, recognize more nuances in them, and share them more openly. These benefits of listening aren't limited to one-on-one interactions—they can also emerge in groups. In experiments across government organizations, tech companies, and schools, people's attitudes became more complex and less extreme after they sat in a listening circle, where one person at a time held a talking stick and everyone else listened attentively. Psychologists recommend practicing this skill by sitting down with people whom we sometimes have a hard time understanding. The idea is to tell them that we're working on being better listeners, we'd like to hear their thoughts, and we'll listen for a few minutes before responding.

Many communicators try to make themselves look smart. Great listeners are more interested in making their audiences feel smart. They help people approach their own views with more humility, doubt, and curiosity. When people have a chance to express themselves out loud, they often discover new thoughts. As the writer E. M. Forster put it, "How can I tell what I think till I see what I say?" That understanding made Forster an unusually dedicated listener. In the words of one biographer, "To speak with him was to be seduced by an inverse charisma, a sense of being listened to with such intensity that you had to be your most honest, sharpest, and best self."

Inverse charisma. What a wonderful turn of phrase to capture the magnetic quality of a great listener. Think about how rare that kind of listening is. Among managers rated as the worst listeners by their employees, 94 percent of them evaluated themselves as good or very good listeners. *Dunning and Kruger might have something to say about that.* In one poll, a third of women said their pets were better listeners than their partners. *Maybe it wasn't just my kids who wanted a cat.* It's common for doctors to interrupt their patients within 11 seconds, even though patients may need only 29 seconds to describe their symptoms. In Quebec, however, Marie-Hélène experienced something very different.

When Marie-Hélène explained that she was concerned about autism and the effects of administering multiple vaccines simultaneously, Arnaud didn't bombard her with a barrage of scientific facts. He asked what her sources were. Like many parents, she said she had read about vaccines on the internet but didn't remember where. He agreed that in a sea of conflicting claims, it's difficult to gain a clear sense of whether immunization is safe.

Eventually, when he understood Marie-Hélène's beliefs, Arnaud asked if he could share some information about vaccines based on his own expertise. "I started a dialogue," he told me. "The aim was to build a trusting relationship. If you present information without permission, no one will listen to you." Arnaud was able to address her fears and misconceptions by explaining that the measles vaccine is a weakened live virus, so the symptoms are typically minimal, and there's no evidence that it increases autism or other syndromes. He wasn't delivering a lecture; he was engaging in a discussion. Marie-Hélène's questions guided the evidence he shared, and they reconstructed her knowledge together. Every step of the way, Arnaud avoided putting pressure on her. Even after talking through the science, he concluded the conversation by telling her he would let her think about it, affirming her freedom to make up her own mind.

In 2020, during the worst snowstorm of the winter, a married couple drove an hour and a half to visit Arnaud. They hadn't vaccinated any of their children, but after forty-five minutes of discussion with him, they decided to vaccinate all four of them. The couple lived in Marie-Hélène's village, and seeing other children vaccinated there made the mother curious enough to seek more information.

The power of listening doesn't lie just in giving people the space to reflect on their views. It's a display of respect and an expression of care. When Arnaud took the time to understand Marie-Hélène's concerns instead of dismissing them, he was showing a sincere interest in her wellbeing and that of her son. When Betty Bigombe stayed with displaced Ugandans in their camps and asked them to air their grievances, she was proving that what they had to say mattered to her. Listening is a way of offering others our scarcest, most precious gift: our attention. Once we've demonstrated that we care about them and their goals, they're more willing to listen to us.

If we can convince a mother to vaccinate her vulnerable children—or a warlord to consider peace talks—it's easy to conclude that the ends justify whatever means are necessary. But it's worth remembering that the means are a measure of our character. When we succeed in changing someone's mind, we shouldn't only ask whether we're proud of what we've achieved. We should also ask whether we're proud of how we've achieved it.

PART III

Collective Rethinking

Creating Communities of Lifelong Learners

CHAPTER 8

Charged Conversations

Depolarizing Our Divided Discussions

□ □ □

When conflict is cliché, complexity is breaking news.

—AMANDA RIPLEY

E ager to have a jaw-clenching, emotionally fraught argument about
abortion? How about immigration, the death penalty, or climate
change? If you think you can handle it, head for the second floor of
a brick building on the Columbia University campus in New York. It's
the home of the Difficult Conversations Lab.

If you're brave enough to visit, you'll be matched up with a stranger
who strongly disagrees with your views on a controversial topic. You'll be
given just twenty minutes to discuss the issue, and then you'll both have
to decide whether you've aligned enough to write and sign a joint statement on your shared views around abortion laws. If you're able to do
so—no small feat—your statement will be posted on a public forum.

For two decades, the psychologist who runs the lab, Peter T. Coleman, has been bringing people together to talk about polarizing issues.
His mission is to reverse-engineer the successful conversations and then
experiment with recipes to make more of them.

To put you in the right mindset before you begin your conversation about abortion, Peter gives you and the stranger a news article about another divisive issue: gun control. What you don't know is that there are different versions of the gun control article, and which one you read is going to have a major impact on whether you land on the same page about abortion.

If the gun control article covers both sides of the issue, making a balanced case for both gun rights and gun legislation, you and your adversary have a decent chance at reaching consensus on abortion. In one of Peter's experiments, after reading a "both-sides" article, 46 percent of pairs were able to find enough common ground to draft and sign a statement together. That's a remarkable result.

But Peter went on to do something far more impressive. He randomly assigned some pairs to read another version of the same article, which led 100 percent of them to generate and sign a joint statement about abortion laws.

That version of the article featured the same information but presented it differently. Instead of describing the issue as a black-and-white disagreement between two sides, the article framed the debate as a complex problem with many shades of gray, representing a number of different viewpoints.

At the turn of the last century, the great hope for the internet was that it would expose us to different views. But as the web welcomed a few billion fresh voices and vantage points into the conversation, it also became a weapon of misinformation and disinformation. By the 2016 elections, as the problem of political polarization became more extreme and more visible, the solution seemed obvious to me. We needed to burst filter bubbles in our news feeds and shatter echo chambers in our networks. If we could just show people the other side of an issue, they would open their minds and become more informed. Peter's research challenges that assumption.

We now know that where complicated issues are concerned, seeing the opinions of the other side is not enough. Social media platforms have exposed us to them, but they haven't changed our minds. Knowing another side exists isn't sufficient to leave preachers doubting whether they're on the right side of morality, prosecutors questioning whether they're on the right side of the case, or politicians wondering whether they're on the right side of history. Hearing an opposing opinion doesn't necessarily motivate you to rethink your own stance; it makes it easier for you to stick to your guns (or your gun bans). Presenting two extremes isn't the solution; it's part of the polarization problem.

Psychologists have a name for this: binary bias. It's a basic human tendency to seek clarity and closure by simplifying a complex continuum into two categories. To paraphrase the humorist Robert Benchley, there are two kinds of people: those who divide the world into two kinds of people, and those who don't.

An antidote to this proclivity is complexifying: showcasing the range of perspectives on a given topic. We might believe we're making progress by discussing hot-button issues as two sides of a coin, but people are actually more inclined to think again if we present these topics through the many lenses of a prism. To borrow a phrase from Walt Whitman, it takes a multitude of views to help people realize that they too contain multitudes.

A dose of complexity can disrupt overconfidence cycles and spur rethinking cycles. It gives us more humility about our knowledge and more doubts about our opinions, and it can make us curious enough to discover information we were lacking. In Peter's experiment, all it took was framing gun control not as an issue with only two extreme positions but rather as one involving many interrelated dilemmas. As journalist Amanda Ripley describes it, the gun control article "read less like a lawyer's opening statement and more like an anthropologist's field notes." Those field notes were enough to help pro-life and pro-choice advocates find some areas of agreement on abortion in only twenty minutes.

The article didn't just leave people open to rethinking their views on abortion; they also reconsidered their positions on other divisive issues like affirmative action and the death penalty.* If people read the binary version of the article, they defended their own perspective more often than they showed an interest in their opponent's. If they read the complexified version, they made about twice as many comments about common ground as about their own views. They asserted fewer opinions and asked more questions. At the end of the conversation, they generated more sophisticated, higher-quality position statements—and both parties came away more satisfied.

For a long time, I struggled with how to handle politics in this book. I don't have any silver bullets or simple bridges across a widening gulf. *I don't really even believe in political parties. As an organizational psychologist, I want to vet candidates' leadership skills before I worry about their policy positions. As a citizen, I believe it's my responsibility to form an independent opinion on each issue.* Eventually, I decided that the best way to stay above the fray was to explore the moments that affect us all as individuals: the charged conversations we have in person and online.

Resisting the impulse to simplify is a step toward becoming more argument literate. Doing so has profound implications for how we communicate about polarizing issues. In the traditional media, it can help journalists open people's minds to uncomfortable facts. On social media, it can help all of us have more productive Twitter tiffs and Facebook fights. At family gatherings, it might not land you on the same page as your least favorite uncle, but it could very well prevent a seemingly innocent conversation from exploding into an emotional inferno. And in discussions of policies that affect all of our lives, it might bring us better, more

---

* When media headlines proclaim a divided America on gun laws, they're missing a lot of complexity. Yes, there's a gap of 47 to 50 percentage points between Republicans and Democrats on support for banning and buying back assault weapons. Yet polls show bipartisan consensus on required background checks (supported by 83 percent of Republicans and 96 percent of Democrats) and mental health screenings (favored by 81 percent of Republicans and 94 percent of Democrats). Psychologists find that showing red vs. blue maps leads people to see America as more divided—and judge people more by their state's stereotypes. "Purple maps" with states in different shades of purple based on proportions of red and blue voters are enough to reduce perceived polarization and stereotypes.

practical solutions sooner. That's what this section of the book is about: applying rethinking to different parts of our lives, so that we can keep learning at every stage of our lives.

SOME INCONVENIENT TRUTHS

In 2006, Al Gore starred in a blockbuster film on climate change, *An Inconvenient Truth*. It won the Academy Award for Best Documentary and spawned a wave of activism, motivating businesses to go green and governments to pass legislation and sign landmark agreements to protect the planet. History teaches us that it sometimes takes a combination of preaching, prosecuting, and politicking to fuel that kind of dramatic swing.

Yet by 2018, only 59 percent of Americans saw climate change as a major threat—and 16 percent believed it wasn't a threat at all. Across many countries in Western Europe and Southeast Asia, higher percentages of the populations had opened their minds to the evidence that climate change is a dire problem. In the past decade in the United States, beliefs about climate change have hardly budged.

This thorny issue is a natural place to explore how we can bring more complexity into our conversations. Fundamentally, that involves drawing attention to the nuances that often get overlooked. It starts with seeking and spotlighting shades of gray.

A fundamental lesson of desirability bias is that our beliefs are shaped by our motivations. What we believe depends on what we *want* to believe. Emotionally, it can be unsettling for anyone to admit that all life as we know it might be in danger, but Americans have some additional reasons to be dubious about climate change. Politically, climate change has been branded in the United States as a liberal issue; in some conservative circles, merely acknowledging the fact that it might exist puts people on a fast track to exile. There's evidence that higher levels of education predict heightened concern about climate change among Democrats but dampened concern among Republicans. Economically, we remain confident that America will be more resilient in response to a changing climate than most of the world, and we're reluctant to sacrifice our current ways of achieving prosperity. These deep-seated beliefs are hard to change.

As a psychologist, I want to zoom in on another factor. It's one we can all control: the way we communicate about climate change. Many people believe that preaching with passion and conviction is necessary for persuasion. A clear example is Al Gore. When he narrowly lost the U.S. presidential election in 2000, one of the knocks against him was his energy—or lack thereof. People called him dry. Boring. Robotic. Fast-forward a few years: his film was riveting and his own platform skills had evolved dramatically. In 2016, when I watched Gore speak in the red circle at TED, his language was vivid, his voice pulsated with emotion, and his passion literally dripped off him in the form of sweat. *If a robot was ever controlling his brain, it short-circuited and left the human in charge.* "Some still doubt that we have the will to act," he boomed, "but I say the will to act is itself a renewable resource." The audience erupted in a standing ovation, and afterward he was called the Elvis of

TED. If it's not his communication style that's failing to reach people, what is?

At TED, Gore was preaching to the choir: his audience was heavily progressive. For audiences with more varied beliefs, his language hasn't always resonated. In *An Inconvenient Truth*, Gore contrasted the "truth" with claims made by "so-called skeptics." In a 2010 op-ed, he contrasted scientists with "climate deniers."

This is binary bias in action. It presumes that the world is divided into two sides: believers and nonbelievers. Only one side can be right, because there is only one truth. I don't blame Al Gore for taking that position; he was presenting rigorous data and representing the consensus of the scientific community. Because he was a recovering politician, seeing two sides to an issue must have been second nature. But when the only available options are black and white, it's natural to slip into a mentality of us versus them and to focus on the sides over the science. For those on the fence, when forced to choose a side, the emotional, political, and economic pressures tilt in favor of disengaging or dismissing the problem.

To overcome binary bias, a good starting point is to become aware of the range of perspectives across a given spectrum. Polls suggest that on climate change, there are at least six camps of thought. Believers represent more than half of Americans, but some are concerned while others are alarmed. The so-called nonbelievers actually range from cautious to disengaged to doubtful to dismissive.

It's especially important to distinguish skeptics from deniers. Skeptics have a healthy scientific stance: They don't believe everything they see, hear, or read. They ask critical questions and update their thinking as they gain access to new information. Deniers are in the dismissive camp, locked in preacher, prosecutor, or politician mode: They don't believe anything that comes from the other side. They ignore or twist facts to support their predetermined conclusions. As the Committee for Skeptical Inquiry put it in a plea to the media, skepticism is "foundational to the scientific method," whereas denial is "the *a priori* rejection of ideas without objective consideration."*

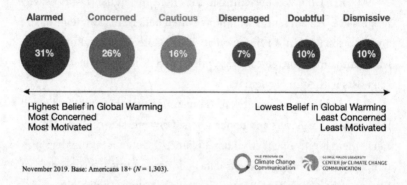

November 2019. Base: Americans 18+ (*N* = 1,303).

The complexity of this spectrum of beliefs is often missing from coverage of climate change. Although no more than 10 percent of Americans are dismissive of climate change, it's these rare deniers who get the most press. In an analysis of some hundred thousand media articles on climate change between 2000 and 2016, prominent climate contrarians received disproportionate coverage: they were featured 49 percent more often than expert scientists. As a result, people end up overestimating how common denial is—which in turn makes them more hesitant to advocate for policies that protect the environment. When the middle of the spectrum is invisible, the majority's will to act vanishes with it. *If other people aren't going to do anything about it, why should I bother?* When they become aware of just how many people are concerned about climate change, they're more prepared to do something about it.

---

* Climatologists go further, noting that within denial there are at least six different categories: arguing that (1) CO2 is not increasing; (2) even if CO2 is increasing, warming is not happening; (3) even if warming is happening, it's due to natural causes; (4) even if humans are causing warming, the impact is minimal; (5) even if the human impact is not trivial, it will be beneficial; and (6) before the situation becomes truly dire, we'll adapt or solve it. Experiments suggest that giving science deniers a public platform can backfire by spreading false beliefs, but rebutting their arguments or their techniques can help.

TALKING ABOUT CHARGED TOPICS

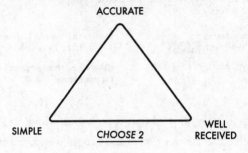

As consumers of information, we have a role to play in embracing a more nuanced point of view. When we're reading, listening, or watching, we can learn to recognize complexity as a signal of credibility. We can favor content and sources that present many sides of an issue rather than just one or two. When we come across simplifying headlines, we can fight our tendency to accept binaries by asking what additional perspectives are missing between the extremes.

This applies when we're the ones producing and communicating information, too. New research suggests that when journalists acknowledge the uncertainties around facts on complex issues like climate change and immigration, it doesn't undermine their readers' trust. And multiple experiments have shown that when experts express doubt, they become more persuasive. When someone knowledgeable admits uncertainty, it surprises people, and they end up paying more attention to the substance of the argument.

Of course, a potential challenge of nuance is that it doesn't seem to go viral. Attention spans are short: we have only a few seconds to capture eyeballs with a catchy headline. It's true that complexity doesn't always make for good sound bites, but it does seed great conversations. And some journalists have found clever ways to capture it in few words.

A few years ago, the media reported on a study of the cognitive consequences of coffee consumption. Although their headlines were drawn from the same data, some newspapers praised the benefits of coffee, while other outlets warned about the costs:

Here's More Evidence That Coffee Is Good For Your Brain Forbes

Study: Increasing Coffee Intake Harmful To Brain ⊚CBS Atlanta

Coffee Guards Against Mild Cognitive Impairment, Says Study BUSTLE

Here's why that extra cup of coffee is bad for your brain INDIA TODAY

The actual study showed that older adults who drank a daily cup or two of coffee had a lower risk of mild cognitive impairment, relative to abstainers, occasional consumers, and heavier consumers. If they increased their consumption by another cup or more per day, they had a higher risk than those who stayed at or below a single cup a day. Each of the one-sided headlines took seven to twelve words to mislead the reader about the effects of drinking coffee. A more accurate headline needed just twelve words to serve up a jolt of instant complexity:

Yesterday's coffee science: It's good for the brain. Today: Not so fast... The Washington Post

Imagine if even this kind of minimal nod to complexity appeared in articles on climate change. Scientists overwhelmingly agree about its human causes, but even they have a range of views on the actual effects—and the potential remedies. It's possible to be alarmed about the situation while recognizing the variety of ways to improve it.*

---

* When reporters and activists discuss the consequences of climate change, complexity is often lacking there as well. The gloom-and-doom message can create a burning platform for those who fear a burning planet. But research across twenty-four countries suggests that people are more motivated to act and advocate when they see the collective benefits of doing so—like economic and scientific advancement and building a more moral and caring community. People across the spectrum of climate skepticism, from alarmed to doubtful, are more determined to take initiative when they believe it would produce identifiable benefits. And instead of just appealing to stereotypical liberal values like compassion and justice, research suggests that journalists can spur more action by emphasizing crosscutting values like defending freedom as well as more conservative values like preserving the purity of nature or protecting the planet as an act of patriotism.

Psychologists find that people will ignore or even deny the existence of a problem if they're not fond of the solution. Liberals were more dismissive of the issue of intruder violence when they read an argument that strict gun control laws could make it difficult for homeowners to protect themselves. Conservatives were more receptive to climate science when they read about a green technology policy proposal than about an emissions restriction proposal.

Featuring shades of gray in discussions of solutions can help to shift attention from why climate change is a problem to how we can do something about it. As we've seen from the evidence on the illusion of explanatory depth, asking "how" tends to reduce polarization, setting the stage for more constructive conversations about action. Here are examples of headlines in which writers have hinted at the complexity of the solutions:

**I WORK IN THE ENVIRONMENTAL MOVEMENT.
I DON'T CARE IF YOU RECYCLE**

**CAN PLANTING A TRILLION TREES STOP CLIMATE CHANGE?
SCIENTISTS SAY IT'S A LOT MORE COMPLICATED**

SOME CAVEATS AND CONTINGENCIES

If you want to get better at conveying complexity, it's worth taking a close look at how scientists communicate. One key step is to include caveats. It's rare that a single study or even a series of studies is conclusive. Researchers typically feature multiple paragraphs about the limitations of each study in their articles. We see them less as holes in our work and more as portholes to future discoveries. When we share the findings with nonscientists, though, we sometimes gloss over these caveats.

That's a mistake, according to recent research. In a series of experiments, psychologists demonstrated that when news reports about science included caveats, they succeeded in capturing readers' interest and keeping their minds open. Take a study suggesting that a poor diet accelerates aging. Readers were just as engaged in the story—but more flexible in their beliefs—when it mentioned that scientists remained hesitant to draw strong causal conclusions given the number of factors that can affect aging. It even helped just to note that scientists believed more work needed to be done in this area.

We can also convey complexity by highlighting contingencies. Every empirical finding raises unanswered questions about when and where results will be replicated, nullified, or reversed. Contingencies are all the places and populations where an effect may change.

Consider diversity: although headlines often say "Diversity is good," the evidence is full of contingencies. Although diversity of background and thought has the potential to help groups think more broadly and process information more deeply, that potential is realized in some situations but not others. New research reveals that people are more likely to promote diversity and inclusion when the message is more nuanced (and more accurate): "Diversity is good, but it isn't easy."* Acknowledging complexity doesn't make speakers and writers less convincing; it makes them more credible. It doesn't lose viewers and readers; it maintains their engagement while stoking their curiosity.

In social science, rather than cherry-picking information to fit our existing narratives, we're trained to ask whether we should rethink and revise those narratives. When we find evidence that doesn't fit neatly into

---

* Even when we try to convey nuance, sometimes the message gets lost in translation. Recently some colleagues and I published an article titled "The Mixed Effects of Online Diversity Training." I thought we were making it abundantly clear that our research revealed how complicated diversity training is, but soon various commentators were heralding it as evidence supporting the value of diversity training—and a similar number were holding it up as evidence that diversity training is a waste of time. Confirmation bias and desirability bias are alive and well.

our belief systems, we're expected to share it anyway.* In some of my past writing for the public, though, I regret not having done enough to emphasize areas where evidence was incomplete or conflicting. I sometimes shied away from discussing mixed results because I didn't want to leave readers confused. Research suggests that many writers fall into the same trap, caught up in trying to "maintain a consistent narrative rather than an accurate record."

A fascinating example is the divide around emotional intelligence. On one extreme is Daniel Goleman, who popularized the concept. He preaches that emotional intelligence matters more for performance than cognitive ability (IQ) and accounts for "nearly 90 percent" of success in leadership jobs. At the other extreme is Jordan Peterson, writing that "There is NO SUCH THING AS EQ" and prosecuting emotional intelligence as "a fraudulent concept, a fad, a convenient band-wagon, a corporate marketing scheme."

Both men hold doctorates in psychology, but neither seems particularly interested in creating an accurate record. If Peterson had bothered to read the comprehensive meta-analyses of studies spanning nearly two hundred jobs, he'd have discovered that—contrary to his claims— emotional intelligence is real and it does matter. Emotional intelligence tests predict performance even after controlling for IQ and personality. If Goleman hadn't ignored those same data, he'd have learned that if you want to predict performance across jobs, IQ is more than twice as important as emotional intelligence (which accounts for only 3 to 8 percent of performance).

I think they're both missing the point. Instead of arguing about *whether* emotional intelligence is meaningful, we should be focusing on

---

* Some experiments show that when people embrace paradoxes and contradictions—rather than avoid them—they generate more creative ideas and solutions. But other experiments show that when people embrace paradoxes and contradictions, they're more likely to persist with wrong beliefs and failing actions. Let that paradox marinate for a while.

the contingencies that explain *when* it's more and less consequential. It turns out that emotional intelligence is beneficial in jobs that involve dealing with emotions, but less relevant—and maybe even detrimental—in work where emotions are less central. If you're a real estate agent, a customer service representative, or a counselor, being skilled at perceiving, understanding, and managing emotions can help you support your clients and address their problems. If you're a mechanic or an accountant, being an emotional genius is less useful and could even become a distraction. *If you're fixing my car or doing my taxes, I'd rather you didn't pay too much attention to my emotions.*

In an effort to set the record straight, I wrote a short LinkedIn post arguing that emotional intelligence is overrated. I did my best to follow my own guidelines for complexity:

Nuance: This isn't to say that emotional intelligence is useless.

Caveats: As better tests of emotional intelligence are designed, our knowledge may change.

Contingencies: For now, the best available evidence suggests that emotional intelligence is not a panacea. Let's recognize it for what it is: a set of skills that can be beneficial in situations where emotional information is rich or vital.

Over a thousand comments poured in, and I was pleasantly surprised that many reacted enthusiastically to the complexified message. Some mentioned that nothing is either/or and that data can help us reexamine even our closely held beliefs. Others were downright hostile. They turned a blind eye to the evidence and insisted that emotional intelligence was the sine qua non of success. It was as if they belonged to an emotional intelligence cult.

From time to time I've run into idea cults—groups that stir up a batch of oversimplified intellectual Kool-Aid and recruit followers to serve it widely. They preach the merits of their pet concept and prosecute anyone who calls for nuance or complexity. In the area of health, idea cults defend detox diets and cleanses long after they've been exposed as snake oil. In education, there are idea cults around learning styles—the notion that instruction should be tailored to each student's preference for learning through auditory, visual, or kinesthetic modes. Some teachers are determined to tailor their instruction accordingly despite decades of evidence that although students might enjoy listening, reading, or doing, they don't actually learn better that way. In psychology, I've inadvertently offended members of idea cults when I've shared evidence that meditation isn't the only way to prevent stress or promote mindfulness; that when it comes to reliability and validity, the Myers-Briggs personality tool falls somewhere between a horoscope and a heart monitor; and that being more authentic can sometimes make us less successful. *If you find yourself saying ___ is always good or ___ is never bad, you may be a member of an idea cult.* Appreciating complexity reminds us that no behavior is always effective and that all cures have unintended consequences.

ARE YOU COMING TO BED?

I CAN'T. THIS IS IMPORTANT.

WHAT?

SOMEONE IS WRONG ON THE INTERNET.

xkcd.com

In the moral philosophy of John Rawls, the veil of ignorance asks us to judge the justice of a society by whether we'd join it without knowing our place in it. I think the scientist's veil of ignorance is to ask whether we'd accept the results of a study based on the methods involved, without knowing what the conclusion will be.

MIXED FEELINGS

In polarized discussions, a common piece of advice is to take the other side's perspective. In theory, putting ourselves in another person's shoes enables us to walk in lockstep with them. In practice, though, it's not that simple.

In a pair of experiments, randomly assigning people to reflect on the intentions and interests of their political opposites made them *less* receptive to rethinking their own attitudes on health care and universal basic income. Across twenty-five experiments, imagining other people's perspectives failed to elicit more accurate insights—and occasionally made participants more confident in their own inaccurate judgments. Perspective-taking consistently fails because we're terrible mind readers. We're just guessing.

If we don't understand someone, we can't have a eureka moment by imagining his perspective. Polls show that Democrats underestimate the number of Republicans who recognize the prevalence of racism and sexism—and Republicans underestimate the number of Democrats who are proud to be Americans and oppose open borders. The greater the distance between us and an adversary, the more likely we are to oversimplify their actual motives and invent explanations that stray far from their reality. What works is not perspective-taking but perspective-seeking: actually talking to people to gain insight into the nuances of their views. That's what good scientists do: instead of drawing conclusions about people based on minimal clues, they test their hypotheses by striking up conversations.

For a long time, I believed that the best way to make those conversations less polarizing was to leave emotions out of them. If only we could keep our feelings off the table, we'd all be more open to rethinking. Then I read evidence that complicated my thinking.

It turns out that even if we disagree strongly with someone on a social issue, when we discover that she cares deeply about the issue, we trust her more. We might still dislike her, but we see her passion for a principle as a sign of integrity. We reject the belief but grow to respect the person behind it.

It can help to make that respect explicit at the start of a conversation. In one experiment, if an ideological opponent merely began by acknowledging that "I have a lot of respect for people like you who stand by their principles," people were less likely to see her as an adversary—and showed her more generosity.

When Peter Coleman brings people together in his Difficult Conversations Lab, he plays them the recording of their discussions afterward. What he wants to learn is how they were feeling, moment by moment, as they listen to themselves. After studying over five hundred of these conversations, he found that the unproductive ones feature a more limited set of both positive and negative emotions, as illustrated below in the image on the left. People get trapped in emotional simplicity, with one or two dominant feelings.

As you can see with the duo on the right, the productive conversations cover a much more varied spectrum of emotions. They're not less

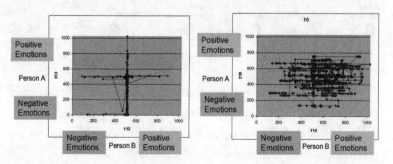

emotional—they're more emotionally complex. At one point, people might be angry about the other person's views, but by the next minute they're curious to learn more. Soon they could be shifting into anxiety and then excitement about considering a new perspective. Sometimes they even stumble into the joy of being wrong.

In a productive conversation, people treat their feelings as a rough draft. Like art, emotions are works in progress. It rarely serves us well to frame our first sketch. As we gain perspective, we revise what we feel. Sometimes we even start over from scratch.

PRODUCTIVE vs. UNPRODUCTIVE CONVERSATION

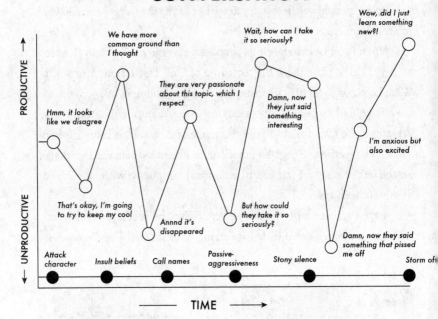

What stands in the way of rethinking isn't the expression of emotion; it's a restricted range of emotion. So how do we infuse our charged conversations with greater emotional variety—and thereby greater potential for mutual understanding and rethinking?

It helps to remember that we can fall victim to binary bias with emotions, not only with issues. Just as the spectrum of beliefs on charged topics is much more complex than two extremes, our emotions are often more mixed than we realize.* If you come across evidence that you might be wrong about the best path to gun safety, you can simultaneously feel upset by and intrigued with what you've learned. If you feel wronged by someone with a different set of beliefs, you can be simultaneously angry about your past interactions and hopeful about a future relationship. If someone says your actions haven't lived up to your antiracist rhetoric, you can experience both defensiveness (*I'm a good person!*) and remorse (*I could've done a lot more*).

In the spring of 2020, a Black man named Christian Cooper was bird-watching in Central Park when a white woman walked by with her dog. He respectfully asked her to put the dog on a leash, as the nearby signs required. When she refused, he stayed calm and started filming her on his phone. She responded by informing him that she was going to call the police and "tell them there's an African American man threatening my life." She went on to do exactly that with a 911 operator.

When the video of the encounter went viral, the continuum of emotional reactions on social media rightfully spanned from moral outrage to sheer rage. The incident called to mind a painful history of false criminal accusations made against Black men by white women, which often ended with devastating consequences. It was appalling that the woman didn't leash her dog—and her prejudice.

---

* It turns out that younger Anglo Americans are more likely than their older or Asian American counterparts to reject mixed emotions, like feeling happy and sad at the same time. The difference seems to lie in comfort accepting dualities and paradoxes. I think it might help if we had richer language to capture ambivalent emotions. For example, Japanese gives us *koi no yokan*, the feeling that it wasn't love at first sight but we could grow to love the person over time. The Inuit have *iktsuarpok*, the mix of anticipation and anxiety when we're awaiting the arrival of a guest at our house. Georgians have *shemomedjamo*, the feeling of being completely full but eating anyway because the meal is so good. My favorite emotion word is German: *kummerspeck*, the extra weight we gain from emotional overeating when we're sad. The literal translation of that one: "grief bacon." I can see that coming in handy in charged conversations: *I didn't mean to insult you. I'm just working through some grief bacon right now.*

"I'm not a racist. I did not mean to harm that man in any way," the woman declared in her public apology. "I think I was just scared." Her simple explanation overlooks the complex emotions that fueled her actions. She could have stopped to ask why she had been afraid—what views about Black men had led her to feel threatened in a polite conversation? She could have paused to consider why she had felt entitled to lie to the police—what power dynamics had made her feel this was acceptable?

Her simple denial overlooks the complex reality that racism is a function of our actions, not merely our intentions. As historian Ibram X. Kendi writes, "Racist and antiracist are not fixed identities. We can be a racist one minute and an antiracist the next." Humans, like polarizing issues, rarely come in binaries.

When asked whether he accepted her apology, Christian Cooper refused to make a simple judgment, offering a nuanced assessment:

> I think her apology is sincere. I'm not sure if in that apology she recognizes that while she may not be or consider herself a racist, that particular act was definitely racist. . . .
>
> Granted, it was a stressful situation, a sudden situation, maybe a moment of spectacularly poor judgment, but she went there. . . .
>
> Is she a racist? I can't answer that—only she can answer that . . . going forward with how she conducts herself, and how she chooses to reflect on the situation and examine it.

Many months later, it became clear that the media had glossed over the complexity of the situation. Other dog walkers—including at least one Black man—had complained about Christian Cooper yelling at them to use leashes and attempting to lure their dogs with treats in his pocket. In his original post about the incident, Christian had mentioned carrying treats for that purpose, but it wasn't clear that others had found his behavior threatening. Being aware of how he had come across in the past could have helped us understand how the woman may have experienced the situation. But it doesn't justify her decision to endanger his life by falsely claiming that he was endangering hers. And it doesn't explain why she didn't just walk away.

I think there's something to be learned from Christian's nuanced refusal to pass a blanket judgment. By expressing his mixed emotions and his uncertainty about the woman's character, Christian signaled his willingness to rethink the situation and encouraged others to rethink their own reactions. You might even be experiencing some complex emotions as you read this.

It shouldn't be up to the victim to inject complexity into a difficult conversation. Rethinking should start with the offender. If the woman had taken responsibility for reevaluating her beliefs and behaviors, she might have become an example to others who recognized a bit of themselves in her reaction. Although she couldn't change what she'd already done, by recognizing the complex power dynamics that breed and perpetuate systemic racism, she might have spurred deeper discussions of the range of possible steps toward justice.

Charged conversations cry out for nuance. When we're preaching, prosecuting, or politicking, the complexity of reality can seem like an inconvenient truth. In scientist mode, it can be an invigorating truth—it means there are new opportunities for understanding and for progress.

CHAPTER 9

Rewriting the Textbook

Teaching Students to Question Knowledge

□ □ □

No schooling was allowed to interfere with my education.

—GRANT ALLEN

A decade ago, if you had told Erin McCarthy she would become a teacher, she would have laughed. When she graduated from college, the last thing she wanted to do was teach. She was fascinated by history but bored by her social studies classes. Searching for a way to breathe life into overlooked objects and forgotten events, Erin started her career working in museums. Before long, she found herself writing a resource manual for teachers, leading school tours, and engaging students in interactive programs. She realized that the enthusiasm she saw on field trips was missing in too many classrooms, and she decided to do something about it.

For the past eight years, Erin has taught social studies in the Milwaukee area. Her mission is to cultivate curiosity about the past, but also to motivate students to update their knowledge in the present. In 2020, she was named Wisconsin's Teacher of the Year.

One day, an eighth grader complained that the reading assignment from a history textbook was inaccurate. If you're a teacher, that kind of criticism could be a nightmare. Using an outdated textbook would be a sign that you don't know your material, and it would be embarrassing if your students noticed the error before you did.

But Erin had assigned that particular reading intentionally. She collects old history books because she enjoys seeing how the stories we tell change over time, and she decided to give her students part of a textbook from 1940. Some of them just accepted the information it presented at face value. Through years of education, they had come to take it for granted that textbooks told the truth. Others were shocked by errors and omissions. It was ingrained in their minds that their readings were filled with incontrovertible facts. The lesson led them to start thinking like scientists and questioning what they were learning: whose story was included, whose was excluded, and what were they missing if only one or two perspectives were shared?

After opening her students' eyes to the fact that knowledge can evolve, Erin's next step was to show them that it's always evolving. To set up a unit on expansion in the West, she created her own textbook section describing what it's like to be a middle-school student today. All the protagonists were women and girls, and all the generic pronouns were female. In the first year she introduced the material, a student raised his hand to point out that the boys were missing. "But there's one boy," Erin replied. "Boys were around. They just weren't doing anything important." It was an aha moment for the student: he suddenly realized what it was like for an entire group to be marginalized for hundreds of years.

My favorite assignment of Erin's is her final one. As a passionate champion of inquiry-based learning, she sends her eighth graders off to do self-directed research in which they inspect, investigate, interrogate, and interpret. Their active learning culminates in a group project: they pick a chapter from their textbook, choosing a time period that interests them and a theme in history that they see as underrepresented. Then they go off to rewrite it.

One group took on the civil rights chapter for failing to cover the original March on Washington, which was called off at the last minute in the early 1940s but inspired Martin Luther King Jr.'s historic march two decades later. Other groups revised the chapter on World War II to include the infantry regiments of Hispanic soldiers and second-generation Japanese soldiers who fought for the U.S. Army. "It's a huge light-bulb moment," Erin told me.

Even if you're not a teacher by profession, you probably have roles in which you spend time educating others—whether as a parent, a mentor, a friend, or a colleague. In fact, every time we try to help someone think again, we're doing a kind of education. Whether we do our instruction in a classroom or in a boardroom, in an office or at our kitchen table, there are ways to make rethinking central to what—and how—we teach.

With so much emphasis placed on imparting knowledge and building confidence, many teachers don't do enough to encourage students to question themselves and one another. To figure out what it takes to change that mindset, I tracked down some extraordinary educators who foster rethinking cycles by instilling intellectual humility, disseminating doubt, and cultivating curiosity. I also tested a few of my own ideas by turning my classroom into something of a living lab.

LEARNING, INTERRUPTED

Looking back on my own early education, one of my biggest disappointments is that I never got to fully experience the biggest upheavals in science. Long before it ever occurred to me to be curious about the cosmos, my teachers started demystifying it in kindergarten. I often wonder how I would have felt if I was a teenager when I first learned that we don't live on a static, flat disc, but on a spinning, moving sphere.

I hope I would have been stunned, and that disbelief would have quickly given way to curiosity and eventually the awe of discovery and the joy of being wrong. I also suspect it would have been a life-changing lesson in confident humility. *If I could be that mistaken about what was under my own two feet, how many other so-called truths were actually question marks?* Sure, I knew that many earlier generations of humans had gotten it wrong, but there's a huge difference between learning about other people's false beliefs and actually learning to unbelieve things ourselves.

I realize this thought experiment is wildly impractical. It's hard enough to keep kids in the dark about Santa Claus or the Tooth Fairy. Even if we could pull off such a delay, there's a risk that some students would seize and freeze on what they learned early on. They could become trapped in an overconfidence cycle where pride in false knowledge fuels conviction, and confirmation and desirability biases lead to validation. Before you know it, we might have a whole nation of flat-earthers.

Evidence shows that if false scientific beliefs aren't addressed in elementary school, they become harder to change later. "Learning counterintuitive scientific ideas [is] akin to becoming a fluent speaker of a second language," psychologist Deborah Kelemen writes. It's "a task that becomes increasingly difficult the longer it is delayed, and one that is almost never achieved with only piecemeal instruction and infrequent practice." That's what kids really need: frequent practice at unlearning, especially when it comes to the mechanisms of how cause and effect work.

FLAT EARTH OVERCONFIDENCE CYCLE

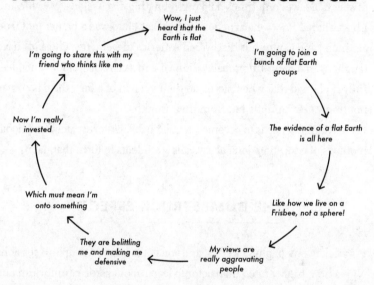

In the field of history education, there's a growing movement to ask questions that don't have a single right answer. In a curriculum developed at Stanford, high school students are encouraged to critically examine what really caused the Spanish-American War, whether the New Deal was a success, and why the Montgomery bus boycott was a watershed moment. Some teachers even send students out to interview people with whom they disagree. The focus is less on being right, and more on building the skills to consider different views and argue productively about them.

That doesn't mean all interpretations are accepted as valid. When the son of a Holocaust survivor came to her class, Erin McCarthy told her students that some people denied the existence of the Holocaust, and taught them to examine the evidence and reject those false claims. This is part of a broader movement to teach kids to think like fact-checkers: the guidelines include (1) "interrogate information instead of simply consuming it," (2) "reject rank and popularity as a proxy for reliability," and (3) "understand that the sender of information is often not its source."

These principles are valuable beyond the classroom. At our family dinner table, we sometimes hold myth-busting discussions. My wife and I have shared how we learned in school that Pluto was a planet (not true anymore) and Columbus discovered America (never true). Our kids have taught us that King Tut probably didn't die in a chariot accident and gleefully explained that when sloths do their version of a fart, the gas comes not from their behinds but from their mouths.

Rethinking needs to become a regular habit. Unfortunately, traditional methods of education don't always allow students to form that habit.

THE DUMBSTRUCK EFFECT

It's week twelve of physics class, and you get to attend a couple of sessions with a new, highly rated instructor to learn about static equilibrium and fluids. The first session is on statics; it's a lecture. The second is on fluids, and it's an active-learning session. One of your roommates has a different, equally popular instructor who does the opposite—using active learning for statics and lecturing on fluids.

In both cases the content and the handouts are identical; the only difference is the delivery method. During the lecture the instructor presents slides, gives explanations, does demonstrations, and solves sample problems, and you take notes on the handouts. In the active-learning session, instead of doing the example problems himself, the instructor sends the class off to figure them out in small groups, wandering around to ask questions and offer tips before walking the class through the solution. At the end, you fill out a survey.

In this experiment the topic doesn't matter: the teaching method is what shapes your experience. I expected active learning to win the day, but the data suggest that you and your roommate will both enjoy the subject more when it's delivered by lecture. You'll also rate the instructor who lectures as more effective—and you'll be more likely to say you wish all your physics courses were taught that way.

Upon reflection, the appeal of dynamic lectures shouldn't be surprising. For generations, people have admired the rhetorical eloquence of poets like Maya Angelou, politicians like John F. Kennedy Jr. and Ronald Reagan, preachers like Martin Luther King Jr., and teachers like Richard Feynman. Today we live in a golden age of spellbinding speaking, where great orators engage and educate from platforms with unprecedented reach. Creatives used to share their methods in small communities; now they can accumulate enough YouTube and Instagram subscribers to populate a small country. Pastors once gave sermons to hundreds at church; now they can reach hundreds of thousands over the internet in megachurches. Professors used to teach small enough classes that they could spend individual time with each student; now their lessons can be broadcast to millions through online courses.

It's clear that these lectures are entertaining and informative. The question is whether they're the ideal method of teaching. In the physics experiment, the students took tests to gauge how much they had learned about statics and fluids. Despite enjoying the lectures more, they actually gained more knowledge and skill from the active-learning session. It required more mental effort, which made it less fun but led to deeper understanding.

For a long time, I believed that we learn more when we're having fun. This research convinced me I was wrong. *It also reminded me of my favorite physics teacher, who got stellar reviews for letting us play Ping-Pong in class, but didn't quite make the coefficient of friction stick.*

Active learning has impact far beyond physics. A meta-analysis compared the effects of lecturing and active learning on students' mastery of the material, cumulating 225 studies with over 46,000 undergraduates in science, technology, engineering, and math (STEM). Active-learning methods included group problem solving, worksheets, and tutorials. On average, students scored half a letter grade worse under traditional lecturing than through active learning—and students were 1.55 times more likely to fail in classes with traditional lecturing. The researchers estimate that if the students who failed in lecture courses had participated in active learning, more than $3.5 million in tuition could have been saved.

It's not hard to see why a boring lecture would fail, but even captivating lectures can fall short for a less obvious, more concerning reason. Lectures aren't designed to accommodate dialogue or disagreement; they turn students into passive receivers of information rather than active thinkers. In the above meta-analysis, lecturing was especially ineffective in debunking known misconceptions—in leading students to think again. And experiments have shown that when a speaker delivers an inspiring message, the audience scrutinizes the material less carefully and forgets more of the content—even while claiming to remember more of it.

Social scientists have called this phenomenon the awestruck effect, but I think it's better described as the dumbstruck effect. The sage-on-the-stage often preaches new thoughts, but rarely teaches us how to think for ourselves. Thoughtful lecturers might prosecute inaccurate arguments and tell us what to think instead, but they don't necessarily show us how to rethink moving forward. Charismatic speakers can put us under a political spell, under which we follow them to gain their approval or affiliate with their tribe. We should be persuaded by the substance of an argument, not the shiny package in which it's wrapped.

To be clear, I'm not suggesting eliminating lectures altogether. I love watching TED talks and have even learned to enjoy giving them. It was attending brilliant lectures that first piqued my curiosity about becoming a teacher, and I'm not opposed to doing some lecturing in my own classes. I just think it's a problem that lectures remain the dominant method of teaching in secondary and higher education. *Expect a lecture on that soon.*

In North American universities, more than half of STEM professors spend at least 80 percent of their time lecturing, just over a quarter incorporate bits of interactivity, and fewer than a fifth use truly student-centered methods that involve active learning. In high schools it seems that half of teachers lecture most or all of the time.* Lectures are not always the best method of learning, and they are not enough to develop students into lifelong learners. If you spend all of your school years being fed information and are never given the opportunity to question it, you won't develop the tools for rethinking that you need in life.

"We'd now like to open the floor to shorter speeches disguised as questions."

Steve Macone/The New Yorker Collection/The Cartoon Bank; © Condé Nast

---

*There's evidence that middle schoolers score higher on math and science competency tests when teachers dedicate more time to lecturing than active learning. It remains to be seen whether lectures are more effective with younger students or whether the gap is driven by the ineffective implementation of active-learning methods.

THE UNBEARABLE LIGHTNESS OF REPEATING

There's only one class I regret missing in college. It was taught by a philosopher named Robert Nozick. One of his ideas became famous thanks
to the movie *The Matrix*: in the 1970s, Nozick introduced a thought
experiment about whether people would choose to enter an "experience
machine" that could provide infinite pleasure but remove them from real
life.* In his classroom, Nozick created his own version of an experience
machine: he insisted on teaching a new class every year. "I do my thinking through the courses I give," he said.

Nozick taught one course on truth; another on philosophy and neuroscience; a third on Socrates, Buddha, and Jesus; a fourth on thinking
about thinking; and a fifth on the Russian Revolution. In four decades of
teaching, he taught only one class a second time: it was on the good life.
"Presenting a completely polished and worked-out view doesn't give students a feel for what it's like to do original work in philosophy and to see
it happen, to catch on to doing it," he explained. Sadly, before I could take
one of his courses, he died of cancer.

What I found so inspiring about Nozick's approach was that he wasn't
content for students to learn from him. He wanted them to learn *with*
him. Every time he tackled a new topic, he would have the opportunity

* Nozick predicted that most of us would ditch the machine because we value doing and being—not
just experiencing—and because we wouldn't want to limit our experiences to what humans could
imagine and simulate. Later philosophers argued that if we did reject the machine, it might not be for
those reasons but due to status quo bias: we would have to walk away from reality as we know it. To
investigate that possibility, they changed the premise and ran an experiment. Imagine that you wake
up one day to learn that your whole life has been an experience machine that you chose years earlier,
and you now get to choose whether to unplug or plug back in. In that scenario, 46 percent of people
said they wanted to plug back in. If they were told that unplugging would take them back to "real life"
as a multimillionaire artist based in Monaco, 50 percent of people still wanted to plug back in. It seems
that many people would rather not abandon a familiar virtual reality for an unfamiliar actual reality—
or maybe some have a distaste for art, wealth, and sovereign principalities.

to rethink his existing views on it. He was a remarkable role model for changing up our familiar methods of teaching—and learning. When I started teaching, I wanted to adopt some of his principles. I wasn't prepared to inflict an entire semester of half-baked ideas on my students, so I set a benchmark: every year I would aim to throw out 20 percent of my class and replace it with new material. If I was doing new thinking every year, we could all start rethinking together.

With the other 80 percent of the material, though, I found myself failing. I was teaching a semester-long class on organizational behavior for juniors and seniors. When I introduced evidence, I wasn't giving them the space to rethink it. After years of wrestling with this problem, it dawned on me that I could create a new assignment to teach rethinking. I assigned students to work in small groups to record their own mini-podcasts or mini–TED talks. Their charge was to question a popular practice, to champion an idea that went against the grain of conventional wisdom, or to challenge principles covered in class.

As they started working on the project, I noticed a surprising pattern. The students who struggled the most were the straight-A students—the perfectionists. It turns out that although perfectionists are more likely than their peers to ace school, they don't perform any better than their colleagues at work. This tracks with evidence that, across a wide range of industries, grades are not a strong predictor of job performance.

Achieving excellence in school often requires mastering old ways of thinking. Building an influential career demands new ways of thinking. In a classic study of highly accomplished architects, the most creative ones graduated with a B average. Their straight-A counterparts were so determined to be right that they often failed to take the risk of rethinking the orthodoxy. A similar pattern emerged in a study of students who graduated at the top of their class. "Valedictorians aren't likely to be the future's visionaries," education researcher Karen

Arnold explains. "They typically settle into the system instead of shaking it up."

That's what I saw with my straight-A students: they were terrified of being wrong. To give them a strong incentive to take some risks, I made the assignment worth 20 percent of their final grade. I had changed the rules: now they were being rewarded for rethinking instead of regurgitating. I wasn't sure if that incentive would work until I reviewed the work of a trio of straight-A students. They gave their mini–TED talk about the problems with TED talks, pointing out the risks of reinforcing short attention spans and privileging superficial polish over deep insight. Their presentation was so thoughtful and entertaining that I played it for the entire class. "If you have the courage to stand up to the trend towards glib, seamless answers," they deadpanned as we laughed, "then stop watching this video right now, and do some real research, like we did."

I made the assignment a staple of the course from then on. The following year I wanted to go further in rethinking the content and format of my class. In a typical three-hour class, I would spend no more than twenty to thirty minutes lecturing. The rest is active learning—students make decisions in simulations and negotiate in role-plays, and then we debrief, discuss, debate, and problem solve. My mistake was treating the syllabus as if it were a formal contract: once I finalized it in September, it was effectively set in stone. I decided it was time to change that and invite the students to rethink part of the structure of the class itself.

On my next syllabus, I deliberately left one class session completely blank. Halfway through the semester, I invited the students to work in small groups to develop and pitch an idea for how we should spend that open day. Then they voted.

One of the most popular ideas came from Lauren McCann, who suggested a creative step toward helping students recognize that rethinking was a useful skill—and one they had already been using in college.

She invited her classmates to write letters to their freshmen selves covering what they wish they had known back then. The students encouraged their younger selves to stay open to different majors, instead of declaring the first one that erased their uncertainty. To be less obsessed with grades, and more focused on relationships. To explore different career possibilities, rather than committing too soon to the one that promised the most pay or prestige.

Lauren collected letters from dozens of students to launch a website, Dear Penn Freshmen. Within twenty-four hours, dearpennfresh.com had over ten thousand visits, and a half dozen schools were starting their own versions to help students rethink their academic, social, and professional choices.

This practice can extend far beyond the classroom. As we approach any life transition—whether it's a first job, a second marriage, or a third child—we can pause to ask people what they wish they'd known before they went through that experience. Once we're on the other side of it, we can share what we ourselves should have rethought.

It's been demonstrated repeatedly that one of the best ways to learn is to teach. It wasn't until I let my students design a day of class that I truly understood how much they had to teach one another—*and* me. They were rethinking not just what they learned, but whom they could learn from.

The following year, the class's favorite idea took that rethinking a step further: the students hosted a day of "passion talks" on which anyone could teach the class about something he or she loved. We learned how to beatbox and design buildings that mesh with nature and make the world more allergy safe. From that point on, sharing passions has been part of class participation. All the students give a passion talk as a way of introducing themselves to their peers. Year after year, they tell me that it injects a heightened level of curiosity into the room, leaving them eager to soak up insights from each of their classmates.

"Writing is ~~communication illumination discovery~~ rewriting."

www.CartoonCollections.com

JACK OF ROUGH DRAFTS, MASTER OF CRAFTS

When I asked a handful of education pioneers to name the best teacher of rethinking they've ever encountered, I kept hearing the same name: Ron Berger. If you invited Ron over for dinner, he's the kind of person who would notice that one of your chairs was broken, ask if you had some tools handy, and fix it on the spot.

For most of his career, Ron was a public-elementary-school teacher in rural Massachusetts. His nurse, his plumber, and his local firefighters were all former students. During the summers and on weekends, he worked as a carpenter. Ron has devoted his life to teaching students an ethic of excellence. Mastering a craft, in his experience, is about constantly revising our thinking. Hands-on craftsmanship is the foundation for his classroom philosophy.

Ron wanted his students to experience the joy of discovery, so he didn't start by teaching them established knowledge. He began the school year by presenting them with "grapples"—problems to work through in phases. The approach was think-pair-share: the kids started individually, updated their ideas in small groups, and then presented their thoughts to the rest of the class, arriving at solutions together. Instead of introducing existing taxonomies of animals, for example, Ron had them develop their own categories first. Some students classified animals by whether they walked on land, swam in water, or flew through the air; others arranged them according to color, size, or diet. The lesson was that scientists always have many options, and their frameworks are useful in some ways but arbitrary in others.

When students confront complex problems, they often feel confused. A teacher's natural impulse is to rescue them as quickly as possible so they don't feel lost or incompetent. Yet psychologists find that one of the hallmarks of an open mind is responding to confusion with curiosity and interest. One student put it eloquently: "I need time for my confusion." Confusion can be a cue that there's new territory to be explored or a fresh puzzle to be solved.

Ron wasn't content to deliver lessons that erased confusion. He wanted students to embrace confusion. His vision was for them to become leaders of their own learning, much like they would in "do it yourself" (DIY) craft projects. He started encouraging students to think like young scientists: they would identify problems, develop hypotheses, and design their own experiments to test them. His sixth graders went around the community to test local homes for radon gas. His third graders created their own maps of amphibian habitats. His first graders got their own group of snails to take care of, and went on to test which of over 140 foods they liked—and whether they preferred hot or cold, dark or light, and wet or dry environments.

For architecture and engineering lessons, Ron had his students create blueprints for a house. When he required them to do at least four different drafts, other teachers warned him that younger students would become discouraged. Ron disagreed—he had already tested the concept with kindergarteners and first graders in art. Rather than asking them to simply draw a house, he announced, "We'll be doing four different *versions* of a drawing of a house."

Some students didn't stop there; many wound up deciding to do eight or ten drafts. The students had a support network of classmates cheering them on in their efforts. "Quality means rethinking, reworking, and polishing," Ron reflects. "They need to feel they will be celebrated, not ridiculed, for going back to the drawing board. . . . They soon began complaining if I didn't allow them to do more than one version."

Ron wanted to teach his students to revise their thinking based on input from others, so he turned the classroom into a challenge network. Every week—and sometimes every day—the entire class would do a critique session. One format was a gallery critique: Ron put everyone's work on display, sent students around the room to observe, and then facilitated a discussion of what they saw as excellent and why. This method wasn't used only for art and science projects; for a writing assignment, they would evaluate a sentence or a paragraph. The other format was an in-depth critique: for a single session, the class would focus on the work of one student or group. The authors would explain their goals and where they needed help, and Ron guided the class through a discussion of strengths and areas for development. He encouraged students to be specific and kind: to critique the work rather than the author. He taught them to avoid preaching and prosecuting: since they were sharing their subjective opinions, not objective assessments, they should say "I think" rather than "This isn't good." He invited them to show humility and curiosity, framing their suggestions in terms of questions like "I'd love to hear why . . ." and "Have you considered . . ."

The class didn't just critique projects. Each day they would discuss what excellence looked like. With each new project they updated their criteria. Along with rethinking their own work, they were learning to continually rethink their standards. To help them further evolve those standards, Ron regularly brought in outside experts. Local architects and scientists would come in to offer their own critiques, and the class would incorporate their principles and vocabularies into future discussions. Long after they'd moved on to middle and high school, it was not uncommon for former students to visit Ron's class and ask for a critique of their work.

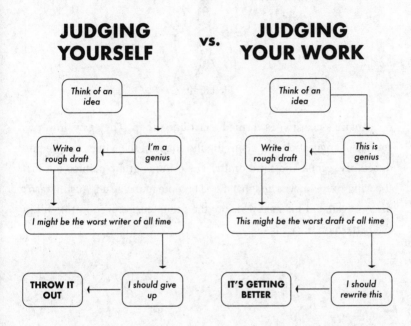

JUDGING YOURSELF vs. JUDGING YOUR WORK

JUDGING YOURSELF

- Think of an idea
- I'm a genius
- Write a rough draft
- I might be the worst writer of all time
- I should give up
- **THROW IT OUT**

JUDGING YOUR WORK

- Think of an idea
- This is genius
- Write a rough draft
- This might be the worst draft of all time
- I should rewrite this
- **IT'S GETTING BETTER**

As soon as I connected with Ron Berger, I couldn't help but wish I had been able to take one of his classes. It wasn't because I had suffered from a lack of exceptional teachers. It was because I had never had the privilege of being in a classroom with a culture like his, with a whole room of students dedicated to questioning themselves and one another.

Ron now spends his days speaking, writing, teaching a course for teachers at Harvard, and consulting with schools. He's the chief academic officer of EL Education, an organization dedicated to reimagining how teaching and learning take place in schools. Ron and his colleagues work directly with 150 schools and develop curricula that have reached millions of students.

At one of their schools in Idaho, a student named Austin was assigned to make a scientifically accurate drawing of a butterfly. This is his first draft:

First draft

Austin's classmates formed a critique group. They gave him two rounds of suggestions for changing the shape of the wings, and he produced his second and third drafts. The critique group pointed out that the wings were uneven and that they'd become round again. Austin wasn't discouraged. On his next revision, the group encouraged him to fill in the pattern on the wings.

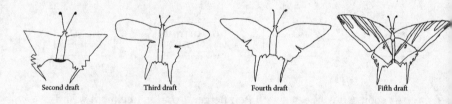

Second draft   Third draft   Fourth draft   Fifth draft

For the final draft, Austin was ready to color it in. When Ron showed the completed drawing to a roomful of elementary school students in Maine, they gasped in awe at his progress and his final product.

Final draft

I gasped, too, because Austin made these drawings when he was in first grade.

Seeing a six-year-old undergo that kind of metamorphosis made me think again about how quickly children can become comfortable rethinking and revising. Ever since, I've encouraged our kids to do multiple drafts of their own drawings. As excited as they were to see their first draft hanging on the wall, they're that much prouder of their fourth version.

Few of us will have the good fortune to learn to draw a butterfly with Ron Berger or rewrite a textbook with Erin McCarthy. Yet all of us have the opportunity to teach more like them. Whomever we're educating, we can express more humility, exude more curiosity, and introduce the children in our lives to the infectious joy of discovery.

I believe that good teachers introduce new thoughts, but great teachers introduce new ways of thinking. Collecting a teacher's knowledge may help us solve the challenges of the day, but understanding how a teacher thinks can help us navigate the challenges of a lifetime. Ultimately, education is more than the information we accumulate in our heads. It's the habits we develop as we keep revising our drafts and the skills we build to keep learning.

CHAPTER 10

That's Not the Way
We've Always Done It

Building Cultures of Learning at Work

□ □ □

If only it weren't for the people . . .
earth would be an engineer's paradise.

—KURT VONNEGUT

As an avid scuba diver, Luca Parmitano was familiar with the risks of drowning. He just didn't realize it could happen in outer space.

Luca had just become the youngest astronaut ever to take a long trip to the International Space Station. In July 2013, the thirty-six-year-old Italian astronaut completed his first spacewalk, spending six hours running experiments, moving equipment, and setting up power and data cables. Now, a week later, Luca and another astronaut, Chris Cassidy, were heading out for a second walk to continue their work and do some maintenance. As they prepared to leave the airlock, they could see the Earth 250 miles below.

After forty-four minutes in space, Luca felt something strange: the back of his head seemed to be wet. He wasn't sure where the water was coming from. It wasn't just a nuisance; it could cut off communication by shorting out his microphone or earphones. He reported the problem to Mission Control in Houston, and Chris asked if he was sweating. "I am sweating," Luca said, "but it feels like a lot of water. It's not going anywhere, it's just in my Snoopy cap. Just FYI." He went back to work.

The officer in charge of spacewalks, Karina Eversley, knew something was wrong. *That's not normal,* she thought, and quickly recruited a team of experts to compile questions for Luca. Was the amount of liquid increasing? Luca couldn't tell. Was he sure it was water? When he stuck out his tongue to capture a few of the drops that were floating in his helmet, the taste was metallic.

Mission Control made the call to terminate the spacewalk early. Luca and Chris had to split up to follow their tethers, which were routed in opposite directions. To get around an antenna, Luca flipped over. Suddenly, he couldn't see clearly or breathe through his nose—globs of water were covering his eyes and filling his nostrils. The water was continuing to accumulate, and if it reached his mouth he could drown. His only hope was to navigate quickly back to the airlock. As the sun set, Luca was surrounded by darkness, with only a small headlight to guide him. Then his comms went down, too—he couldn't hear himself or anyone else speak.

Luca managed to find his way back to the outer hatch of the airlock, using his memory and the tension in his tether. He was still in grave danger: before he could remove his helmet, he would have to wait for Chris to close the hatch and repressurize the airlock. For several agonizing minutes of silence, it was unclear whether he would survive. When it was finally safe to remove his helmet, a quart and a half of water was in it, but Luca was alive. Months later, the incident would be called the "scariest wardrobe malfunction in NASA history."

The technical updates followed swiftly. The spacesuit engineers traced the leak to a fan/pump/separator, which they replaced moving forward. They also added a breathing tube that works like a snorkel and a pad to absorb water inside the helmet. Yet the biggest error wasn't technical—it was human.

When Luca had returned from his first spacewalk a week earlier, he had noticed some droplets of water in his helmet. He and Chris assumed they were the result of a leak in the bag that provided drinking water in his suit, and the crew in Houston agreed. Just to be safe, they replaced the bag, but that was the end of the discussion.

The space station chief engineer, Chris Hansen, led the eventual investigation into what had gone wrong with Luca's suit. "The occurrence of minor amounts of water in the helmet was normalized," Chris told me. In the space station community, the "perception was that drink bags leak, which led to an acceptance that it was a likely explanation without digging deeper into it."

Luca's scare wasn't the first time that NASA's failure at rethinking had proven disastrous. In 1986, the space shuttle *Challenger* exploded after a catastrophically shallow analysis of the risk that circular gaskets called O-rings could fail. Although this had been identified as a launch constraint, NASA had a track record of overriding it in prior missions without any problems occurring. On an unusually cold launch day, the O-ring sealing the rocket booster joints ruptured, allowing hot gas to burn through the fuel tank, killing all seven *Challenger* astronauts.

In 2003, the space shuttle *Columbia* disintegrated under similar circumstances. After takeoff, the team on the ground noticed that some foam had fallen from the ship, but most of them assumed it wasn't a major issue since it had happened in past missions without incident. They failed to rethink that assumption and instead started discussing what repairs would be done to the ship to reduce the turnaround time for the next mission. The foam loss was, in fact, a critical issue: the damage it caused to the wing's leading edge let hot gas leak into the shuttle's wing upon reentry into the atmosphere. Once again, all seven astronauts lost their lives.

Rethinking is not just an individual skill. It's a collective capability, and it depends heavily on an organization's culture. NASA had long been a prime example of a performance culture: excellence of execution was the paramount value. Although NASA accomplished extraordinary things, they soon became victims of overconfidence cycles. As people took pride in their standard operating procedures, gained conviction in their routines, and saw their decisions validated through their results, they missed opportunities for rethinking.

Rethinking is more likely to happen in a learning culture, where growth is the core value and rethinking cycles are routine. In learning cultures, the norm is for people to know what they don't know, doubt their existing practices, and stay curious about new routines to try out. Evidence shows that in learning cultures, organizations innovate more and make fewer mistakes. After studying and advising change initiatives at NASA and the Gates Foundation, I've learned that learning cultures thrive under a particular combination of psychological safety and accountability.

Tradition
(n.)

Peer pressure from
dead people.

I ERR, THEREFORE I LEARN

Years ago, an engineer turned management professor named Amy Edmondson became interested in preventing medical errors. She went into a hospital and surveyed its staff about the degree of psychological safety they experienced in their teams—could they take risks without the fear of being punished? Then she collected data on the number of medical errors each team made, tracking serious outcomes like potentially fatal doses of the wrong medication. She was surprised to find that the more psychological safety a team felt, the higher its error rates.

It appeared that psychological safety could breed complacency. When trust runs deep in a team, people might not feel the need to question their colleagues or double-check their own work.

But Edmondson soon recognized a major limitation of the data: the errors were all self-reported. To get an unbiased measure of mistakes, she sent a covert observer into the units. When she analyzed those data, the results flipped: psychologically safe teams *reported* more errors, but they actually *made* fewer errors. By freely admitting their mistakes, they were then able to learn what had caused them and eliminate them moving forward. In psychologically unsafe teams, people hid their mishaps to avoid penalties, which made it difficult for anyone to diagnose the root causes and prevent future problems. They kept repeating the same mistakes.

Since then, research on psychological safety has flourished. When I was involved in a study at Google to identify the factors that distinguish teams with high performance and well-being, the most important differentiator wasn't who was on the team or even how meaningful their work was. What mattered most was psychological safety.

Over the past few years, psychological safety has become a buzzword in many workplaces. Although leaders might understand its significance, they often misunderstand exactly what it is and how to create it. Edmondson is quick to point out that psychological safety is not a matter of relaxing standards, making people comfortable, being nice and agreeable, or giving unconditional praise. It's fostering a climate of respect, trust, and openness in which people can raise concerns and suggestions without fear of reprisal. It's the foundation of a learning culture.

In performance cultures, the emphasis on results often undermines psychological safety. When we see people get punished for failures and mistakes, we become worried about proving our competence and protecting our careers. We learn to engage in self-limiting behavior, biting our tongues rather than voicing questions and concerns. Sometimes that's due to power distance: we're afraid of challenging the big boss at the top. The pressure to conform to authority is real, and those who dare to deviate run the risk of backlash. In performance cultures, we also censor ourselves in the presence of experts who seem to know all the answers—especially if we lack confidence in our own expertise.

PSYCHOLOGICAL SAFETY

WHEN YOU HAVE IT	WHEN YOU DON'T
See mistakes as opportunities to learn	See mistakes as threats to your career
Willing to take risks and fail	Unwilling to rock the boat
Speaking your mind in meetings	Keeping your ideas to yourself
Openly sharing your struggles	Only touting your strengths
Trust in your teammates and supervisors	Fear of your teammates and supervisors
Sticking your neck out	Having your head chopped off

A lack of psychological safety was a persistent problem at NASA. Before the *Challenger* launch, some engineers did raise red flags but were silenced by managers; others were ignored and ended up silencing themselves. After the *Columbia* launch, an engineer asked for clearer photographs to inspect the damage to the wing, but managers didn't supply them. In a critical meeting to evaluate the condition of the shuttle after takeoff, the engineer didn't speak up.

About a month before that *Columbia* launch, Ellen Ochoa became the deputy director of flight crew operations. In 1993, Ellen had made history by becoming the first Latina in space. Now, the first flight she supported in a management role had ended in tragedy. After breaking the news to the space station crew and consoling the family members of the fallen astronauts, she was determined to figure out how she could personally help to prevent this kind of disaster from ever happening again. Ellen recognized that at NASA, the performance culture was eroding psychological safety. "People pride themselves on their engineering expertise and excellence," she told me. "They fear their expertise will be questioned in a way that's embarrassing to them. It's that basic fear of looking like a fool, asking questions that people just dismiss, or being told you don't know what you're talking about." To combat that problem and nudge the culture toward learning, she started carrying a 3 × 5 note card in her pocket with questions to ask about every launch and important operational decision. Her list included:

- What leads you to that assumption? Why do you think it is correct? What might happen if it's wrong?
- What are the uncertainties in your analysis?
- I understand the advantages of your recommendation. What are the disadvantages?

A decade later, though, the same lessons about rethinking would have to be relearned in the context of spacewalk suits. As flight controllers first became aware of the droplets of water in Luca Parmitano's helmet, they made two faulty assumptions: the cause was the drink bag, and the effect was inconsequential. It wasn't until the second spacewalk, when Luca was in actual danger, that they started to question whether those assumptions were wrong.

When engineer Chris Hansen took over as the manager of the extravehicular activity office, he inaugurated a norm of posing questions like Ellen's: "All anybody would've had to ask is, 'How do you know the drink bag leaked?' The answer would've been, 'Because somebody told us.' That response would've set off red flags. It would've taken ten minutes to check, but nobody asked. It was the same for *Columbia*. Boeing came in and said, 'This foam, we think we know what it did.' If somebody had asked how they knew, nobody could've answered that question."

How do you know? It's a question we need to ask more often, both of ourselves and of others. The power lies in its frankness. It's nonjudgmental—a straightforward expression of doubt and curiosity that doesn't put people on the defensive. Ellen Ochoa wasn't afraid to ask that question, but she was an astronaut with a doctorate in engineering, serving in a senior leadership role. For too many people in too many workplaces, the question feels like a bridge too far. Creating psychological safety is easier said than done, so I set out to learn about how leaders can establish it.

SAFE AT HOME GATES

When I first arrived at the Gates Foundation, people were whispering about the annual strategy reviews. It's the time when program teams across the foundation meet with the cochairs—Bill and Melinda Gates—and the CEO to give progress reports on execution and collect feedback. Although the foundation employs some of the world's leading experts in areas ranging from eradicating disease to promoting educational equity, these experts are often intimidated by Bill's knowledge base, which seems impossibly broad and deep. What if he spots a fatal flaw in my work? Will it be the end of my career here?

A few years ago, leaders at the Gates Foundation reached out to see if I could help them build psychological safety. They were worried that the pressure to present airtight analyses was discouraging people from taking risks. They often stuck to tried-and-true strategies that would make incremental progress rather than daring to undertake bold experiments that might make a bigger dent in some of the world's most vexing problems.

The existing evidence on creating psychological safety gave us some starting points. I knew that changing the culture of an entire organization is daunting, while changing the culture of a team is more feasible. It starts with modeling the values we want to promote, identifying and praising others who exemplify them, and building a coalition of colleagues who are committed to making the change.

The standard advice for managers on building psychological safety is to model openness and inclusiveness. Ask for feedback on how you can improve, and people will feel safe to take risks. To test whether that recommendation would work, I launched an experiment with a doctoral student, Constantinos Coutifaris. In multiple companies, we randomly assigned some managers to ask their teams for constructive criticism. Over the following week, their teams reported higher psychological safety, but as we anticipated, it didn't last. Some managers who asked for feedback didn't like what they heard and got defensive. Others found the feedback useless or felt helpless to act on it, which discouraged them from continuing to seek feedback and their teams from continuing to offer it.

Another group of managers took a different approach, one that had less immediate impact in the first week but led to sustainable gains in psychological safety a full year later. Instead of asking them to seek feedback, we had randomly assigned those managers to share their past experiences with receiving feedback and their future development goals. We advised them to tell their teams about a time when they benefited from constructive criticism and to identify the areas that they were working to improve now.

By admitting some of their imperfections out loud, managers demonstrated that they could take it—and made a public commitment to remain open to feedback. They normalized vulnerability, making their teams more comfortable opening up about their own struggles. Their employees gave more useful feedback because they knew where their managers were working to grow. That motivated managers to create practices to keep the door open: they started holding "ask me anything" coffee chats, opening weekly one-on-one meetings by asking for constructive criticism, and setting up monthly team sessions where everyone shared their development goals and progress.

Creating psychological safety can't be an isolated episode or a task to check off on a to-do list. When discussing their weaknesses, many of the managers in our experiment felt awkward and anxious at first. Many of their team members were surprised by that vulnerability and unsure of how to respond. Some were skeptical: they thought their managers might be fishing for compliments or cherry-picking comments that made them look good. It was only over time—as managers repeatedly demonstrated humility and curiosity—that the dynamic changed.

At the Gates Foundation, I wanted to go a step further. Instead of just having managers open up with their own teams about how they had previously been criticized, I wondered what would happen if senior leaders shared their experiences across the entire organization. It dawned on me that I had a memorable way to make that happen.

A few years earlier, our MBA students at Wharton decided to create a video for their annual comedy show. It was inspired by "Mean Tweets," the late-night segment on *Jimmy Kimmel Live!* in which celebrities read cruel tweets about themselves out loud. Our version was Mean Reviews, where faculty members read harsh comments from student course evaluations. "This is possibly the worst class I've ever taken in my life," one professor read, looking defeated before saying, "Fair enough." Another read, "This professor is a b*tch. But she's a nice b*tch," adding with chagrin: "That's sweet." One of my own was "You remind me of a Muppet." The kicker belonged to a junior faculty member: "Prof acts all down with pop culture, but secretly thinks Ariana Grande is a font in Microsoft Word."

I made it a habit to show that video in class every fall, and afterward the floodgates would open. Students seemed to be more comfortable sharing their criticisms and suggestions for improvement after seeing that although I take my work seriously, I don't take myself too seriously.

I sent the video to Melinda Gates, asking if she thought something similar might help with psychological safety in her organization. She not only said yes; she challenged the entire executive leadership team to participate and volunteered to be the first to take the hot seat. Her team compiled criticisms from staff surveys, printed them on note cards, and had her react in real time in front of a camera. She read one employee's complaint that she was like Mary F***ing Poppins—the first time anyone could remember hearing Melinda curse—and explained how she was working on making her imperfections more visible.

To test the impact of her presentation, we randomly assigned one group of employees to watch Melinda engage with the tough comments, a second to watch a video of her talking about the culture she wanted to create in more general terms, and a third to serve as a pure control group. The first group came away with a stronger learning orientation—they were inspired to recognize their shortcomings and work to overcome them. Some of the power distance evaporated—they were more likely to reach out to Melinda and other senior leaders with both criticism and compliments. One employee commented:

> In that video Melinda did something that I've not yet seen happen at the foundation: she broke through the veneer. It happened for me when she said, "I go into so many meetings where there are things I don't know." I had to write that down because I was shocked and grateful at her honesty. Later, when she laughed, like really belly-laughed, and then answered the hard comments, the veneer came off again and I saw that she was no less of Melinda Gates, but actually, a whole lot more of Melinda Gates.

It takes confident humility to admit that we're a work in progress. It shows that we care more about improving ourselves than proving ourselves.* If that mindset spreads far enough within an organization, it can give people the freedom and courage to speak up.

But mindsets aren't enough to transform a culture. Although psychological safety erases the fear of challenging authority, it doesn't necessarily motivate us to question authority in the first place. To build a

---

* Sharing our imperfections can be risky if we haven't yet established our competence. In studies of lawyers and teachers searching for jobs, expressing themselves authentically increased the odds of getting job offers if they were rated in the 90th percentile or above in competence, but backfired if they were less competent. Lawyers at or below the 50th percentile in competence—and teachers at or below the 25th—actually did worse when they were candid. Experiments show that people who haven't yet proven their competence are respected less if they admit their weaknesses. They aren't just incompetent; they seem insecure, too.

learning culture, we also need to create a specific kind of accountability—one that leads people to think again about the best practices in their workplaces.

THE WORST THING ABOUT BEST PRACTICES

In performance cultures, people often become attached to best practices. The risk is that once we've declared a routine the best, it becomes frozen in time. We preach about its virtues and stop questioning its vices, no longer curious about where it's imperfect and where it could improve. Organizational learning should be an ongoing activity, but best practices imply it has reached an endpoint. We might be better off looking for better practices.

At NASA, although teams routinely debriefed after both training simulations and significant operational events, what sometimes stood in the way of exploring better practices was a performance culture that held people accountable for *outcomes*. Every time they delayed a scheduled launch, they faced widespread public criticism and threats to funding.

Each time they celebrated a flight that made it into orbit, they were encouraging their engineers to focus on the fact that the launch resulted in a success rather than on the faulty processes that could jeopardize future launches. That left NASA rewarding luck and repeating problematic practices, failing to rethink what qualified as an acceptable risk. *It wasn't for a lack of ability. After all, these were rocket scientists.* As Ellen Ochoa observes, "When you are dealing with people's lives hanging in the balance, you rely on following the procedures you already have. This can be the best approach in a time-critical situation, but it's problematic if it prevents a thorough assessment in the aftermath."

Focusing on results might be good for short-term performance, but it can be an obstacle to long-term learning. Sure enough, social scientists find that when people are held accountable only for whether the outcome was a success or failure, they are more likely to continue with ill-fated courses of action. Exclusively praising and rewarding results is dangerous because it breeds overconfidence in poor strategies, incentivizing people to keep doing things the way they've always done them. It isn't until a high-stakes decision goes horribly wrong that people pause to reexamine their practices.

We shouldn't have to wait until a space shuttle explodes or an astronaut nearly drowns to determine whether a decision was successful. Along with outcome accountability, we can create process accountability by evaluating how carefully different options are considered as people make decisions. A bad decision process is based on shallow thinking. A good process is grounded in deep thinking and rethinking, enabling people to form and express independent opinions. Research shows that when we have to explain the procedures behind our decisions in real time, we think more critically and process the possibilities more thoroughly.

Process accountability might sound like the opposite of psychological safety, but they're actually independent. Amy Edmondson finds that when psychological safety exists without accountability, people tend to stay within their comfort zone, and when there's accountability but not safety, people tend to stay silent in an anxiety zone. When we combine the two, we create a learning zone. People feel free to experiment—and to poke holes in one another's experiments in service of making them better. They become a challenge network.

One of the most effective steps toward process accountability that I've seen is at Amazon, where important decisions aren't made based on simple PowerPoint presentations. They're informed by a six-page memo that lays out a problem, the different approaches that have been considered in the past, and how the proposed solutions serve the customer. At the start of the meeting, to avoid groupthink, everyone reads the memo silently. This isn't practical in every situation, but it's paramount when choices are both consequential and irreversible. Long before the results of the decision are known, the quality of the process can be evaluated based on the rigor and creativity of the author's thinking in the memo and in the thoroughness of the discussion that ensues in the meeting.

In learning cultures, people don't stop keeping score. They expand the scorecard to consider processes as well as outcomes:

THE RETHINKING SCORECARD

Decision Outcome

	POSITIVE	NEGATIVE
SHALLOW	Luck	Failure
DEEP	Improvement	Experiment

(Decision Process)

Even if the outcome of a decision is positive, it doesn't necessarily qualify as a success. If the process was shallow, you were lucky. If the decision process was deep, you can count it as an improvement: you've discovered a better practice. If the outcome is negative, it's a failure only if the decision process was shallow. If the result was negative but you evaluated the decision thoroughly, you've run a smart experiment.

The ideal time to run those experiments is when decisions are relatively inconsequential or reversible. In too many organizations, leaders look for guarantees that the results will be favorable before testing or investing in something new. It's the equivalent of telling Gutenberg you'd only bankroll his printing press once he had a long line of satisfied customers—or announcing to a group of HIV researchers that you'd only fund their clinical trials after their treatments worked.

Requiring proof is an enemy of progress. This is why companies like Amazon use a principle of disagree and commit. As Jeff Bezos explained it in an annual shareholder letter, instead of demanding convincing results, experiments start with asking people to make bets. "Look, I know we disagree on this but will you gamble with me on it?" The goal in a learning culture is to welcome these kinds of experiments, to make rethinking so familiar that it becomes routine.

Process accountability isn't just a matter of rewards and punishments. It's also about who has decision authority. In a study of California banks, executives often kept approving additional loans to customers who'd already defaulted on a previous one. Since the bankers had signed off on the first loan, they were motivated to justify their initial decision. Interestingly, banks were more likely to identify and write off problem loans when they had high rates of executive turnover. If you're not the person who greenlit the initial loan, you have every incentive to rethink the previous assessment of that customer. *If they've defaulted on the past nineteen loans, it's probably time to adjust.* Rethinking is more likely when we separate the initial decision makers from the later decision evaluators.

A SPECTRUM OF REASONS FOR FAILURE

exploratory testing
an experiment conducted to expand knowledge and investigated possibility leads to an undesired result

uncertainty
a lack of clarity about future events causes people to take seemingly reasonable actions that produce undesired results

task challenge
an individual faces a task too difficult to be executed reliably every time.

lack of ability
an individual doesn't have the skills, conditions or training to execute a job

deviance
an individual chooses to violate a prescribed process or practice

Praiseworthy ←→ **Blameworthy**

hypothesis testing
an experiment conducted to prove that an idea or a design will succeed fails

process complexity
a process composed of many elements breaks down when it encounters novel interactions

process inadequacy
a competent individual adheres to a prescribed but faulty or incomplete process

inattention
an individual inadvertently deviates from specifications

© Hayley Lewis, Sketchnote summary of *A Spectrum of Reasons for Failure*.
From "Strategies for Learning from Failure" by Amy Edmondson, *Harvard Business Review*, April 2011.
Illustration drawn May 2020. London, United Kingdom. Copyright © 2020 by HALO Psychology Limited.

For years, NASA had failed to create that separation. Ellen Ochoa recalls that traditionally "the same managers who were responsible for cost and schedule were the ones who also had the authority to waive technical requirements. It's easy to talk yourself into something on a launch day."

The *Columbia* disaster reinforced the need for NASA to develop a stronger learning culture. On the next space shuttle flight, a problem surfaced with the sensors in an external engine tank. It reoccurred several more times over the next year and a half, but it didn't create any observable problems. In 2006, on the day of a countdown in Houston, the whole mission management team held a vote. There was overwhelming consensus that the launch should go forward. Only one outlier had voted no: Ellen Ochoa.

In the old performance culture, Ellen might've been afraid to vote against the launch. In the emerging learning culture, "it's not just that we're encouraged to speak up. It's our responsibility to speak up," she explains. "Inclusion at NASA is not only a way to increase innovation and engage employees; it directly affects safety since people need to feel valued and respected in order to be comfortable speaking up." In the past, the onus would've been on her to prove it was *not* safe to launch. Now the onus was on the team to prove it *was* safe to launch. That meant approaching their expertise with more humility, their decision with more doubt, and their analysis with more curiosity about the causes and potential consequences of the problem.

After the vote, Ellen received a call from the NASA administrator in Florida, who expressed surprising interest in rethinking the majority opinion in the room. "I'd like to understand your thinking," he told her. They went on to delay the launch. "Some people weren't happy we didn't launch that day," Ellen reflects. "But people did not come up to me and berate me in any way or make me feel bad. They didn't take it out on me personally." The following day all the sensors worked properly, but NASA ended up delaying three more launches over the next few months due to intermittent sensor malfunctions. At that point, the manager of the shuttle program called for the team to stand down until they identified the root cause. Eventually they figured out that the sensors were working fine; it was the cryogenic environment that was causing a faulty connection between the sensors and computers.

Ellen became the deputy director and then the director of the Johnson Space Center, and NASA went on to execute nineteen consecutive successful space shuttle missions before retiring the program. In 2018, when Ellen retired from NASA, a senior leader approached her to tell her how her vote to delay the launch in 2006 had affected him. "I never said anything to you twelve years ago," he said, but "it made me rethink how I approached launch days and whether I'm doing the right thing."

We can't run experiments in the past; we can only imagine the counterfactual in the present. We can wonder whether the lives of fourteen astronauts would have been saved if NASA had gone back to rethink the risks of O-ring failures and foam loss before it was too late. We can wonder why those events didn't make them as careful in reevaluating problems with spacesuits as they had become with space shuttles. In cultures of learning, we're not weighed down with as many of these questions—which means we can live with fewer regrets.

It's a mistake to follow traditions because the status quo is familiar. We're better off questioning whether past routines are serving us well in the present and guiding us toward a better future.

PART IV

Conclusion

CHAPTER 11

Escaping Tunnel Vision

Reconsidering Our Best-Laid Career and Life Plans

□ □ □

A malaise set in within a couple hours of my arriving.
I thought getting a job might help. It turns out I have a lot
of relatives in Hell, and, using connections, I became the
assistant to a demon who pulls people's teeth out. It wasn't
actually a job, more of an internship. But I was eager. And
at first it was kind of interesting. After a while, though,
you start asking yourself: Is this what I came to Hell for,
to hand different kinds of pliers to a demon?

—JACK HANDEY

What do you want to be when you grow up? As a kid, that was my least favorite question. I dreaded conversations with adults because they always asked it—and no matter how I replied, they never liked my answer. When I said I wanted to be a superhero, they laughed. My next goal was to make the NBA, but despite countless hours of shooting hoops on my driveway, I was cut from middle school basketball tryouts three years in a row. I was clearly aiming too high.

In high school, I became obsessed with springboard diving and decided I wanted to become a diving coach. Adults scoffed at that plan: they told me I was aiming too low. In my first semester of college, I decided to major in psychology, but that didn't open any doors—it just gave me a few to close. I knew I didn't want to be a therapist (not patient enough) or a psychiatrist (too squeamish for med school). I was still aimless, and I envied people who had a clear career plan.

From the time he was in kindergarten, my cousin Ryan knew exactly what he wanted to be when he grew up. Becoming a doctor wasn't just the American dream—it was the family dream. Our great-grandparents emigrated from Russia and barely scraped by. Our grandmother was a secretary, and our grandfather worked in a factory, but it wasn't enough to support five children, so he worked a second job delivering milk. Before his kids were teenagers, he had taught them to drive the milk truck so they could finish their 4:00 a.m. delivery cycle before the school day and workday started. When none of their children went on to med school (or milk delivery), my grandparents hoped our generation would bring the prestige of a Dr. Grant to the family.

The first seven grandchildren didn't become doctors. I was the eighth, and I worked multiple jobs to pay for college and to keep my options open. My grandparents were proud when I ended up getting my doctorate in psychology, but they still hoped for a *real* doctor. For the ninth grandchild, Ryan, who arrived four years after me, an M.D. was practically preordained.

Ryan checked all the right boxes: along with being precocious, he had a strong work ethic. He set his sights on becoming a neurosurgeon. He was passionate about the potential to help people and ready to persist in the face of whatever obstacles would come into his path.

When Ryan was looking at colleges, he came to visit me. As we started talking about majors, he expressed a flicker of doubt about the premed track and asked if he should study economics instead. There's a term in psychology that captures Ryan's personality: blirtatiousness. *Yep, that's an actual research concept, derived from the combination of blurting and flirting.* When "blirters" meet people, their responses tend to be fast and effusive. They typically score high in extraversion and impulsiveness—and low in shyness and neuroticism. Ryan could push himself to study for long hours, but it drained him. Drawn to something more active and social, he toyed with the idea of squeezing in an economics major along with premed, but abandoned that idea when he got to college. *Gotta stay on track.*

Ryan sailed through the premed curriculum and became a teaching assistant for undergrads while he was still an undergrad himself. When he showed up at exam review sessions and saw how stressed the students were, he refused to start covering the material until they stood up and danced. When he was accepted to an Ivy League medical school, he asked me if he should do a joint M.D.–M.B.A. program. He hadn't lost his interest in business, but he was afraid to divide his attention. *Gotta stay on track.*

In his last year of med school, Ryan dutifully applied to neurosurgery residencies. It takes a focused brain to slice into the brain of another human. He wasn't sure if he was cut out for it—or if the career would leave any space for him to have a life. He wondered if he should start a health-care company instead, but when he was admitted to Yale, he opted for the residency. *Gotta stay on track.*

Partway through his residency, the grueling hours and the intense focus began to take their toll, and Ryan burned out. He felt that if he died that very day, no one in the system would really care or even notice. He regularly suffered from the heartache of losing patients and the headache of dealing with abusive attending surgeons, and there was no end in sight. Although it was his childhood dream and our grandparents' dream, his work left little time for anything else. The sheer exhaustion left him questioning whether he should quit.

Ryan decided that he couldn't give up. He had gone too far to change course, so he finished the seven-year neurosurgery residency. When he submitted the paperwork for his credentials, the hospital denied him because he had placed the dates on his résumé on the right instead of the left. He was so fed up with the system that, out of principle, he refused to move them. After winning that battle with bureaucracy, he added another feather to his cap, doing an eighth year of a fellowship in complex, minimally invasive spinal surgery.

Today Ryan is a neurosurgeon at a major medical center. In his midthirties, he's still in debt from student loans more than a decade after graduating from med school. Even though he enjoys helping people and caring for patients, the long hours and red tape undercut his enthusiasm. He tells me that if he could do it over, he would have gone a different route. I've often wondered what it would have taken to convince him to rethink his chosen line of work—and what he truly wanted out of a career.

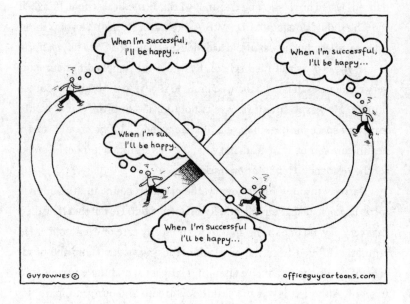

We all have notions of who we want to be and how we hope to lead our lives. They're not limited to careers; from an early age, we develop ideas about where we'll live, which school we'll attend, what kind of person we'll marry, and how many kids we'll have. These images can inspire us to set bolder goals and guide us toward a path to achieve them. The danger of these plans is that they can give us tunnel vision, blinding us to alternative possibilities. We don't know how time and circumstances will change what we want and even who we want to be, and locking our life GPS onto a single target can give us the right directions to the wrong destination.

GOING INTO FORECLOSURE

When we dedicate ourselves to a plan and it isn't going as we hoped, our first instinct isn't usually to rethink it. Instead, we tend to double down and sink more resources in the plan. This pattern is called escalation of commitment. Evidence shows that entrepreneurs persist with failing strategies when they should pivot, NBA general managers and coaches keep investing in new contracts and more playing time for draft busts, and politicians continue sending soldiers to wars that didn't need to be fought in the first place. Sunk costs are a factor, but the most important causes appear to be psychological rather than economic. Escalation of commitment happens because we're rationalizing creatures, constantly searching for self-justifications for our prior beliefs as a way to soothe our egos, shield our images, and validate our past decisions.

Escalation of commitment is a major factor in preventable failures. Ironically, it can be fueled by one of the most celebrated engines of success: grit. Grit is the combination of passion and perseverance, and research shows that it can play an important role in motivating us to accomplish long-term goals. When it comes to rethinking, though, grit may have a dark side. Experiments show that gritty people are more likely to keep playing beyond their planned limits in roulette and more willing to stay the course in tasks at which they're failing and success is impossible. Researchers have even suggested that gritty mountaineers are more likely to die on expeditions, because they're determined to do whatever it takes to reach the summit. There's a fine line between heroic persistence and foolish stubbornness. Sometimes the best kind of grit is gritting our teeth and turning around.

Ryan escalated his commitment to medical training for sixteen years. If he had been less tenacious, he might have changed tracks sooner. Early on, he had fallen victim to what psychologists call identity foreclosure—when we settle prematurely on a sense of self without enough due diligence, and close our minds to alternative selves.

In career choices, identity foreclosure often begins when adults ask kids: what do you want to be when you grow up? Pondering that question can foster a fixed mindset about work and self. "I think it's one of the most useless questions an adult can ask a child," Michelle Obama writes. *"What do you want to be when you grow up?* As if growing up is finite. As if at some point you become something and that's the end."*

Some kids dream too small. They foreclose on following in family footsteps and never really consider alternatives. You probably know some people who faced the opposite problem. They dreamed too big, becoming attached to a lofty vision that wasn't realistic. Sometimes we lack the talent to pursue our callings professionally, leaving them unanswered; other times there's little hope that our passions can pay the bills. "You can be anything you wanna be?!" the comedian Chris Rock quipped. "Tell the kids the truth. . . . You can be anything you're good at . . . as long as they're hiring."

Even if kids get excited about a career path that does prove realistic, what they thought was their dream job can turn out to be a nightmare. Kids might be better off learning about careers as actions to take rather than as identities to claim. When they see work as what they do rather than who they are, they become more open to exploring different possibilities.

---

*I have another objection to this question: it encourages kids to make work the main event of their identities. When you're asked what you want to be, the only socially acceptable response is a job. Adults are waiting for kids to wax poetic about becoming something grand like an astronaut, heroic like a firefighter, or inspired like a filmmaker. There's no room to say you just want job security, let alone that you hope to be a good father or a great mother—or a caring and curious person. Although I study work for a living, I don't think it should define us.

SHOULD YOU ASK "WHAT DO YOU WANT TO BE WHEN YOU GROW UP?"

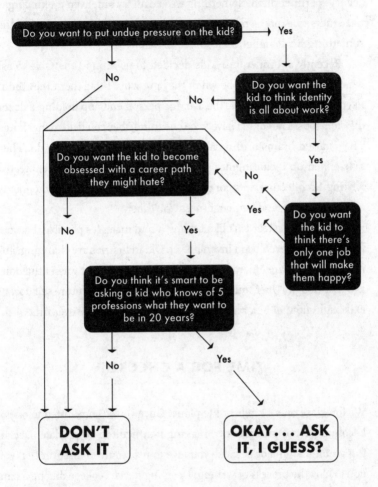

Although children are often fascinated by science from a young age, over the course of elementary school, they tend to lose interest and confidence in their potential to be scientists. Recent studies show that it's possible to maintain their enthusiasm by introducing them to science differently. When second and third graders learned about "doing science" rather than "being scientists," they were more excited about pursuing science. Becoming a scientist might seem out of reach, but the act of experimenting is something we can all try out. Even prekindergarten students express more interest in science when it's presented as something we *do* rather than someone we *are*.

Recently at dinner, our kids decided to go around the table to ask what everyone wanted to be when they grew up. I told them they didn't need to choose one career; the average person ends up holding a dozen different jobs. They didn't have to be one thing; they could do many things. They started brainstorming about all the things they love to do. Their lists ended up including designing Lego sets, studying space, creative writing, architecture, interior design, teaching gymnastics, photography, coaching soccer, and being a fitness YouTuber.

Choosing a career isn't like finding a soul mate. It's possible that your ideal job hasn't even been invented yet. Old industries are changing, and new industries are emerging faster than ever before: it wasn't that long ago that Google, Uber, and Instagram didn't exist. Your future self doesn't exist right now, either, and your interests might change over time.

TIME FOR A CHECKUP

We foreclose on all kinds of life plans. Once you've committed to one, it becomes part of your identity, making it difficult to de-escalate. Declaring an English major because you love to read, only to discover that you don't enjoy the process of writing. Deciding to start college during a pandemic, only to conclude later that you should have considered a gap year. *Gotta stay on track.* Ending a romantic relationship because you don't want kids, only to realize years down the road that you might after all.

Identity foreclosure can stop us from evolving. In a study of amateur musicians, those who had settled on music as a professional calling were more likely to ignore career advice from a trusted adviser over the course of the following seven years. They listened to their hearts and tuned out their mentors. In some ways, identity foreclosure is the opposite of an identity crisis: instead of accepting uncertainty about who we want to become, we develop compensatory conviction and plunge head over heels into a career path. I've noticed that the students who are the most certain about their career plans at twenty are often the ones with the deepest regrets by thirty. They haven't done enough rethinking along the way.*

Sometimes it's because they're thinking too much like politicians, eager to earn the approval of parents and peers. They become seduced by status, failing to see that no matter how much an accomplishment or affiliation impresses someone else, it's still a poor choice if it depresses them. In other cases it's because they're stuck in preacher mode, and they've come to see a job as a sacred cause. And occasionally they pick careers in prosecutor mode, where they charge classmates with selling their souls to capitalism and hurl themselves into nonprofits in the hopes of saving the world.

Sadly, they often know too little about the job—and too little about their evolving selves—to make a lifelong commitment. They get trapped in an overconfidence cycle, taking pride in pursuing a career identity and surrounding themselves with people who validate their conviction. By the time they discover it was the wrong fit, they feel it's too late to think again. The stakes seem too high to walk away; the sacrifices of salary, status, skill, and time seem too great. *For the record, I think it's better to lose the past two years of progress than to waste the next twenty.* In hindsight, identity foreclosure is a Band-Aid: it covers up an identity crisis, but fails to cure it.

My advice to students is to take a cue from health-care professions. Just as they make appointments with the doctor and the dentist even

---

*There's evidence that graduates of universities in England and Wales were more likely to change career paths than those who studied in Scotland. It isn't a culture effect—it's a timing effect. In England and Wales, students had to start specializing in high school, which limited their options for exploring alternatives throughout college. In Scotland, students weren't allowed to specialize until their third year of college, which gave them more opportunities to rethink their plans and develop new interests. They ended up being more likely to major in subjects that weren't covered in high school—and more likely to find a match.

when nothing is wrong, they should schedule checkups on their careers. I encourage them to put a reminder in their calendars to ask some key questions twice a year. When did you form the aspirations you're currently pursuing, and how have you changed since then? Have you reached a learning plateau in your role or your workplace, and is it time to consider a pivot? Answering these career checkup questions is a way to periodically activate rethinking cycles. It helps students maintain humility about their ability to predict the future, contemplate doubts about their plans, and stay curious enough to discover new possibilities or reconsider previously discarded ones.

A TYPICAL WORKWEEK AFTER IDENTITY FORECLOSURE

MON.	TUES.	WED.	THURS.	FRI.

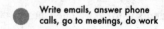

Write emails, answer phone calls, go to meetings, do work

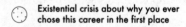

Existential crisis about why you ever chose this career in the first place

I had one student, Marissa Shandell, who scored a coveted job at a prestigious consulting firm and planned on climbing up the ladder. She kept getting promoted early but found herself working around the clock. Instead of continuing to just grit and bear it, she and her husband had a career checkup conversation every six months, talking not just about the growth trajectory of their companies but also about the growth trajectory of their jobs. After being promoted to associate partner well ahead of schedule, Marissa realized she had reached a learning plateau (and a lifestyle plateau) and decided to pursue a doctorate in management.*

Deciding to leave a current career path is often easier than identifying a new one. My favorite framework for navigating that challenge comes from a management professor, Herminia Ibarra. She finds that as people consider career choices and transitions, it helps to think like scientists. A first step is to entertain possible selves: identify some people you admire within or outside your field, and observe what they actually do at work day by day. A second step is to develop hypotheses about how these paths might align with your own interests, skills, and values. A third step is to test out the different identities by running experiments: do informational interviews, job shadowing, and sample projects to get a taste of the work. The goal is not to confirm a particular plan but to expand your repertoire of possible selves—which keeps you open to rethinking.

Checkups aren't limited to careers—they're relevant to the plans we make in every domain of our lives. A few years ago, a former student called for romantic advice. *Caveat: I'm not that kind of psychologist.* He'd been dating a woman for just over a year, and although it was the most fulfilling relationship he'd ever had, he was still questioning whether it was the right match. He had always imagined himself marrying a woman who was ambitious in her career or passionate about improving the world, and his girlfriend seemed less driven and more relaxed in her approach to life.

It was an ideal time for a checkup. I asked him how old he was when he formed that vision of a partner and how much he'd changed since then.

---

* I originally recommended career checkups for students to avoid tunnel vision, but I've learned that they can also be useful for students at the opposite end of the rethinking spectrum: overthinkers. They often report back that when they're dissatisfied at work, knowing a reminder will pop up twice a year helps them resist the temptation to think about quitting every day.

He said he'd held it since he was a teenager and had never paused to rethink it. As we talked, he started to realize that if he and his girlfriend were happy together, ambition and passion might not be as important to him in a partner as they had been in the past. He came to understand that he was inspired by women who were highly motivated to succeed and serve because that was who he wanted to be.

Two and a half years later, he reached out with an update. He had decided to let go of his preconceived image of who his partner should be:

> I decided to open up and talk to her about how she's different from the person I'd imagined being with. Surprisingly, she told me the same thing! I wasn't who she imagined she'd end up with either—she expected to end up with a guy who was more of a creative, someone who was more gregarious. We accepted it and moved on. I'm thrilled to have left my old ideas behind to make space for the full her and everything our relationship could bring.

Just before the pandemic, he proposed to her, and they're now engaged.

A successful relationship requires rethinking. Psychologists find that doing an annual relationship health checkup improves satisfaction in married couples. Sometimes being considerate means reconsidering something as simple as our habits. *Learning not to be fashionably late to everything. Retiring that wardrobe of ratty conference T-shirts. Rolling over to snore in the other direction.* At other times being supportive means opening our minds to bigger life changes—moving to a different country, a different community, or a different job to support our partner's priorities. In my student's case, it meant rethinking who his fiancée would be, but also staying open to who she might become. She eventually switched jobs and became passionate about both her work and a personal cause of fighting educational inequity. When we're willing to update our ideas of who our partners are, it can give them freedom to evolve and our relationships room to grow.

Whether we do checkups with our partners, our parents, or our mentors, it's worth pausing once or twice a year to reflect on how our aspirations have changed. As we identify past images of our lives that are no longer relevant to our future, we can start to rethink our plans. That can set us up for happiness—as long as we're not too fixated on finding it.

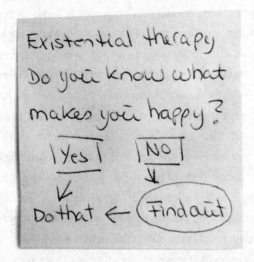

WHEN CHASING HAPPINESS CHASES IT AWAY

When we think about how to plan our lives, there are few things that take priority over happiness. The kingdom of Bhutan has a Gross National Happiness index. In the United States, the pursuit of happiness is so prized that it's one of the three unalienable rights in our Declaration of Independence. If we're not careful, though, the pursuit of happiness can become a recipe for misery.

Psychologists find that the more people value happiness, the less happy they often become with their lives. It's true for people who naturally care about happiness and for people who are randomly assigned to reflect on why happiness matters. There's even evidence that placing a great deal of importance on happiness is a risk factor for depression. Why?

One possibility is that when we're searching for happiness, we get too busy evaluating life to actually experience it. Instead of savoring our moments of joy, we ruminate about why our lives aren't *more* joyful. A second likely culprit is that we spend too much time striving for peak happiness, overlooking the fact that happiness depends more on the frequency of positive emotions than their intensity. A third potential factor is that when we hunt for happiness, we overemphasize pleasure at the expense of purpose. This theory is consistent with data suggesting that meaning is healthier than happiness, and that people who look for purpose in their work are more successful in pursuing their passions—and less likely to quit their jobs—than those who look for joy. While enjoyment waxes and wanes, meaning tends to last. A fourth explanation is that Western conceptions of happiness as an individual state leave us feeling lonely. In more collectivistic Eastern cultures, that pattern is reversed: pursuing happiness predicts higher well-being, because people prioritize social engagement over independent activities.

Last fall a student stopped by my office hours for some advice. She explained that when she chose Wharton, she had focused too much on getting into the best school and too little on finding the best fit. She wished she had picked a college with a more carefree culture and a stronger sense of community. Now that she was clear on her values, she was considering a transfer to a school that would make her happier.

A few weeks later she told me that a moment in class had helped her rethink her plan. It wasn't the research on happiness that we discussed, the values survey she took, or the decision-making activity we did. It was a comedy sketch I showed from *Saturday Night Live*.

The scene stars Adam Sandler as a tour guide. In a mock commercial advertising his company's Italian tours, he mentions that customer reviews sometimes express disappointment. He takes the opportunity to remind customers about what a vacation can and can't do for them:

There's a lot a vacation can do: help you unwind, see some different-looking squirrels, but it cannot fix deeper issues, like how you behave in group settings.

We can take you on a hike. We cannot turn you into someone who likes hiking.

Remember, you're still gonna be *you* on vacation. If you are sad where you are, and then you get on a plane to Italy, the you in Italy will be the same sad you from before, just in a new place.

© *Saturday Night Live*/NBC

When we pursue happiness, we often start by changing our surroundings. We expect to find bliss in a warmer climate or a friendlier dorm, but any joy that those choices bring about is typically temporary. In a series of studies, students who changed their environments by adjusting their living arrangements or course schedules quickly returned to their baseline levels of happiness. As Ernest Hemingway wrote, "You can't get away from yourself by moving from one place to another." Meanwhile, students who changed their actions by joining a new club, adjusting their study habits, or starting a new project experienced lasting gains in happiness. Our happiness often depends more on what we do than where we are. It's our actions—not our surroundings—that bring us meaning and belonging.

My student decided not to transfer. Instead of rethinking where she went to school, she would rethink how she spent her time. She might not be able to change the culture of an entire institution, but she could create a new subculture. She started doing weekly coffee chats with classmates and invited the ones who shared her interests and values over for weekly tea. A few months later, she reported that she had formed several close friendships and was thrilled with her decision to stay. The impact didn't stop there: her tea gatherings became a tradition for welcoming students who felt out of place. Instead of transferring to a new community, they built their own microcommunity. They weren't focusing on happiness—they were looking for contribution and connection.

LIFE, LIBERTY, AND THE PURSUIT OF MEANING

To be clear, I wouldn't encourage anyone to stay in a role, relationship, or place they hated unless they had no other alternatives. Still, when it comes to careers, instead of searching for the job where we'll be happiest, we might be better off pursuing the job where we expect to learn and contribute the most.

Psychologists find that passions are often developed, not discovered. In a study of entrepreneurs, the more effort they put into their startups, the more their enthusiasm about their businesses climbed each week. Their passion grew as they gained momentum and mastery. Interest doesn't always lead to effort and skill; sometimes it follows them. By investing in learning and problem solving, we can develop our passions—and build the skills necessary to do the work and lead the lives we find worthwhile.

As we get older, we become more focused on searching for meaning—and we're most likely to find it in actions that benefit others. My favorite test of meaningful work is to ask: if this job didn't exist, how much worse off would people be? It's near midlife that this question often begins to loom large. At around this time, in both work and life, we feel we have more to give (and less to lose), and we're especially keen to share our knowledge and skills with the next generation.

When my students talk about the evolution of self-esteem in their careers, the progression often goes something like this:

Phase 1: I'm not important
Phase 2: I'm important
Phase 3: I want to contribute to something important

I've noticed that the sooner they get to phase 3, the more impact they have and the more happiness they experience. It's left me thinking about happiness less as a goal and more as a by-product of mastery and meaning. "Those only are happy," philosopher John Stuart Mill wrote, "who have their minds fixed on some object other than their own happiness; on the happiness of others, on the improvement of mankind, even on some art or pursuit, followed not as a means, but as itself an ideal end. Aiming thus at something else, they find happiness by the way."

Careers, relationships, and communities are examples of what scientists call open systems—they're constantly in flux because they're not closed off from the environments around them. We know that open systems are governed by at least two key principles: there are always multiple paths to the same end (equifinality), and the same starting point can be a path to many different ends (multifinality). We should be careful to avoid getting too attached to a particular route or even a particular destination. There isn't one definition of success or one track to happiness.

My cousin Ryan finally wound up rethinking his career arc. Five years into his neurosurgery residency, he did his own version of a career checkup and decided to scratch his entrepreneurial itch. He cofounded a fast-growing, venture-backed startup called Nomad Health, which creates a marketplace to match clinicians with medical facilities. He also advised several medical device startups, filed medical device patents, and is now working on multiple startups to improve health care. Looking back, he still regrets that he foreclosed so early on an identity as a neurosurgeon and escalated his commitment to that career.

At work and in life, the best we can do is plan for what we want to learn and contribute over the next year or two, and stay open to what might come next. To adapt an analogy from E. L. Doctorow, writing out a plan for your life "is like driving at night in the fog. You can only see as far as your headlights, but you can make the whole trip that way."

□ □ □

WE DON'T HAVE TO UPEND our entire paths to rethink some of our plans. Some people are perfectly content with their fields of work but dissatisfied with their current roles. Others may be too risk averse to make a geographic move for a job or a partner. And many don't have the luxury of making a pivot: being economically dependent on a job or emotionally attached to an extended family can limit the options available. Whether or not we have the opportunity or appetite for major changes in our lives, it's still possible to make smaller adjustments that breathe new meaning into our days.

My colleagues Amy Wrzesniewski and Jane Dutton find that in every line of work, there are people who become active architects of their own jobs. They rethink their roles through job crafting—changing their daily actions to better fit their values, interests, and skills. One of the places Amy and Jane studied job crafting was in the University of Michigan health-care system.

If you visited a certain floor of the hospital, it wouldn't be long before cancer patients told you how grateful they were for Candice Walker. Her mission was not only to protect their fragile immune systems—it was also to care for their fragile emotions. She called the chemotherapy center the House of Hope.

Candice was often the first one to console families when their loved ones went through treatment; she showed up with bagels and coffee. She would make patients laugh by telling stories about her cats drinking her milk or showing them that she had accidentally put on one brown sock and one blue sock. One day she saw a patient on the floor of an elevator writhing in pain, and the staff members nearby weren't sure what to do. Candice immediately took charge, rushed the woman into a wheelchair, and took her up in the elevator for urgent treatment. The patient later called her "my savior."

Candice Walker wasn't a doctor or a nurse. She wasn't a social worker, either. She was a custodian. Her official job was to keep the cancer center clean.

Candice and her fellow custodians were all hired to do the same job, but some of them ended up rethinking their roles. One cleaner on a long-term intensive care unit took it upon herself to regularly rearrange the paintings on the walls, hoping that a change of scenery might spark some awareness among patients in comas. When asked about it, she said, "No, it's not part of my job, but it's part of me."

Our identities are open systems, and so are our lives. We don't have to stay tethered to old images of where we want to go or who we want to be. The simplest way to start rethinking our options is to question what we do daily.

It takes humility to reconsider our past commitments, doubt to question our present decisions, and curiosity to reimagine our future plans. What we discover along the way can free us from the shackles of our familiar surroundings and our former selves. Rethinking liberates us to do more than update our knowledge and opinions—it's a tool for leading a more fulfilling life.

Epilogue

□ □ □

"What I believe" is a process rather than a finality.

—EMMA GOLDMAN

When reading fiction, my favorite part has always been the conclusion. As long as I can remember, whether I was devouring sci-fi like *Ender's Game* or mystery like *The Westing Game,* the twist at the end wasn't just the highlight of the story. It transformed the story, making me rethink everything I'd read before.

In writing about ideas, though, I've never liked conclusions. Can't the final chapter just serve as the end? *It's a book, not a book report. If I had something else worth saying, I would've already said it.*

What bothers me most about a conclusion is the finality. If a topic is important enough to deserve an entire book, it shouldn't end. It should be open-ended.

That's an inherent challenge for *Think Again.* I don't want the conclusion to bring closure. I want my thinking to keep evolving. To symbolize that openness, I decided to make the epilogue a blank page. Literally.

I think the absurdity was best captured by humorist Richard Brautigan: "Expressing a human need, I always wanted to write a book that ended with the word Mayonnaise." He wrote that line in the penultimate chapter of a book, and delightfully went on to end the book with the word—but deliberately misspelled it "mayonaise" to deprive the reader of closure. *Human need, unfulfilled.*

My challenge network unanimously rejected that concept. Two of my most insightful students convinced me that although it might represent an endpoint for me as a writer, it's a starting point for you as a reader—a springboard to new thoughts and a bridge to new conversations. Then they proposed a way to honor the spirit of the book: I could take a cue from Ron Berger's classroom and show some of my rethinking of the conclusion from one draft to the next.

I loved the idea. ~~For a book about rethinking, it seemed delightfully meta. Like the *Seinfeld* coffee table book about coffee tables—or the time when Ryan Gosling wore a shirt with a photo of Macaulay Culkin, and Macaulay Culkin one-upped him by wearing a shirt with a picture of Ryan Gosling wearing that shirt.~~

The conclusion seemed like the perfect place to show a few key moments of rethinking, but I still didn't know what to cover. I went back to my challenge network, and they suggested one more way to synthesize key themes and provide an update on what I'm rethinking right now.

~~The first thing that came to mind was a moment in the fact-checking process, when I learned that scientists have revised their thinking about the purported plumage of the tyrannosaurus family. If you were picturing a feathered *T. rex* in chapter 1, so was I, but the current consensus is that a typical *T. rex* was covered mostly in scales. If you're devastated by that update, please flip to the index and look up *joy of being wrong, the*. Actually, I have some good news: there's another tyrannosaur, the yutyrannus, that scientists believe was covered in vibrant feathers to stay cool.~~

<u>Lately, I've been thinking again about how rethinking happens. For thousands of years, much of the rethinking that people did unfolded invisibly in groups over time.</u>

Margin notes:

Had thought earlier about showing my edits throughout the book, but didn't want to inflict that on you. Slogging through half-baked ideas and falsified hypotheses wouldn't be the best use of your time. Even if you're a huge fan of *Hamilton*, you probably wouldn't love the first draft—it's much more exciting to engage with the product of rethinking than the process.

Too whimsical. Early readers want more gravitas here—several have reported that they're handling dissent differently now. When they confront information that challenges their opinions, instead of rejecting it or begrudgingly engaging with it, they're taking it as an opportunity to learn something new: "Maybe I should rethink that!"

Challenge network says updating a "fun fact" from the book is too trivial.

Before the printing press, a great deal of knowledge was transmitted orally. Human history was one long game of telephone, where each sender would remember and convey information differently, and each receiver would have no way of knowing how the story had changed. By the time an idea traveled across a land, it could be completely reimagined without anyone's being aware of it. As more information began to be recorded in books and then newspapers, we could begin to track the different ways in which knowledge and beliefs evolved. Today, although we can see every revision made in Wikipedia, the individuals making the changes often wind up in edit wars, refusing to concede that others were right or that they were wrong. Codifying knowledge might help us track it, but it doesn't necessarily lead us to open our minds.

Many great thinkers have argued that rethinking is a task for each generation, not each person—even in science. As the eminent physicist Max Planck put it, "A new scientific truth does not triumph by convincing its opponents and making them see the light, but rather because its opponents eventually die." From this perspective, generations are replaced faster than people change their views.

I no longer believe that has to be the case. We all have the capacity to think again—we just don't use it often enough, because we don't think like scientists often enough.

The scientific method can be traced back several millennia, at least as far back as Aristotle and the ancient Greeks. I was surprised to learn, then, that the word *scientist* is relatively new: it wasn't coined until 1833. For centuries, there was no general term for people whose profession was to discover knowledge through developing hypotheses, designing experiments, and collecting data. I hope we don't wait that long to recognize that this way of thinking applies to every line of work—and any walk of life.

Even as this book goes to press, I'm still rethinking. One key question is what to rethink. The case for being quick to rethink taken-for-granted assumptions, intuitions, and opinions is clear. It's less obvious how we should approach deeper knowledge, core beliefs, and sacred values. On the one hand, it would be a mistake to recklessly abandon what's core to your sense of self. I'd hate to see you walk away from a good job after one bad day or a good marriage after one bad fight. On the other hand, sometimes our most important rethinking happens when we question the ideas and ideals that we've been most reluctant to give up. Failing to reconsider "settled science" has stalled progress at too many times in history.

A second dilemma is when to think again. Before making a decision, it's worth considering two questions: how high are the stakes, and how reversible is it? If a choice is inconsequential, it makes sense to be decisive: the early bird gets the worm. If you're about to walk through a revolving door, it's fine to act quickly too: you can always rethink it later. But if the stakes are high and the door is going to lock behind you, it pays to do your rethinking up front. It really matters, and it won't be so easy to undo.

A third puzzle is how much rethinking to do. Yes, overthinking is a problem, but underthinking is a bigger problem. I feel for people who get stuck in analysis paralysis. I worry about people who don't do the analysis in the first place. I'd rather see you embrace the discomfort of doubt than live with the regret of foolish conviction. For me, the difference between reflection and rumination is whether you're still learning. If you're pondering a familiar problem without gaining fresh insights, it's time to seek new information or reach out to your challenge network.

In making the case for thinking like a scientist, something has been nagging at me. I wonder if I've devoted too little attention to the situations in which it's productive to preach, prosecute, and politick. When it comes to rethinking our own views, the weight of the evidence favors the scientist mode as giving us the best odds. But the ideal mode is less clear cut when it comes to opening other people's minds. I tried to capture the nuances in the value of each approach, exploring how preaching can be effective in debates with people who are receptive to our viewpoint or aren't invested in the issue; prosecuting can get through to audiences who aren't determined to be in control; and simplicity can persuade our own political tribe. But even after reviewing these data points, I still wasn't sure whether I'd done enough to qualify my argument.

Then the coronavirus pandemic happened, and I became curious about how leaders communicate during crisis. How do they give people a sense of security in the present and hope for the future? Preaching the virtues of their plans and prosecuting alternative proposals could reduce uncertainty. Making a political case might rally the base around shared goals.

For me, the most instructive example came from the governor of New York. In an early speech in the spring, as his state and the nation faced an unprecedented crisis, he announced, "It is common sense to take a method and try it: If it fails, admit it frankly and try another. But above all, try something."

The New York Times quickly eviscerated the governor's speech, noting that "something unspecified is no better than

A big unanswered question here is when rethinking should end—where should we draw the line? I think the answer is different for every person in every situation, but my sense is that most of us are operating too far to the left of the curve. The most relevant data I've seen were in chapter 3 on superforecasters: they updated their predictions an average of four times per question instead of twice per question. This suggests that it doesn't take much rethinking to benefit from it, and the downsides are minimal. Rethinking doesn't always have to change our minds. Like students rethinking their answers on tests, even if we decide not to pivot on a belief or a decision, we still come away knowing we've reflected more thoughtfully.

nothing." Whereas other leaders were "precise, concrete, positive," the governor was "indefinite, abstract, irresolute." It wasn't just the media that trashed the speech—one of the governor's own advisers apparently described it as an act of political stupidity.

It's easy to see the appeal of a confident leader who offers a clear vision, a strong plan, and a definitive forecast for the future. But in times of crisis as well as times of prosperity, what we need more is a leader who accepts uncertainty, acknowledges mistakes, learns from others, and rethinks plans. That's what this particular governor was offering, and the early critics were wrong about how his proposed approach would unfold.

This didn't happen during the coronavirus pandemic, and the governor wasn't Andrew Cuomo. It occurred the last time unemployment in America was so high: during the Great Depression. It was 1932, and the governor of New York was Franklin Delano Roosevelt. He delivered his "try something" message as the country was reeling from the Great Depression, in a commencement speech at a small university in Georgia. In the most memorable line from the speech, FDR argued that "the country demands bold, persistent experimentation." That principle became a touchstone of his leadership. Although economists are still debating which of the resulting reforms lifted the country out of a historic depression, FDR's trial-and-error method of formulating policy was popular enough that Americans elected him president four times.

In his commencement speech, FDR wasn't preaching, prosecuting, or appealing to politics. He spoke with the same kind of confident humility that you'd expect from a scientist. There's a lot we don't know about how to communicate confident humility. When people lack knowledge about a complex topic—like stopping a pandemic or reinvigorating an economy—they might be comfortable with leaders admitting what they don't know today and doubting the statements they made yesterday. When people feel more informed and the problem is simpler, they might dismiss leaders who acknowledge uncertainty and change their minds as flip-floppers.

I'm still curious about when each mode is most effective for persuasion, but on balance, I'd love to see more people do their rethinking out loud, as FDR did. As valuable as rethinking is, we don't do it enough—whether we're grappling with the pivotal decisions of our lives or the great quandaries of our time. Complex problems like pandemics, climate change, and political polarization call on us to stay mentally flexible. In the face of any number of unknown and evolving threats, humility, doubt, and curiosity are vital to discovery. Bold, persistent experimentation might be our best tool for rethinking.

We can all improve at thinking again. Whatever conclusion we reach, I think the world would be a better place if everyone put on scientist goggles a little more often. I'm curious: do you agree? If not, what evidence would change your mind?

Actions for Impact

□ □ □

If you're interested in working on your rethinking skills, here are my top thirty practical takeaways.

I. INDIVIDUAL RETHINKING

A. Develop the Habit of Thinking Again

1. ***Think like a scientist.*** When you start forming an opinion, resist the temptation to preach, prosecute, or politick. Treat your emerging view as a hunch or a hypothesis and test it with data. Like the entrepreneurs who learned to approach their business strategies as experiments, you'll maintain the agility to pivot. For a free assessment of your habits of thinking like a preacher, prosecutor, politician, and scientist, visit www.adamgrant.net/quiz.

2. ***Define your identity in terms of values, not opinions.*** It's easier to avoid getting stuck to your past beliefs if you don't become attached to them as part of your present self-concept. See yourself as someone who values

curiosity, learning, mental flexibility, and searching for knowledge. As you form opinions, keep a list of factors that would change your mind.

3. *Seek out information that goes against your views.* You can fight confirmation bias, burst filter bubbles, and escape echo chambers by actively engaging with ideas that challenge your assumptions. An easy place to start is to follow people who make you think—even if you usually disagree with what they think.

B. Calibrate Your Confidence

4. *Beware of getting stranded at the summit of Mount Stupid.* Don't confuse confidence with competence. The Dunning-Kruger effect is a good reminder that the better you think you are, the greater the risk that you're overestimating yourself—and the greater the odds that you'll stop improving. To prevent overconfidence in your knowledge, reflect on how well you can explain a given subject.

5. *Harness the benefits of doubt.* When you find yourself doubting your ability, reframe the situation as an opportunity for growth. You can have confidence in your capacity to learn while questioning your current solution to a problem. Knowing what you don't know is often the first step toward developing expertise.

6. *Embrace the joy of being wrong.* When you find out you've made a mistake, take it as a sign that you've just discovered something new. Don't be afraid to laugh at yourself. It helps you focus less on proving yourself—and more on improving yourself.

C. Invite Others to Question Your Thinking

7. *Learn something new from each person you meet.* Everyone knows more than you about something. Ask people what they've been rethinking lately, or start a conversation about times you've changed your mind in the past year.

8. *Build a challenge network, not just a support network.* It's helpful to have cheerleaders encouraging you, but you also need critics to challenge you. Who are your most thoughtful critics? Once you've identified them, invite them to question your thinking. To make sure they know you're open to dissenting views, tell them why you respect their pushback—and where they usually add the most value.

9. *Don't shy away from constructive conflict.* Disagreements don't have to be disagreeable. Although relationship conflict is usually counterproductive, task conflict can help you think again. Try framing disagreement as a debate: people are more likely to approach it intellectually and less likely to take it personally.

II. INTERPERSONAL RETHINKING

A. Ask Better Questions

10. *Practice the art of persuasive listening.* When we're trying to open other people's minds, we can frequently accomplish more by listening than by talking. How can you show an interest in helping people crystallize their own views and uncover their own reasons for change? A good way to start is to increase your question-to-statement ratio.

11. *Question how rather than why.* When people describe *why* they hold extreme views, they often intensify their commitment and double down. When they try to explain *how* they would make their views a reality, they often realize the limits of their understanding and start to temper some of their opinions.

12. *Ask "What evidence would change your mind?"* You can't bully someone into agreeing with you. It's often more effective to inquire about what would open their minds, and then see if you can convince them on their own terms.

13. *Ask how people originally formed an opinion.* Many of our opinions, like our stereotypes, are arbitrary; we've developed them without rigorous data or deep reflection. To help people reevaluate, prompt them to consider how they'd believe different things if they'd been born at a different time or in a different place.

B. Approach Disagreements as Dances, Not Battles

14. *Acknowledge common ground.* A debate is like a dance, not a war. Admitting points of convergence doesn't make you weaker—it shows that you're willing to negotiate about what's true, and it motivates the other side to consider your point of view.

15. *Remember that less is often more.* If you pile on too many different reasons to support your case, it can make your audiences defensive—and cause them to reject your entire argument based on its least compelling points. Instead of diluting your argument, lead with a few of your strongest points.

16. *Reinforce freedom of choice.* Sometimes people resist not because they're dismissing the argument but because they're rejecting the feeling of their behavior being controlled. It helps to respect their autonomy by reminding them that it's up to them to choose what they believe.

17. *Have a conversation about the conversation.* If emotions are running hot, try redirecting the discussion to the process. Like the expert negotiators who comment on their feelings and test their understanding of the other side's feelings, you can sometimes make progress by expressing your disappointment or frustration and asking people if they share it.

III. COLLECTIVE RETHINKING

A. Have More Nuanced Conversations

18. *Complexify contentious topics.* There are more than two sides to every story. Instead of treating polarizing issues like two sides of a coin, look at them through the many lenses of a prism. Seeing the shades of gray can make us more open.

19. *Don't shy away from caveats and contingencies.* Acknowledging competing claims and conflicting results doesn't sacrifice interest or credibility. It's an effective way to engage audiences while encouraging them to stay curious.

20. *Expand your emotional range.* You don't have to eliminate frustration or even indignation to have a productive conversation. You just need to mix in a broader set of emotions along with them—you might try showing some curiosity or even admitting confusion or ambivalence.

B. Teach Kids to Think Again

21. *Have a weekly myth-busting discussion at dinner.* It's easier to debunk false beliefs at an early age, and it's a great way to teach kids to become comfortable with rethinking. Pick a different topic each week—one day it might be dinosaurs, the next it could be outer space—and rotate responsibility around the family for bringing a myth for discussion.

22. *Invite kids to do multiple drafts and seek feedback from others.* Creating different versions of a drawing or a story can encourage kids to learn the value of revising their ideas. Getting input from others can also help them to continue evolving their standards. They might learn to embrace confusion—and to stop expecting perfection on the first try.

23. *Stop asking kids what they want to be when they grow up.* They don't have to define themselves in terms of a career. A single identity can close the door to alternatives. Instead of trying to narrow their options, help them broaden their possibilities. They don't have to be one thing—they can do many things.

C. Create Learning Organizations

24. *Abandon best practices.* Best practices suggest that the ideal routines are already in place. If we want people to keep rethinking the way they work, we might be better off adopting process accountability and continually striving for better practices.

25. *Establish psychological safety.* In learning cultures, people feel confident that they can question and challenge the status quo without being punished. Psychological safety often starts with leaders role-modeling humility.

26. *Keep a rethinking scorecard.* Don't evaluate decisions based only on the results; track how thoroughly different options are considered in the process. A bad process with a good outcome is luck. A good process with a bad outcome might be a smart experiment.

D. Stay Open to Rethinking Your Future

27. *Throw out the ten-year plan.* What interested you last year might bore you this year—and what confused you yesterday might become exciting tomorrow. Passions are developed, not just discovered. Planning just one step ahead can keep you open to rethinking.

28. *Rethink your actions, not just your surroundings.* Chasing happiness can chase it away. Trading one set of circumstances for another isn't always enough. Joy can wax and wane, but meaning is more likely to last. Building a sense of purpose often starts with taking actions to enhance your learning or your contribution to others.

29. *Schedule a life checkup.* It's easy to get caught in escalation of commitment to an unfulfilling path. Just as you schedule health checkups with your doctor, it's worth having a life checkup on your calendar once or twice a year. It's a way to assess how much you're learning, how your beliefs and goals are evolving, and whether your next steps warrant some rethinking.

30. *Make time to think again.* When I looked at my calendar, I noticed that it was mostly full of doing. I set a goal of spending an hour a day thinking and learning. Now I've decided to go further: I'm scheduling a weekly time for rethinking and unlearning. I reach out to my challenge network and ask what ideas and opinions they think I should be reconsidering. Recently, my wife, Allison, told me that I need to rethink the way I pronounce the word *mayonnaise*.

ACKNOWLEDGMENTS

The expression of gratitude is something that probably needs less re-thinking and more doing. I want to start by commending literary agent extraordinaire Richard Pine for inspiring me to rethink my audience and continue broadening my lens beyond work, and editor par excellence Rick Kot for believing in and developing the potential of these ideas. As always, it was a dream to work with the two of them, and they offered the ideal blend of challenge and support.

The accuracy of this book was enhanced by the meticulous work of two professional fact-checkers. Paul Durbin applied his eagle eye to every sentence, working with remarkable thoroughness and alacrity. Andy Young carefully reviewed every page and followed up with a number of key sources.

The content and tone of the book benefited immeasurably from the early readers in my challenge network. Marissa Shandell and Karren Knowlton were exceedingly generous in reading more chapter drafts than any human should endure and unfailingly brilliant in improving them. I cannot thank them enough for enriching every section of the book with leads on characters, suggestions on flow, and refinements on language.

Marissa went the extra mile to enliven concepts and synthesize practical takeaways. Karren went above and beyond to amplify complexity and diversify thought.

Reb Rebele, whose taste in ideas and prose is second to none, dished out the tough love that the early chapters needed and brought the seasoning that was missing from the denouements. Queen of signposting Grace Rubenstein offered sage guidance for helping readers see the forest in the trees and recognize thinking again as a habit that's both timely and timeless. Dan O'Donnell helped me de-escalate my commitment to a series of dead ends and composed the written version of jaunty music to animate several key studies and stories.

Lindsay Miller—the human equivalent of the corpus callosum—led the cheer for more conversational snippets and richer illustrations of how the preacher, prosecutor, politician, and scientist waltz into our psyches. Nicole Granet expanded my thinking around how rethinking is relevant to every domain of life. Sheryl Sandberg sharpened the structure by convincing me to introduce the core idea before the organizing framework, and underscoring the value of well-placed bookends. Constantinos Coutifaris made the vital point that I needed to explore when it's persuasive to preach, prosecute, and politick. Natalia Villarman, Neal Stewart, and Will Fields shared their expertise on antiracism. Michael Choo motivated me to go back to the drawing board on a chapter that wasn't working. Justin Berg lent his creative forecasting skills to select and develop my most novel and useful insights, and also introduced me to the satisfaction of reverse alliteration (where sequential words share a last letter or syllable). Susan Grant, ever the English teacher, corrected grammar, caught typos, and fought with me about the Oxford comma. *Sorry, Mom, that's one thing I don't plan to rethink.*

Impact Lab reminded me once again how much teachers can learn from students. Vanessa Wanyandeh challenged me to consider how power imbalances affect which groups should be doing the majority of the rethinking and highlight whose responsibility it is to fight prejudice. Akash Pulluru fearlessly obliterated weak arguments and debated the principles of good debate. Graelin Mandel called for more information about when and why task conflict causes relationship conflict, and Zach Sweeney made a passionate case for expanding the role of the rethinking cycle. Jordan Lei pushed me to delve more deeply into the first-instinct fallacy, and Shane Goldstein took the lead in talking me out of the blank-page epilogue and into showing some edits and margin notes. Nicholas Strauch requested more context on how to ask good questions and defended the frog, and Madeline Fagen suggested more clarity on the distinction between beliefs and values. Wendy Lee advised me to go into more detail on expressing confident humility, Kenny Hoang suggested I demonstrate some of the interpersonal rethinking principles in my writing, and Lizzie Youshaei called for more analysis of when and why people are open to being wrong. Meg Sreenivas pointed out extraneous details, Aaron Kahane clarified confusing arguments, and Shaheel Mitra suggested the Edgar Mitchell quote.

I was lucky to have the support of top-notch teams at InkWell (shout-out to Alexis Hurley, Nathaniel Jacks, and Eliza Rothstein) and Viking (a group of people whose curiosity I miss every week I'm not writing or launching a book). Special thanks to Carolyn Coleburn, Whitney Peeling, Lindsay Prevette, and Bel Banta for their publicity prowess; Kate Stark, Lydia Hirt, and Mary Stone for their creative marketing; Tricia Conley, Tess Espinoza, Bruce Giffords, and Fabiana Van Arsdell for their editorial and production expertise; Jason Ramirez for art direction; Camille LeBlanc for wrangling; and Brian Tart, Andrea Schulz, Madeline McIntosh, Allison Dobson, and speed demon Markus Dohle for their ongoing support. Also, it was a delight to collaborate with Matt Shirley on the charts. Along with lending his characteristic cleverness and humor, he showed impressive patience in working to make sure they fit the content and tone of the book.

A number of colleagues contributed to this book through conversations. As always, Dan Pink gave excellent input on framing the idea and tips on relevant research. My colleagues at Wharton—especially Rachel Arnett, Sigal Barsade, Drew Carton, Stephanie Creary, Angela Duckworth, Cade Massey, Samir Nurmohamed, and Nancy Rothbard—modeled many of the principles in the book and led me to think again about many of the points I was making. I am also grateful to Phil Tetlock for the preacher-prosecutor-politician framework and referrals to Kjirste Morrell and Jean-Pierre Beugoms; Eva Chen, Terry Murray, and Phil Rescober for the analysis of Jean-Pierre's forecasts; Bob Sutton for putting Brad Bird on my radar and analyzing his *Incredibles* leadership so perceptively, as well as Jamie Woolf and Chris Wiggum for opening the Pixar door; Karl Weick for introducing me to Mann Gulch; Shannon Sedgwick Davis and Laren Poole for putting me in touch with Betty Bigombe and sharing background on her story; Jeff Ashby and Mike Bloomfield for the referrals to Chris Hansen and Ellen Ochoa; Eoghan Sheehy for the connection to Harish Natarajan; and Douglas Archibald for recommending Ron Berger (props to Noah Devereaux and the Strive Challenge for that serendipitous conversation). Early on, Eric Best showed me how rethinking could help people raise the bar, and Brian Little, Jane Dutton, Richard Hackman, and Sue Ashford taught me to see rethinking as one of the great joys of being an organizational psychologist.

Every day, being a parent shows me that we all have the innate capacity to change our minds. As I finished writing this book during the pandemic, Henry wondered if the water supply might be affected and was eager to rethink where we get running water (*Is there a tube that connects the ocean to our house? We might get an octopus!*). When I asked how she convinces me to rethink things, Elena opened my eyes to a persuasion technique I had completely overlooked (*Puppy dog eyes! Works every time!*). When we were considering various optical illusions for the jacket of this book, Joanna came up with a better idea (*What about a candle with a flame that's water instead of fire?*). I came away rethinking where creative ideas come from: if our twelve-year-old can come up with the perfect image for my book jacket, what else can kids do? I love how happily and effortlessly our children think again—and how they coax me to do it more often, too.

My deep gratitude goes to Allison Sweet Grant for her love, advice, and humor every step of the way. As always, she helped me rethink many of my assumptions and put up with countless trivial questions, random requests, and unnecessary debates. I still pronounce it *man-aze*, not *may-o-naze*, but she makes a compelling point that no one says "Please pass the man"; it's "Please pass the mayo." For the record, I don't even like mayonnaise.

NOTES

Prologue

2 **The smarter you are:** Frank L. Schmidt and John Hunter, "General Mental Ability in the World of Work: Occupational Attainment and Job Performance," *Journal of Personality and Social Psychology* 86 (2004): 162–73.

2 **the faster you can solve them:** David C. Geary, "Efficiency of Mitochondrial Functioning as the Fundamental Biological Mechanism of General Intelligence (G)," *Psychological Review* 15 (2018): 1028–50.

2 **the ability to think and learn:** Neel Burton, "What Is Intelligence?," *Psychology Today*, November 28, 2018, www.psychologytoday.com/us/blog/hide-and-seek/201811/what-is-intelligence; Charles Stangor and Jennifer Walinga, *Introduction to Psychology* (Victoria, BC: BCcampus, 2014); Frank L. Schmidt, "The Role of Cognitive Ability and Job Performance: Why There Cannot Be a Debate," *Human Performance* 15 (2002): 187–210.

3 **"exercise great caution if you decide to change":** *A Systematic Approach to the GRE* (New York: Kaplan, 1999).

3 **the majority of answer revisions:** Ludy T. Benjamin Jr., Timothy A. Cavell, and William R. Shallenberger III, "Staying with Initial Answers on Objective Tests: Is It a Myth?," *Teaching of Psychology* 11 (1984): 133–41.

3 **counted eraser marks:** Justin Kruger, Derrick Wirtz, and Dale T. Miller, "Counterfactual Thinking and the First Instinct Fallacy," *Journal of Personality and Social Psychology* 88 (2005): 725–35.

3 **those who do rethink their first answers:** Yongnam Kim, "Apples to Oranges: Causal Effects of Answer Changing in Multiple-Choice Exams," arXiv:1808.10577v4, last revised October 14, 2019, arxiv.org/abs/1808.10577.

3 **considering whether you should change it:** Justin J. Couchman et al., "The Instinct Fallacy: The Metacognition of Answering and Revising during College Exams," *Metacognition and Learning* 11 (2016): 171–85.

3 **The speaker taught them:** Charles M. Slem, "The Effects of an Educational Intervention on Answer Changing Behavior," *Annual Convention of the American Psychological Association*, August 1985, eric.ed.gov/?id=ED266395.

4 **we're mental misers:** Susan T. Fiske and Shelley E. Taylor, *Social Cognition: From Brains to Culture*, 2nd ed. (Los Angeles: Sage, 2013).

4 **seizing and freezing:** Arie W. Kruglanski and Donna M. Webster, "Motivated Closing of the Mind: 'Seizing' and 'Freezing,'" *Psychological Review* 103 (1996): 263–83.

4 **better off in the slow-boiling pot:** James Fallows, "The Boiled-Frog Myth: Stop the Lying Now!," *The Atlantic*, September 16, 2006, www.theatlantic.com/technology/archive/2006/09/the-boiled-frog-myth-stop-the-lying-now/7446/.

5 **"On a big fire":** Norman Maclean, *Young Men and Fire*, 25th anniversary ed. (Chicago: University of Chicago Press, 2017); see also www.nifc.gov/safety/mann_gulch/event_timeline/event6.htm.

5 **Under acute stress, people typically revert:** Barry M. Staw, Lance E. Sandelands, and Jane E. Dutton, "Threat Rigidity Effects in Organizational Behavior: A Multilevel Analysis," *Administrative Science Quarterly* 26 (1981): 501–24; Karl E. Weick, "The Collapse of Sense-Making in Organizations: The Mann Gulch Disaster," *Administrative Science Quarterly* 38 (1993): 628–52.

6 **twenty-three wildland firefighters perished:** Ted Putnam, "Findings from the Wildland Firefighters Human Factors Workshop," United States Department of Agriculture, Forest Service, Technology & Development Program, November 1995.

6 **Storm King Mountain:** John N. Maclean, *Fire on the Mountain: The True Story of the South Canyon Fire* (New York: HarperPerennial, 2009).

6 **could have moved 15 to 20 percent faster:** Ted Putnam, "Analysis of Escape Efforts and Personal Protective Equipment on the South Canyon Fire," *Wildfire* 4 (1995): 34–39.

6 **"Most would have lived":** Ted Putnam, "The Collapse of Decision Making and Organizational Structure on Storm King Mountain," *Wildfire* 4 (1995): 40–45.

6 **"dropped their packs":** Report of the South Canyon Fire Accident Investigation Team, August 17, 1994.

7 **"Without my tools, who am I?":** Karl E. Weick, "Drop Your Tools: An Allegory for Organizational Studies," *Administrative Science Quarterly* 41 (1996): 301–13.

8 **in an "e-group":** Elizabeth Widdicombe, "Prefrosh E-group Connected Class of '03," *Harvard Crimson*, June 5, 2003, www.thecrimson.com/article/2003/6/5/prefrosh-e-group-connected-class-of-03; Scott A. Golder, "Re: 'Alone in Annenberg? First-Years Take Heart,'" *Harvard Crimson*, September 17, 1999, www.thecrimson.com/article/1999/9/17/letters-begroup-an-important-link-connecting.

10 **rethink their views on racial injustice:** Nate Cohn and Kevin Quealy, "How Public Opinion Has Moved on Black Lives Matter," *New York Times*, June 10, 2020, www.nytimes.com/interactive/2020/06/10/upshot/black-lives-matter-attitudes.html.

11 **role that wildfires play in the life cycles of forests:** Kathryn Schulz, "The Story That Tore Through the Trees," *New York Magazine*, September 9, 2014, nymag.com/arts/books/features/mann-gulch-norman-maclean-2014-9/index.html.

Chapter 1. A Preacher, a Prosecutor, a Politician, and a Scientist Walk into Your Mind

15 **"Progress is impossible without change":** George Bernard Shaw, *Everybody's Political What's What?* (London: Constable, 1944).

15 **Mike Lazaridis has had a defining:** Jacquie McNish and Sean Silcoff, *Losing the Signal: The Untold Story behind the Extraordinary Rise and Spectacular Fall of BlackBerry* (New York: Flatiron Books, 2015).

16 **the fastest-growing company:** "100 Fastest-Growing Companies," CNN Money, August 31, 2009, money.cnn.com/magazines/fortune/fortunefastestgrowing/2009/snapshots/1.html.

17 **five times as much information:** Richard Alleyne, "Welcome to the Information Age—174 Newspapers a Day," *Daily Telegraph*, February 11, 2011, www.telegraph.co.uk/news/science/science-news/8316534/Welcome-to-the-information-age-174-newspapers-a-day.html.

17 **medical knowledge was doubling:** Peter Densen, "Challenges and Opportunities Facing Medical Education," *Transactions of the American Clinical and Climatological Association* 122 (2011): 48–58.

17 **become more extreme:** Joshua J. Clarkson, Zakary L. Tormala, and Christopher Leone, "A Self-Validation Perspective on the Mere Thought Effect," *Journal of Experimental Social Psychology* 47 (2011): 449–54.

17 **and more entrenched:** Jamie Barden and Richard E. Petty, "The Mere Perception of Elaboration Creates Attitude Certainty: Exploring the Thoughtfulness Heuristic," *Journal of Personality and Social Psychology* 95 (2008): 489–509.

17 **such subjects as Cleopatra's roots:** W. Ralph Eubanks, "How History and Hollywood Got 'Cleopatra' Wrong," NPR, November 1, 2010, www.npr.org/templates/story/story.php?storyId=130976125.

17 **tyrannosaurs had colorful feathers:** Jason Farago, "T. Rex Like You Haven't Seen Him: With Feathers," *New York Times*, March 7, 2019, www.nytimes.com/2019/03/07/arts/design/t-rex-exhibition-american-museum-of-natural-history.html; Brigit Katz, "T. Rex Was Likely Covered in Scales, Not Feathers," *Smithsonian*, June 8, 2017, www.smithsonianmag.com/smart-news/t-rex-skin-was-not-covered-feathers-study-says-180963603.

17 **sound waves can activate the visual cortex:** Alix Spiegel and Lulu Miller, "How to Become Batman," *Invisibilia*, NPR, January 23, 2015, www.npr.org/programs/invisibilia/378577902/how-to-become-batman.

17 **"blowing smoke up your arse":** Sterling Haynes, "Special Feature: Tobacco Smoke Enemas," *BC Medical Journal* 54 (2012): 496–97.

18 **the Ponzi scheme:** Stephen Greenspan, "Why We Keep Falling for Financial Scams," *Wall Street Journal*, January 3, 2009, www.wsj.com/articles/SB123093987596650197.

18 **mindsets of three different professions:** Philip E. Tetlock, "Social Functionalist Frameworks for Judgment and Choice: Intuitive Politicians, Theologians, and Prosecutors," *Psychological Review* 109 (2002): 451–71.

18 **we marshal arguments:** Hugo Mercier and Dan Sperber, "Why Do Humans Reason? Arguments from an Argumentative Theory," *Behavioral and Brain Sciences* 34 (2011): 57–74.

19 **guilty of "knee-jerk cynicism":** Stephen Greenspan, "Fooled by Ponzi (and Madoff): How Bernard Madoff Made Off with My Money," eSkeptic, December 23, 2008, www.skeptic.com/eskeptic/08-12-23/#feature.

19 **why we get duped:** Greg Griffin, "Scam Expert from CU Expertly Scammed," *Denver Post*, March 2, 2009, www.denverpost.com/2009/03/02/scam-expert-from-cu-expertly-scammed.

20 **scientist is not just a profession:** George A. Kelly, *The Psychology of Personal Constructs*, vol. 1, *A Theory of Personality* (New York: Norton, 1955); Brian R. Little, *Who Are You, Really? The Surprising Puzzle of Personality* (New York: Simon & Schuster, 2017).

20 **view startups through a scientist's goggles:** Arnaldo Camuffo et al., "A Scientific Approach to Entrepreneurial Decision Making: Evidence from a Randomized Control Trial," *Management Science* 66 (2020): 564–86.

21 **when business executives compete:** Mark Chussil, "Slow Deciders Make Better Strategists," *Harvard Business Review*, July 8, 2016, hbr.org/2016/07/slow-deciders-make-better-strategists.

22 **"To punish me":** Walter Isaacson, *Einstein: His Life and Universe* (New York: Simon & Schuster, 2007).

24 **faster at recognizing patterns:** David J. Lick, Adam L. Alter, and Jonathan B. Freeman, "Superior Pattern Detectors Efficiently Learn, Activate, Apply, and Update Social Stereotypes," *Journal of Experimental Psychology: General* 147 (2018): 209–27.

24 **the smarter you are:** Dan M. Kahan, Ellen Peters, Erica C. Dawson, and Paul Slovic, "Motivated Numeracy and Enlightened Self-Government," *Behavioural Public Policy* 1 (2017): 54–86.

25 **One is confirmation bias:** Raymond S. Nickerson, "Confirmation Bias: A Ubiquitous Phenomenon in Many Guises," *Review of General Psychology* 2 (1998): 175–220.

25 **The other is desirability bias:** Ben M. Tappin, Leslie van der Leer, and Ryan T. McKay, "The Heart Trumps the Head: Desirability Bias in Political Belief Revision," *Journal of Experimental Psychology: General* 146 (2017): 1143–49; Ziva Kunda, "The Case for Motivated Reasoning," *Psychological Bulletin* 108 (1990): 480–98.

25 **"I'm not biased" bias:** Emily Pronin, Daniel Y. Lin, and Lee Ross, "The Bias Blind Spot: Perceptions of Bias in Self versus Others," *Personality and Social Psychology Bulletin* 28 (2002): 369–81.

25 **smart people are more likely:** Richard F. West, Russell J. Meserve, and Keith E. Stanovich, "Cognitive Sophistication Does Not Attenuate the Bias Blind Spot," *Journal of Personality and Social Psychology* 103 (2012): 506–19.

25 **being *actively* open-minded:** Keith E. Stanovich and Maggie E. Toplak, "The Need for Intellectual Diversity in Psychological Science: Our Own Studies of Actively Open-Minded Thinking as a Case Study," *Cognition* 187 (2019): 156–66; Jonathan Baron et al., "Why Does the Cognitive Reflection Test (Sometimes) Predict Utilitarian Moral Judgment (and Other Things)?," *Journal of Applied Research in Memory and Cognition* 4 (2015): 265–84.

25 **sharper logic and stronger data:** Neil Stenhouse et al., "The Potential Role of Actively Open-Minded Thinking in Preventing Motivated Reasoning about Controversial Science," *Journal of Environmental Psychology* 57 (2018): 17–24.

27 **"to move from one extreme":** Mihaly Csikszentmihalyi, *Creativity: Flow and the Psychology of Discovery and Invention* (New York: HarperCollins, 1996).

27 **study of highly creative architects:** Donald W. Mackinnon, "The Nature and Nurture of Creative Talent," *American Psychologist* 17 (1962): 484–95.

27 **Experts assessed American presidents:** Dean Keith Simonton, "Presidential IQ, Openness, Intellectual Brilliance, and Leadership: Estimates and Correlations for 42 U.S. Chief Executives," *Political Psychology* 27 (2006): 511–26.

29 **the fat-cat syndrome:** Jane E. Dutton and Robert B. Duncan, "The Creation of Momentum for Change through the Process of Strategic Issue Diagnosis," *Strategic Management Journal* (May/June 1987): 279–95.

29 **"It's an iconic product":** Jacquie McNish, "RIM's Mike Lazaridis Walks Out of BBC Interview," *Globe and Mail*, April 13, 2011, www.theglobeandmail.com/globe-investor/rims-mike-lazaridis-walks-out-of-bbc-interview/article1322202.

29 **"The keyboard is one of the reasons":** Sean Silcoff, Jacquie McNish, and Steve Laurantaye, "How BlackBerry Blew It," *Globe and Mail*, September 27, 2013, www.theglobeandmail.com/report-on-business/the-inside-story-of-why-blackberry-is-failing/article14563602/.

29 **"We laughed and said":** Jonathan S. Geller, "Open Letter to BlackBerry Bosses: Senior RIM Exec Tells All as Company Crumbles Around Him," *BGR*, June 30, 2011, bgr.com/2011/06/30/open-letter-to-blackberry-bosses-senior-rim-exec-tells-all-as-company-crumbles-around-him.

29 **what resurrected Apple:** Personal interviews with Tony Fadell, June 1, 2020, and Mike Bell, November 14, 2019; Brian Merchant, *The One Device: The Secret History of the iPhone* (New York: Little, Brown, 2017).

Chapter 2. The Armchair Quarterback and the Impostor

33 **"Ignorance more frequently":** Charles Darwin, *The Descent of Man* (London: Penguin Classics, 1871/2004).

34 **"mentally blind to her blindness":** Gabriel Anton, "On the Self-Awareness of Focal Drain Diseases by the Patient in Cortical Blindness and Cortical Deafness," *Archiv für Psychiatrie und Nervenkrankheiten* 32 (1899): 86–127.

34 **"One of the most striking features":** Frederick C. Redlich and Joseph F. Dorsey, "Denial of Blindness by Patients with Cerebral Disease," *Archives of Neurology & Psychiatry* 53 (1945): 407–17.

35 **the Roman philosopher Seneca:** Charles André, "Seneca and the First Description of Anton Syndrome," *Journal of Neuro-Ophthalmology* 38 (2018): 511–13.

35 **a deficit of self-awareness:** Giuseppe Vallar and Roberta Ronchi, "Anosognosia for Motor and Sensory Deficits after Unilateral Brain Damage: A Review," *Restorative Neurology and Neuroscience* 24 (2006): 247–57; Howard C. Hughes, Robert Fendrich, and Sarah E. Streeter, "The Diversity of the Human Visual Experience," in *Perception and Its Modalities*, ed. Dustin Stokes, Moham Matthen, and Stephen Biggs (New York: Oxford University Press, 2015); David Dunning, *Self-Insight: Roadblocks and Detours on the Path to Knowing Thyself* (New York: Psychology Press, 2005); Costanza Papagno and Giuseppe Vallar, "Anosognosia for Left Hemiplegia: Babinski's (1914) Cases," in *Classic Cases in Neuropsychology*, vol. 2, ed. Christopher Code et al. (New York: Psychology Press, 2003); Jiann-Jy Chen et al., "Anton-Babinski Syndrome in an Old Patient: A Case Report and Literature Review," *Psychogeriatrics* 15 (2015): 58–61; Susan M. McGlynn, "Impaired Awareness of Deficits in a Psychiatric Context: Implications for Rehabilitation," in *Metacognition in Educational Theory and Practice*, ed. Douglas J. Hacker, John Dunlosky, and Arthur C. Graesser (Mahwah, NJ: Erlbaum, 1998).

37 **"My experience and knowledge":** Agence France Presse, "Iceland's Crisis-Era Central Bank Chief to Run for President," Yahoo! News, May 8, 2016, www.yahoo.com/news/icelands-crisis-era-central-bank-chief-run-president-152717120.html.

37 **women typically underestimated:** Samantha C. Paustian-Underdahl, Lisa Slattery Walker, and David J. Woehr, "Gender and Perceptions of Leadership Effectiveness: A Meta-analysis of Contextual Moderators," *Journal of Applied Psychology* 99 (2014): 1129–45.

37 **competence exceeds confidence:** Mark R. Leary et al., "The Impostor Phenomenon: Self-Perceptions, Reflected Appraisals, and Interpersonal Strategies," *Journal of Personality* 68 (2000): 725–56; Karina K. L. Mak, Sabina Kleitman, and Maree J. Abbott, "Impostor Phenomenon Measurement Scales: A Systematic Review," *Frontiers in Psychology* 10 (2019): 671.

38 **Ig™ Nobel Prize:** Improbable, "The 2000 Ig™ Nobel Prize Ceremony," October 5, 2000, www.improbable.com/ig/2000.

38 **original Dunning-Kruger studies:** Justin Kruger and David Dunning, "Unskilled and Unaware of It: How Difficulties in Recognizing One's Own Incompetence Lead to Inflated Self-Assessments," *Journal of Personality and Social Psychology* 77 (1999): 1121–34.

39 **The less intelligent we are:** John D. Mayer, A. T. Panter, and David R. Caruso, "When People Estimate Their Personal Intelligence Who Is Overconfident? Who Is Accurate?," *Journal of Personality* (May 19, 2020).

39 **when economists evaluated:** Nicholas Bloom, Renata Lemos, Raffaella Sadun, Daniela Scur, and John Van Reenen, "JEEA-FBBVA Lecture 2013: The New Empirical Economics of Management," *Journal of the European Economic Association* 12 (2014): 835–76, https://doi.org/10.1111/jeea.12094.

40 **it was most rampant:** Xavier Cirera and William F. Maloney, *The Innovation Paradox* (Washington, DC: The World Bank, 2017); Nicholas Bloom et al., "Management Practices across Firms and Countries," *Academy of Management Perspectives* 26 (2012): 12–33.

40 **The more superior participants:** Michael P. Hall and Kaitlin T. Raimi, "Is Belief Superiority Justified by Superior Knowledge?," *Journal of Experimental Social Psychology* 76 (2018): 290–306.

40 **"The first rule of the Dunning-Kruger club":** Brian Resnick, "Intellectual Humility: The Importance of Knowing You Might Be Wrong," *Vox*, January 4, 2019, www.vox.com/science-and-health/2019/1/4/17989224/intellectual-humility-explained-psychology-replication.

40 **claim knowledge about fictional topics:** John Jerrim, Phil Parker, and Nikki Shure, "Bullshitters. Who Are They and What Do We Know about Their Lives?," IZA Institute of Labor Economics, DP No. 12282, April 2019, ftp.iza.org/dp12282.pdf; Christopher Ingraham, "Rich Guys Are Most Likely to Have No Idea What They're Talking About, Study Suggests," *Washington Post*, April 26, 2019, www.washingtonpost.com/business/2019/04/26/rich-guys-are-most-likely-have-no-idea-what-theyre-talking-about-study-finds.

40 **"giving a tidy demonstration":** Nina Strohminger (@NinaStrohminger), January 8, 2019, twitter.com/NinaStrohminger/status/1082651708617039875?s=20.

41 **On the questions above:** Mark L. Wolraich, David B. Wilson, and J. Wade White, "The Effect of Sugar on Behavior and Cognition in Children: A Meta-analysis," *Journal of the American Medical Association* 274 (1995): 1617–21; see also Konstantinos Mantantzis et al., "Sugar Rush or Sugar Crash? A Meta-analysis of Carbohydrate Effects on Mood," *Neuroscience & Biobehavioral Reviews* 101 (2019): 45–67.

42 **people who scored the lowest:** Oliver J. Sheldon, David Dunning, and Daniel R. Ames, "Emotionally Unskilled, Unaware, and Uninterested in Learning More: Reactions to Feedback about Deficits in Emotional Intelligence," *Journal of Applied Psychology* 99 (2014): 125–37.

42 **Yet motivation is only part:** Gilles E. Gignac and Marcin Zajenkowski, "The Dunning-Kruger Effect Is (Mostly) a Statistical Artefact: Valid Approaches to Testing the Hypothesis with Individual Differences Data," *Intelligence* 80 (2020): 101449; Tal Yarkoni, "What the Dunning-Kruger Effect Is and Isn't," July 7, 2010, www.talyarkoni.org/blog/2010/07/07/what-the-dunning-kruger-effect-is-and-isnt.

42 **when they're offered a $100 bill:** Joyce Ehrlinger et al., "Why the Unskilled Are Unaware: Further Explorations of (Absent) Self-Insight among the Incompetent," *Organizational Behavior and Human Decision Processes* 105 (2008): 98–121.

43 **We tend to overestimate ourselves:** Spencer Greenberg and Seth Stephens-Davidowitz, "You Are Not as Good at Kissing as You Think. But You Are Better at Dancing," *New York Times*, April 6, 2019, www.nytimes.com/2019/04/06/opinion/sunday/overconfidence-men-women.html.

44 **simulated zombie apocalypse:** Carmen Sanchez and David Dunning, "Overconfidence among Beginners: Is a Little Learning a Dangerous Thing?," *Journal of Personality and Social Psychology* 114 (2018): 10–28.

45 **patient mortality rates:** John Q. Young et al., "'July Effect': Impact of the Academic Year-End Changeover on Patient Outcomes," *Annals of Internal Medicine* 155 (2011): 309–15; Sarah Kliff, "The July Effect Is Real: New Doctors Really Do Make Hospitals More Dangerous," *Vox*, July 13, 2014, www.vox.com/2014/7/13/5893653/the-july-effect-is-real-new-doctors-really-do-make-hospitals-more.

45 **"fiercely loyal henchmen":** Roger Boyes, *Meltdown Iceland: Lessons on the World Financial Crisis from a Small Bankrupt Island* (New York: Bloomsbury, 2009).

45 **"arrogance, his absolute conviction":** Boyes, *Meltdown Iceland*; "Cracks in the Crust," *Economist*, December 11, 2008, www.economist.com/briefing/2008/12/11/cracks-in-the-crust; Heather Farmbrough, "How Iceland's Banking Collapse Created an Opportunity," *Forbes*, December 23, 2019, www.forbes.com/sites/heatherfarmbrough/2019/12/23/how-icelands-banking-collapse-created-an-opportunity/#72693f035e97; "25 People to Blame for the Financial Crisis," *Time*, February 10, 2009, content.time.com/time/specials/packages/article/0,28804,1877351_1877350_1877340,00.html; John L. Campbell and John A. Hall, *The Paradox of Vulnerability: States, Nationalism & the Financial Crisis* (Princeton, NJ: Princeton University Press, 2017); Robert H. Wade and Silla Sigurgeirsdottir, "Iceland's Meltdown: The Rise and Fall of International Banking in the North Atlantic," *Brazilian Journal of Political Economy* 31 (2011): 684–97; Report of the Special Investigation Commission, April 12, 2010, www.rna.is/eldri-nefndir/addragandi-og-orsakir-falls-islensku-bankanna-2008/skyrsla-nefndarinnar/english; Daniel Chartier, *The End of Iceland's Innocence: The Image of Iceland in the Foreign Media during the Financial Crisis* (Ottawa, ON: University of Ottawa Press, 2011); "Excerpts: Iceland's Oddsson," *Wall Street Journal*, October 17, 2008, www.wsj.com/articles/SB122418335729241577; Geir H. Haarde, "Icelandic Leaders Accused of Negligence," *Financial Times*, April 12, 2010, www.ft.com/content/82bb2296-4637-11df-8769-00144feab49a; "Report on Iceland's Banking Collapse Blasts Ex-Officials," *Wall Street Journal*, April 13, 2010, www.wsj.com/articles/SB10001424052702303828304575179722049591754.

45 **"Arrogance is ignorance plus conviction":** Tim Urban, "The Thinking Ladder," *Wait but Why* (blog), September 27, 2019, waitbutwhy.com/2019/09/thinking-ladder.html.

46 **that's distinct from how much you believe in your methods:** Dov Eden, "Means Efficacy: External Sources of General and Specific Subjective Efficacy," in *Work Motivation in the Context of a Globalizing Economy,* ed. Miriam Erez, Uwe Kleinbeck, and Henk Thierry (Mahwah, NJ: Erlbaum, 2001); Dov Eden et al., "Augmenting Means Efficacy to Boost Performance: Two Field Experiments," *Journal of Management* 36 (2008): 687–713.

47 **Spanx founder Sara Blakely:** Personal interview with Sara Blakely, September 12, 2019; see also Clare O'Connor, "How Sara Blakely of Spanx Turned $5,000 into $1 Billion," *Forbes,* March 26, 2012, www.forbes.com/global/2012/0326/billionaires-12-feature-united -states-spanx-sara-blakely-american-booty.html; "How Spanx Got Started," *Inc.,* January 20, 2012, www.inc.com/sara-blakely/how-sara-blakley-started-spanx.html.

48 **Confident humility can be taught:** Tenelle Porter, "The Benefits of Admitting When You Don't Know," *Behavioral Scientist,* April 30, 2018, behavioralscientist.org/the-benefits-of -admitting-when-you-dont-know.

48 **In college and graduate school:** Thomas Gatzka and Benedikt Hell, "Openness and Post-Secondary Academic Performance: A Meta-analysis of Facet-, Aspect-, and Dimension-Level Correlations," *Journal of Educational Psychology* 110 (2018): 355–77.

48 **In high school:** Tenelle Porter et al., "Intellectual Humility Predicts Mastery Behaviors When Learning," *Learning and Individual Differences* 80 (2020): 101888.

48 **contributing more to their teams:** Bradley P. Owens, Michael D. Johnson, and Terence R. Mitchell, "Expressed Humility in Organizations: Implications for Performance, Teams, and Leadership," *Organization Science* 24 (2013): 1517–38.

48 **more attention to how strong evidence is:** Mark R. Leary et al., "Cognitive and Interpersonal Features of Intellectual Humility," *Personality and Social Psychology Bulletin* 43 (2017): 793–813.

48 **more time reading material that contradicts:** Samantha A. Deffler, Mark R. Leary, and Rick H. Hoyle, "Knowing What You Know: Intellectual Humility and Judgments of Recognition Memory," *Personality and Individual Differences* 96 (2016): 255–59.

48 **most effective leaders score high in both:** Bradley P. Owens, Angela S. Wallace, and David A. Waldman, "Leader Narcissism and Follower Outcomes: The Counterbalancing Effect of Leader Humility," *Journal of Applied Psychology* 100 (2015): 1203–13; Hongyu Zhang et al., "CEO Humility, Narcissism and Firm Innovation: A Paradox Perspective on CEO Traits," *Leadership Quarterly* 28 (2017): 585–604.

49 **Halla Tómasdóttir was polling:** Personal interview with Halla Tómasdóttir, February 27, 2019.

50 **more than half the people you know have felt like impostors:** Jaruwan Sakulku, "The Impostor Phenomenon," *International Journal of Behavioral Science* 6 (2011): 75–97.

50 **common among women and marginalized groups:** Dena M. Bravata et al., "Prevalence, Predictors, and Treatment of Impostor Syndrome: A Systematic Review," *Journal of General Internal Medicine* 35 (2020): 1252–75.

50 **the more often they felt like impostors:** Basima Tewfik, "Workplace Impostor Thoughts: Theoretical Conceptualization, Construct Measurement, and Relationships with Work-Related Outcomes," *Publicly Accessible Penn Dissertations* (2019): 3603.

51 **I've found that confidence can:** Adam M. Grant and Amy Wrzesniewski, "I Won't Let You Down . . . or Will I? Core Self-Evaluations, Other-Orientation, Anticipated Guilt and Gratitude, and Job Performance," *Journal of Applied Psychology* 95 (2010): 108–21.

52 **we have something to prove:** See Christine L. Porath and Thomas S. Bateman, "Self-Regulation: From Goal Orientation to Job Performance," *Journal of Applied Psychology* 91 (2006): 185–92; Samir Nurmohamed, "The Underdog Effect: When Low Expectations Increase Performance," *Academy of Management Journal* (July 26, 2020), doi.org/10.5465 /amj.2017.0181.

52 **make us better learners:** See Albert Bandura and Edwin A. Locke, "Negative Self-Efficacy and Goal Effects Revisited," *Journal of Applied Psychology* 88 (2003): 87–99.

52 **"Learning requires the humility":** Elizabeth J. Krumrei-Mancuso et al., "Links between Intellectual Humility and Acquiring Knowledge," *Journal of Positive Psychology* 15 (2020): 155–70.
 52 **seek out second opinions:** Danielle V. Tussing, "Hesitant at the Helm: The Effectiveness-Emergence Paradox of Reluctance to Lead" (Ph.D. diss., University of Pennsylvania, 2018).
 53 **the result of progress:** Edwin A. Locke and Gary P. Latham, "Building a Practically Useful Theory of Goal Setting and Task Motivation: A 35-Year Odyssey," *American Psychologist* 57 (2002): 705–17; M. Travis Maynard et al., "Modeling Time-Lagged Psychological Empowerment-Performance Relationships," *Journal of Applied Psychology* 99 (2014): 1244–53; Dana H. Lindsley, Daniel J. Brass, and James B. Thomas, "Efficacy-Performance Spirals: A Multilevel Perspective," *Academy of Management Review* 20 (1995): 645–78.

Chapter 3. The Joy of Being Wrong

 55 **"I have a degree":** *Frasier*, season 2, episode 12, "Roz in the Doghouse," January 3, 1995, NBC.
 55 **a wildly unethical study:** Henry A. Murray, "Studies of Stressful Interpersonal Disputations," *American Psychologist* 18 (1963): 28–36.
 57 **"Some may have found the experience":** Richard G. Adams, "Unabomber," *The Atlantic*, September 2000, "Letters," www.theatlantic.com/magazine/archive/2000/09/letters/378379.
 57 **events as "highly agreeable":** Alston Chase, *A Mind for Murder: The Education of the Unabomber and the Origins of Modern Terrorism* (New York: W. W. Norton, 2004).
 59 **What makes an idea interesting:** Murray S. Davis, "That's Interesting!: Toward a Phenomenology of Sociology and a Sociology of Phenomenology," *Philosophy of Social Science* 1 (1971): 309–44.
 59 **moon might originally have formed:** Sarah T. Stewart, "Where Did the Moon Come From? A New Theory," TED Talks, February 2019, www.ted.com/talks/sarah_t_stewart_where _did_the_moon_come_from_a_new_theory.
 59 **narwhal's tusk is actually a tooth:** Lesley Evans Ogden, "The Tusks of Narwhals Are Actually Teeth That Are Inside-Out," BBC, October 26, 2015, www.bbc.com/earth/story /20151026-the-tusks-of-narwhals-are-actually-teeth-that-are-inside-out.
 59 **miniature dictator living inside our heads:** Anthony G. Greenwald, "The Totalitarian Ego: Fabrication and Revision of Personal History," *American Psychologist* 35 (1980): 603–18.
 59 **"You must not fool yourself":** Richard P. Feynman, *"Surely You're Joking, Mr. Feynman!": Adventures of a Curious Character* (New York: W. W. Norton, 1985), and "Cargo Cult Science," Caltech Commencement, 1974, calteches.library.caltech.edu/51/2/CargoCult.htm.
 60 **"The Industrial Revolution and its consequences":** "Text of Unabomber Manifesto," *New York Times*, May 26, 1996, archive.nytimes.com/www.nytimes.com/library/national/una bom-manifesto-1.html.
 60 **when our core beliefs are challenged:** Jonas T. Kaplan, Sarah I. Gimbel, and Sam Harris, "Neural Correlates of Maintaining One's Political Beliefs in the Face of Counterevidence," *Scientific Reports* 6 (2016): 39589.
 60 **trigger the amygdala, the primitive "lizard brain":** Joseph LeDoux, *The Emotional Brain: The Mysterious Underpinnings of Emotional Life* (New York: Simon & Schuster, 1998); Joseph Cesario, David J. Johnson, and Heather L. Eisthen, "Your Brain Is Not an Onion with a Tiny Reptile Inside," *Current Directions in Psychological Science* 29 (2020): 255–60.
 60 **"Presented with someone else's argument":** Elizabeth Kolbert, "Why Facts Don't Change Our Minds," *New Yorker*, February 27, 2017, www.newyorker.com/magazine/2017/02/27 /why-facts-dont-change-our-minds.
 61 **First, our wrong opinions:** Eli Pariser, *The Filter Bubble: How the New Personalized Web Is Changing What We Read and How We Think* (New York: Penguin, 2011).
 61 **I gave a speech:** ideas42 Behavioral Summit, New York, NY, October 13, 2016.
 61 **He told me afterward:** Personal interview with Daniel Kahneman, June 13, 2019.
 63 **Even positive changes:** Corey Lee M. Keyes, "Subjective Change and Its Consequences for Emotional Well-Being," *Motivation and Emotion* 24 (2000): 67–84.

63 **evolving your identity:** Anthony L. Burrow et al., "Derailment: Conceptualization, Measurement, and Adjustment Correlates of Perceived Change in Self and Direction," *Journal of Personality and Social Psychology* 118 (2020): 584–601.

63 **you can tell a coherent story:** Michael J. Chandler et al., "Personal Persistence, Identity Development, and Suicide: A Study of Native and Non-Native North American Adolescents," *Monographs of the Society for Research in Child Development* 68 (2003): 1–138.

63 **when people felt detached:** Kaylin Ratner et al., "Depression and Derailment: A Cyclical Model of Mental Illness and Perceived Identity Change," *Clinical Psychological Science* 7 (2019): 735–53.

63 **"If you don't look back":** Personal interview with Ray Dalio, October 11, 2017; "How to Love Criticism," *WorkLife with Adam Grant*, February 28, 2018.

65 **meet Jean-Pierre Beugoms:** Personal interviews with Jean-Pierre Beugoms, June 26 and July 22, 2019.

66 **only 6 percent:** Nate Silver, "How I Acted Like a Pundit and Screwed Up on Donald Trump," FiveThirtyEight, May 18, 2016, fivethirtyeight.com/features/how-i-acted-like-a-pundit-and-screwed-up-on-donald-trump.

66 **Trump had a 68 percent chance:** Andrew Sabisky, "Just-World Bias Has Twisted Media Coverage of the Donald Trump Campaign," *International Business Times*, March 9, 2016, www.ibtimes.co.uk/just-world-bias-has-twisted-media-coverage-donald-trump-campaign-1547151.

66 **It's possible to change:** Daryl R. Van Tongeren et al., "Religious Residue: Cross-Cultural Evidence That Religious Psychology and Behavior Persist Following Deidentification," *Journal of Personality and Social Psychology* (March 12, 2020).

67 **"Mastery at manipulating the media":** Jean-Pierre Beugoms, "Who Will Win the Republican Party Nomination for the U.S. Presidential Election?," Good Judgment Open, November 18, 2015, www.gjopen.com/comments/44283.

67 **forecasting skill is less:** Philip E. Tetlock and Dan Gardner, *Superforecasting: The Art and Science of Prediction* (New York: Random House, 2015); Philip E. Tetlock, *Expert Political Judgment: How Good Is It? How Can We Know?* (Princeton, NJ: Princeton University Press, 2005).

67 **grit and ambition:** Uriel Haran, Ilana Ritov, and Barbara A. Mellers, "The Role of Actively Open-Minded Thinking in Information Acquisition, Accuracy, and Calibration," *Judgment and Decision Making* 8 (2013): 188–201.

67 **The single most important driver:** Barbara Mellers et al., "The Psychology of Intelligence Analysis: Drivers of Prediction Accuracy in World Politics," *Journal of Experimental Psychology: Applied* 21 (2015): 1–14.

67 **The superforecasters updated their predictions:** Barbara Mellers et al., "Identifying and Cultivating Superforecasters as a Method of Improving Probabilistic Predictions," *Perspectives on Psychological Science* 10 (2015): 267–81.

67 **As journalist Kathryn Schulz observes:** Kathryn Schulz, *Being Wrong: Adventures in the Margin of Error* (New York: HarperCollins, 2010).

68 **They saw their opinions:** Keith E. Stanovich and Richard F. West, "Reasoning Independently of Prior Belief and Individual Differences in Actively Open-Minded Thinking," *Journal of Educational Psychology* 89 (1997): 342–57.

68 **"It's not a lie":** *Seinfeld*, season 6, episode 16, "The Beard," February 9, 1995, NBC.

68 **world's top forecasters is Kjirste Morrell:** Personal interview with Kjirste Morrell, May 21, 2019.

70 **identifying even a single reason why:** Asher Koriat, Sarah Lichtenstein, and Baruch Fischhoff, "Reasons for Confidence," *Journal of Experimental Psychology: Human Learning and Memory* 6 (1980): 107–18.

72 **the more frequently we make fun of ourselves:** "Self-Defeating Humor Promotes Psychological Well-Being, Study Reveals," *ScienceDaily*, February 8, 2018, www.sciencedaily.com/releases/2018/02/180208104225.htm.

72 **"People who are right a lot"**: Mark Sullivan, "Jeff Bezos at re:MARS," *Fast Company*, June 6, 2019, www.fastcompany.com/90360687/jeff-bezos-business-advice-5-tips-from-amazons -remars?_ga=2.101831750.679949067.1593530400-358702464.1558396776.

72 **When men make self-deprecating jokes**: Jonathan B. Evans et al., "Gender and the Evaluation of Humor at Work," *Journal of Applied Psychology* 104 (2019): 1077–87.

73 **British physicist Andrew Lyne**: John Noble Wilford, "Astronomer Retracts His Discovery of Planet," *New York Times*, January 16, 1992, www.nytimes.com/1992/01/16/us/astronomer-retracts-his-discovery-of-planet.html.

73 **"the most honorable thing I've ever seen"**: Michael D. Lemonick, "When Scientists Screw Up," *Slate*, October 15, 2012, slate.com/technology/2012/10/scientists-make-mistakes-how -astronomers-and-biologists-correct-the-record-when-theyve-screwed-up.html.

73 **admitting we were wrong**: Adam K. Fetterman and Kai Sassenberg, "The Reputational Consequences of Failed Replications and Wrongness Admission Among Scientists," *PLoS ONE* 10 (2015): e0143723.

73 **display of honesty**: Adam K. Fetterman et al., "On the Willingness to Admit Wrongness: Validation of a New Measure and an Exploration of Its Correlates," *Personality and Individual Differences* 138 (2019): 193–202.

73 **"whose fault it is"**: Will Smith, "Fault vs Responsibility," YouTube, January 31, 2018, www.youtube.com/watch?v=USsqkd-E9ag.

75 **"It was a highly unpleasant experience"**: Chase, *A Mind for Murder*.

75 **unsettled by the content or the structure**: See James Q. Wilson, "In Search of Madness," *New York Times*, January 15, 1998, www.nytimes.com/1998/01/15/opinion/in-search-of -madness.html.

Chapter 4. The Good Fight Club

77 **"Arguments are extremely vulgar"**: Oscar Wilde, "The Remarkable Rocket," in *The Happy Prince and Other Stories*, ed. L. Carr (London: Heritage Illustrated Publishing, 1888/2014).

77 **Wilbur and Orville Wright**: David McCullough, *The Wright Brothers* (New York: Simon & Schuster, 2015); Tom D. Crouch, *The Bishop's Boys: A Life of Wilbur and Orville Wright* (New York: W. W. Norton, 2003); James Tobin, *To Conquer the Air* (New York: Free Press, 2003); Peter L. Jakab and Rick Young, eds., *The Published Writings of Wilbur and Orville Wright* (Washington, DC: Smithsonian, 2000); Fred Howard, *Wilbur and Orville: A Biography of the Wright Brothers* (New York: Ballantine, 1988).

78 **Tina Fey and Amy Poehler**: Jesse David Fox, "The History of Tina Fey and Amy Poehler's Best Friendship," *Vulture*, December 15, 2015, www.vulture.com/2013/01/history-of-tina -and-amys-best-friendship.html.

78 **Paul McCartney was teaching**: Michael Gallucci, "The Day John Lennon Met Paul McCartney," Ultimate Classic Rock, July 6, 2015, ultimateclassicrock.com/john-lennon-meets -paul-mccartney.

78 **Ben & Jerry's Ice Cream**: Rosanna Greenstreet, "How We Met: Ben Cohen and Jerry Greenfield," *Independent*, May 28, 1995, www.independent.co.uk/arts-entertainment/how -we-met-ben-cohen-and-jerry-greenfield-1621559.html.

78 **what Etty calls relationship conflict**: Karen A. Jehn, "A Multimethod Examination of the Benefits and Detriments of Intragroup Conflict," *Administrative Science Quarterly* 40 (1995): 256–82.

78 *I hate your stinking guts*: Penelope Spheeris et al., *The Little Rascals*, directed by Penelope Spheeris, Universal Pictures, 1994.

78 *you warthog-faced buffoon*: William Goldman, *The Princess Bride*, directed by Rob Reiner, 20th Century Fox, 1987.

78 *You bob for apples in the toilet*: David Mickey Evans and Robert Gunter, *The Sandlot*, directed by David Mickey Evans, 20th Century Fox, 1993.

80 **more than a hundred studies:** Frank R. C. de Wit, Lindred L. Greer, and Karen A. Jehn, "The Paradox of Intragroup Conflict: A Meta-analysis," *Journal of Applied Psychology* 97 (2012): 360–90.

80 **more original ideas in Chinese technology companies:** Jiing-Lih Farh, Cynthia Lee, and Crystal I. C. Farh, "Task Conflict and Creativity: A Question of How Much and When," *Journal of Applied Psychology* 95 (2010): 1173–80.

80 **innovate more in Dutch delivery services:** Carsten K. W. De Dreu, "When Too Little or Too Much Hurts: Evidence for a Curvilinear Relationship between Task Conflict and Innovation in Teams," *Journal of Management* 32 (2006): 83–107.

80 **make better decisions in American hospitals:** Robert S. Dooley and Gerald E. Fryxell, "Attaining Decision Quality and Commitment from Dissent: The Moderating Effects of Loyalty and Competence in Strategic Decision-Making Teams," *Academy of Management Journal* 42 (1999): 389–402.

80 **"The absence of conflict":** Kathleen M. Eisenhardt, Jean L. Kahwajy, and L. J. Bourgeois III, "How Management Teams Can Have a Good Fight," *Harvard Business Review*, July–August 1997, 77–85.

80 **Kids whose parents clash constructively:** Kathleen McCoy, E. Mark Cummings, and Patrick T. Davies, "Constructive and Destructive Marital Conflict, Emotional Security and Children's Prosocial Behavior," *Journal of Child Psychology and Psychiatry* 50 (2009): 270–79.

80 **architects were more likely:** Donald W. Mackinnon, "Personality and the Realization of Creative Potential," *American Psychologist* 20 (1965): 273–81.

81 **"tense but secure":** Paula Olszewski, Marilynn Kulieke, and Thomas Buescher, "The Influence of the Family Environment on the Development of Talent: A Literature Review," *Journal for the Education of the Gifted* 11 (1987): 6–28.

81 **"The creative person-to-be":** Robert S. Albert, ed., *Genius & Eminence* (Oxford: Pergamon Press, 1992).

81 **It's called agreeableness:** Lauri A. Jensen-Campbell, Jennifer M. Knack, and Haylie L. Gomez, "The Psychology of Nice People," *Social and Personality Psychology Compass* 4 (2010): 1042–56; Robert R. McCrae and Antonio Terraciano, "National Character and Personality," *Current Directions in Psychological Science* 15 (2006): 156–61.

82 **to become engineers and lawyers:** Henk T. van der Molen, Henk G. Schmidt, and Gerard Kruisman, "Personality Characteristics of Engineers," *European Journal of Engineering Education* 32 (2007): 495–501; Gidi Rubinstein, "The Big Five among Male and Female Students of Different Faculties," *Personality and Individual Differences* 38 (2005): 1495–503.

82 **If you're highly disagreeable:** Stéphane Côté and D. S. Moskowitz, "On the Dynamic Covariation between Interpersonal Behavior and Affect: Prediction from Neuroticism, Extraversion, and Agreeableness," *Journal of Personality and Social Psychology* 75 (1998): 1032–46.

82 **When I studied Pixar:** Personal interviews with Brad Bird, November 8, 2018, and April 28, 2020; Nicole Grindle, October 19, 2018, and March 17, 2020; and John Walker, November 21, 2018, and March 24, 2020; "The Creative Power of Misfits," *WorkLife with Adam Grant*, March 5, 2019; Hayagreeva Rao, Robert Sutton, and Allen P. Webb, "Innovation Lessons from Pixar: An Interview with Oscar-Winning Director Brad Bird," *McKinsey Quarterly*, April 1, 2008, www.mckinsey.com/business-functions/strategy-and-corporate-finance/our-insights/innovation-lessons-from-pixar-an-interview-with-oscar-winning-director-brad-bird; *The Making of "The Incredibles,"* directed by Rick Butler, Pixar, 2005; Alec Bojalad, *"The Incredibles 2*: Brad Bird on Family, Blu-Ray Extras, and More," Den of Geek, October 24, 2018, www.denofgeek.com/tv/the-incredibles-2-brad-brad-bird-on-family-blu-ray-extras-and-more.

82 **analysis of over 40 million tweets:** Bryor Snefjella, Daniel Schmidtke, and Victor Kuperman, "National Character Stereotypes Mirror Language Use: A Study of Canadian and American Tweets," *PLoS ONE* 13 (2018): e0206188.

83 **disagreeable people speak up more frequently:** Jeffery A. LePine and Linn Van Dyne, "Voice and Cooperative Behavior as Contrasting Forms of Contextual Performance: Evidence of Differential Relationships with Big Five Personality Characteristics and Cognitive Ability," *Journal of Applied Psychology* 86 (2001): 326–36.

83 **especially when leaders aren't receptive:** Samuel T. Hunter and Lily Cushenbery, "Is Being a Jerk Necessary for Originality? Examining the Role of Disagreeableness in the Sharing and Utilization of Original Ideas," *Journal of Business and Psychology* 30 (2015): 621–39.

83 **foster more task conflict:** Leslie A. DeChurch and Michelle A. Marks, "Maximizing the Benefits of Task Conflict: The Role of Conflict Management," *International Journal of Conflict Management* 12 (2001): 4–22.

84 **dissatisfaction promotes creativity only:** Jing Zhou and Jennifer M. George, "When Job Dissatisfaction Leads to Creativity: Encouraging the Expression of Voice," *Academy of Management Journal* 44 (2001): 682–96.

84 **cultural misfits are:** Amir Goldberg et al., "Fitting In or Standing Out? The Tradeoffs of Structural and Cultural Embeddedness," *American Sociological Review* 81 (2016): 1190–222.

84 **In building a team:** Joeri Hofmans and Timothy A. Judge, "Hiring for Culture Fit Doesn't Have to Undermine Diversity," *Harvard Business Review*, September 18, 2019, hbr.org /2019/09/hiring-for-culture-fit-doesnt-have-to-undermine-diversity.

85 **CEOs who indulge flattery:** Sun Hyun Park, James D. Westphal, and Ithai Stern, "Set Up for a Fall: The Insidious Effects of Flattery and Opinion Conformity toward Corporate Leaders," *Administrative Science Quarterly* 56 (2011): 257–302.

86 **when employees received tough feedback:** Francesca Gino, "Research: We Drop People Who Give Us Critical Feedback," *Harvard Business Review*, September 16, 2016, hbr.org /2016/09/research-we-drop-people-who-give-us-critical-feedback.

86 **"murder boards" to stir up:** William Safire, "On Language: Murder Board at the Skunk Works," *New York Times*, October 11, 1987, www.nytimes.com/1987/10/11/magazine/on -language-murder-board-at-the-skunk-works.html.

86 **At X, Google's "moonshot factory":** Derek Thompson, "Google X and the Science of Radical Creativity," *The Atlantic*, November 2017, www.theatlantic.com/magazine/archive/2017 /11/x-google-moonshot-factory/540648.

87 **"The most essential gift":** *The Cambridge Companion to Hemingway*, ed. Scott Donaldson (Cambridge: Cambridge University Press, 1996).

87 **How well we take criticism:** David Yeager et al., "Breaking the Cycle of Mistrust: Wise Interventions to Provide Critical Feedback across the Racial Divide," *Journal of Experimental Psychology: General* 143 (2014): 804–24.

88 **people who lack power or status:** Elizabeth W. Morrison, "Employee Voice Behavior: Integration and Directions for Future Research," *Academy of Management Annals* 5 (2011): 373–412; Charlan Jeanne Nemeth, *In Defense of Troublemakers: The Power of Dissent in Life and Business* (New York: Basic Books, 2018).

89 **Agreeable people were significantly more:** Jennifer A. Chatman and Sigal G. Barsade, "Personality, Organizational Culture, and Cooperation: Evidence from a Business Simulation," *Administrative Science Quarterly* 40 (1995): 423–43.

91 **A major problem with task conflict:** De Wit, Greer, and Jehn, "The Paradox of Intragroup Conflict."

91 **framing a dispute as a debate:** Ming-Hong Tsai and Corinne Bendersky, "The Pursuit of Information Sharing: Expressing Task Conflicts as Debates vs. Disagreements Increases Perceived Receptivity to Dissenting Opinions in Groups," *Organization Science* 27 (2016): 141–56.

92 **why they favor particular policies:** Philip M. Fernbach et al., "Political Extremism Is Supported by an Illusion of Understanding," *Psychological Science* 24 (2013): 939–46. Subsequent studies suggest that explaining how makes people more aware of their ignorance but doesn't always make their beliefs less extreme: see Jarret T. Crawford and John Ruscio, "Asking People to Explain Complex Policies Does Not Increase Political Moderation:

Three Preregistered Failures to Closely Replicate Fernbach, Rogers, Fox, and Sloman's (2013) Findings," *Psychological Science* 32 (2021): 611–21; Jan G. Voelkel, Mark J. Brandt, and Matteo Colombo, "I Know That I Know Nothing: Can Puncturing the Illusion of Explanatory Depth Overcome the Relationship between Attitudinal Dissimilarity and Prejudice?," *Comprehensive Results in Social Psychology* 3 (2018): 56–78; Ethan A. Meyers, Martin H. Turpin, Michael Bialek, Jonathan A. Fugelsang, and Derek J. Koehler, "Inducing Feelings of Ignorance Makes People More Receptive to Expert (Economist) Opinion," *Judgment and Decision Making* 15 (2020): 909–25.

92 **illusion of explanatory depth:** Leonid Rozenblit and Frank Keil, "The Misunderstood Limits of Folk Science: An Illusion of Explanatory Depth," *Cognitive Science* 26 (2002): 521–62.

93 **surprised by how much they struggle:** Matthew Fisher and Frank Keil, "The Curse of Expertise: When More Knowledge Leads to Miscalibrated Explanatory Insight," *Cognitive Science* 40 (2016): 1251–69.

93 **how little they actually know:** Dan R. Johnson, Meredith P. Murphy, and Riley M. Messer, "Reflecting on Explanatory Ability: A Mechanism for Detecting Gaps in Causal Knowledge," *Journal of Experimental Psychology: General* 145 (2016): 573–88.

Chapter 5. Dances with Foes

97 **"Exhausting someone in argument":** Tim Kreider, *We Learn Nothing: Essays* (New York: Simon & Schuster, 2012).

98 **introduced to Harish:** Personal interview with Harish Natarajan, May 23, 2019; "Live Debate: IBM Project Debater," IntelligenceSquared Debates, YouTube, February 11, 2019, www.youtube.com/watch?v=m3u-1yttrVw.

98 **evidence that early access to education:** Nicholas Kristof, "Too Small to Fail," *New York Times*, June 2, 2016, www.nytimes.com/2016/06/02/opinion/building-childrens-brains.html.

104 **It's more like a dance:** George Lakoff and Mark Johnson, *Metaphors We Live By* (Chicago: University of Chicago Press, 1980).

104 **what expert negotiators do differently:** Neil Rackham, "The Behavior of Successful Negotiators," in *Negotiation: Readings, Exercises, and Cases*, ed. Roy Lewicki, Bruce Barry, and David Saunders (New York: McGraw-Hill, 1980/2007).

106 **having even one negotiator who brings:** Femke S. Ten Velden, Bianca Beersma, and Carsten K. W. De Dreu, "It Takes One to Tango: The Effects of Dyads' Epistemic Motivation Composition in Negotiations," *Personality and Social Psychology Bulletin* 36 (2010): 1454–66.

107 **We can demonstrate openness:** Maria Popova, "How to Criticize with Kindness: Philosopher Daniel Dennett on the Four Steps to Arguing Intelligently," BrainPickings, March 28, 2014, www.brainpickings.org/2014/03/28/daniel-dennett-rapoport-rules-criticism.

107 **When we concede that someone else:** Fabrizio Butera, Nicolas Sommet, and Céline Darnon, "Sociocognitive Conflict Regulation: How to Make Sense of Diverging Ideas," *Current Directions in Psychological Science* 28 (2019): 145–51.

107 **Her official name is Project Debater:** IBM Research Editorial Staff, "Think 2019 Kicks Off with Live Debate between Man and Machine," *IBM Research Blog*, February 12, 2019, www.ibm.com/blogs/research/2019/02/ai-debate-recap-think-2019; Paul Teich, "IBM Project Debater Speaks to the Future of AI," The Next Platform, March 27, 2019, www.nextplatform.com/2019/03/27/ibm-project-debater-speaks-to-the-future-of-ai; Dieter Bohn, "What It's Like to Watch an IBM AI Successfully Debate Humans," The Verge, June 18, 2018, www.theverge.com/2018/6/18/17477686/ibm-project-debater-ai.

108 **the steel man:** Conor Friedersdorf, "The Highest Form of Disagreement," *The Atlantic*, June 26, 2017, www.theatlantic.com/politics/archive/2017/06/the-highest-form-of-disagreement/531597.

110 **people tend to see quantity:** Kate A. Ranganath, Barbara A. Spellman, and Jennifer A. Joy-Gaba, "Cognitive 'Category-Based Induction' Research and Social 'Persuasion' Research Are Each about What Makes Arguments Believable: A Tale of Two Literatures," *Perspectives on Psychological Science* 5 (2010): 115–22.

111 **the quality of reasons matters:** Richard E. Petty and Duane T. Wegener, "The Elaboration Likelihood Model: Current Status and Controversies," in *Dual-Process Theories in Social Psychology*, ed. Shelly Chaiken and Yaacov Trope (New York: Guilford, 1999).

111 **piling on justifications:** John Biondo and A. P. MacDonald Jr., "Internal-External Locus of Control and Response to Influence Attempts," *Journal of Personality* 39 (1971): 407–19.

111 **convince thousands of resistant alumni:** Daniel C. Feiler, Leigh P. Tost, and Adam M. Grant, "Mixed Reasons, Missed Givings: The Costs of Blending Egoistic and Altruistic Reasons in Donation Requests," *Journal of Experimental Social Psychology* 48 (2012): 1322–28.

112 **are you planning to attend?:** Rachel (Penny) Breuhaus, "Get in the Game: Comparing the Effects of Self-Persuasion and Direct Influence in Motivating Attendance at UNC Men's Basketball Games" (honors thesis, University of North Carolina at Chapel Hill, 2009).

112 **the person most likely to persuade you:** Elliot Aronson, "The Power of Self-Persuasion," *American Psychologist* 54 (1999): 875–84.

113 **paying them more:** David G. Allen, Phillip C. Bryant, and James M. Vardaman, "Retaining Talent: Replacing Misconceptions with Evidence-Based Strategies," *Academy of Management Perspectives* 24 (2017): 48–64.

114 **hierarchy of disagreement:** Paul Graham, "How to Disagree," PaulGraham.com, March 2008, www.paulgraham.com/disagree.html.

114 **Beethoven and Mozart:** Aaron Kozbelt, "Longitudinal Hit Ratios of Classical Composers: Reconciling 'Darwinian' and Expertise Acquisition Perspectives on Lifespan Creativity," *Psychology of Aesthetics, Creativity, and the Arts* 2 (2008): 221–35; Adam Grant, "The Surprising Habits of Original Thinkers," TED Talk, February 2016, www.ted.com/talks/adam_grant_the_surprising_habits_of_original_thinkers.

116 **If we hold an:** See Michael Natkin, "Strong Opinions Loosely Held Might Be the Worst Idea in Tech," *The Glowforge Blog*, May 1, 2019, blog.glowforge.com/strong-opinions-loosely-held-might-be-the-worst-idea-in-tech.

117 **in courtrooms, expert witnesses:** Robert J. Cramer, Stanley L. Brodsky, and Jamie DeCoster, "Expert Witness Confidence and Juror Personality: Their Impact on Credibility and Persuasion in the Courtroom," *Journal of the American Academy of Psychiatry and Law* 37 (2009) 63–74; Harvey London, Dennis McSeveney, and Richard Tropper, "Confidence, Overconfidence and Persuasion," *Human Relations* 24 (1971): 359–69.

117 **expressing some doubts:** Mohamed A. Hussein and Zakary L. Tormala, "Undermining Your Case to Enhance Your Impact: A Framework for Understanding the Effects of Acts of Receptiveness in Persuasion," *Personality and Social Psychology Review* 25 (2021): 229–50.

117 **woman named Michele Hansen:** Personal interview with Michele Hansen, February 23, 2018; "The Problem with All-Stars," *WorkLife with Adam Grant*, March 14, 2018.

117 **two-sided messages were more convincing:** Mike Allen, "Meta-analysis Comparing the Persuasiveness of One-Sided and Two-Sided Messages," *Western Journal of Speech Communication* 55 (1991): 390–404.

118 **"I work too hard, I care too much":** *The Office*, season 3, episode 23, "Beach Games," May 10, 2007, NBC.

118 **"My name is George":** *Seinfeld*, season 5, episode 22, "The Opposite," May 19, 1994, NBC.

119 **candidates who acknowledge legitimate weaknesses:** Ovul Sezer, Francesca Gino, and Michael I. Norton, "Humblebragging: A Distinct—and Ineffective—Self-Presentation Strategy," *Journal of Personality and Social Psychology* 114 (2018): 52–74.

Chapter 6. Bad Blood on the Diamond

121 **"I hated the Yankees with all my heart, even to the point":** Doris Kearns Goodwin, *MLB Pro Blog*, doriskearnsgoodwin.mlblogs.com.

121 **Daryl Davis arrived:** Personal communications with Daryl Davis, April 10, 2020; Daryl Davis, "What Do You Do When Someone Just Doesn't Like You?," TEDxCharlottesville, November 2017, www.ted.com/talks/daryl_davis_what_do_you_do_when_someone

_just_doesn_t_like_you; Dwane Brown, "How One Man Convinced 200 Ku Klux Klan Members to Give Up Their Robes," NPR, August 20, 2017, www.npr.org/transcripts /544861933; Craig Phillips, "Reformed Racists: Is There Life after Hate for Former White Supremacists?," PBS, February 9, 2017, www.pbs.org/independentlens/blog/reformed -racists-white-supremacists-life-after-hate; *The Joe Rogan Experience*, #1419, January 30, 2020; Jeffrey Fleishman, "A Black Man's Quixotic Quest to Quell the Racism of the KKK, One Robe at a Time," *Los Angeles Times*, December 8, 2016, www.latimes.com/entertain ment/movies/la-ca-film-accidental-courtesy-20161205-story.html.

123 **most popular T-shirts:** Amos Barshad, "Yankees Suck! Yankees Suck!" *Grantland*, September 1, 2015, http://grantland.com/features/yankees-suck-t-shirts-boston-red-sox.

123 **When asked how much money:** Steven A. Lehr, Meghan L. Ferreira, and Mahzarin R. Banaji, "When Outgroup Negativity Trumps Ingroup Positivity: Fans of the Boston Red Sox and New York Yankees Place Greater Value on Rival Losses Than Own-Team Gains," *Group Processes & Intergroup Relations* 22 (2017): 26–42.

123 **when Red Sox fans see the Yankees fail:** Mina Cikara and Susan T. Fiske, "Their Pain, Our Pleasure: Stereotype Content and Schadenfreude," *Annals of the New York Academy of Sciences* 1299 (2013): 52–59.

123 **well beyond Boston:** Eduardo Gonzalez, "Most Hated Baseball Team on Twitter?," *Los Angeles Times*, July 1, 2019, www.latimes.com/sports/mlb/la-sp-most-hated-mlb-teams -twitter-yankees-cubs-dodgers-20190701-story.html.

124 **families self-segregated:** Hannah Schwär, "Puma and Adidas' Rivalry Has Divided a Small German Town for 70 Years—Here's What It Looks Like Now," *Business Insider Deutschland*, October 1, 2018; Ellen Emmerentze Jervell, "Where Puma and Adidas Were Like Hatfields and McCoys," *Wall Street Journal*, December 30, 2014, www.wsj.com /articles/where-adidas-and-pumas-were-like-hatfields-and-mccoys-1419894858; Allan Hall, "Adidas and Puma Bury the Hatchet after 60 Years of Brothers' Feud after Football Match," *Daily Telegraph*, September 22, 2009, www.telegraph.co.uk/news/worldnews /europe/germany/6216728/Adidas-and-Puma-bury-the-hatchet-after-60-years-of -brothers-feud-after-football-match.html.

124 **we disidentify with our adversaries:** Kimberly D. Elsbach and C. B. Bhattacharya, "Defining Who You Are by What You're Not: Organizational Disidentification and the National Rifle Association," *Organization Science* 12 (2001): 393–413.

125 **if they were willing to lie:** Gavin J. Kilduff et al., "Whatever It Takes to Win: Rivalry Increases Unethical Behavior," *Academy of Management Journal* 59 (2016): 1508–34.

125 **even when the boundaries between them are trivial:** Michael Diehl, "The Minimal Group Paradigm: Theoretical Explanations and Empirical Findings," *European Review of Social Psychology* 1 (1990): 263–92.

125 **a seemingly innocuous question: is a hot dog a sandwich?:** Dave Hauser (@DavidJHauser), December 5, 2019, twitter.com/DavidJHauser/status/1202610237934592000.

126 **Identifying with a group:** Philip Furley, "What Modern Sports Competitions Can Tell Us about Human Nature," *Perspectives on Psychological Science* 14 (2019): 138–55.

126 **after their team won a football game:** Robert B. Cialdini et al., "Basking in Reflected Glory: Three (Football) Field Studies," *Journal of Personality and Social Psychology* 34 (1976): 366–75.

126 **Rivalries are most likely to develop:** Gavin J. Kilduff, Hillary Anger Elfenbein, and Barry M. Staw, "The Psychology of Rivalry: A Relationally Dependent Analysis of Competition," *Academy of Management Journal* 53 (2010): 943–69.

126 **The two teams also have more fans:** Seth Stephens-Davidowitz, "They Hook You When You're Young," *New York Times*, April 19, 2014, www.nytimes.com/2014/04/20/opinion /sunday/they-hook-you-when-youre-young.html; J. Clement, "Major League Baseball Teams with the Most Facebook Fans as of June 2020," Statista, June 16, 2020, www.statista.com /statistics/235719/facebook-fans-of-major-league-baseball-teams.

126 **subject of extensive debate:** John K. Ashton, Robert Simon Hudson, and Bill Gerrard, "Do National Soccer Results Really Impact on the Stock Market?," *Applied Economics* 43 (2011):

3709–17; Guy Kaplanski and Haim Levy, "Exploitable Predictable Irrationality: The FIFA World Cup Effect on the U.S. Stock Market," *Journal of Financial and Quantitative Analysis* 45 (2010): 535–53; Jerome Geyer-Klingeberg et al., "Do Stock Markets React to Soccer Games? A Meta-regression Analysis," *Applied Economics* 50 (2018): 2171–89.

126 **when their favorite soccer team loses:** Panagiotis Gkorezis et al., "Linking Football Team Performance to Fans' Work Engagement and Job Performance: Test of a Spillover Model," *Journal of Occupational and Organizational Psychology* 89 (2016): 791–812.

127 **pairs of reality goggles:** George A. Kelly, *The Psychology of Personal Constructs*, vol. 1, *A Theory of Personality* (New York: Norton, 1955).

127 **phenomenon is called group polarization:** Daniel J. Isenberg, "Group Polarization: A Critical Review and Meta-analysis," *Journal of Personality and Social Psychology* 50 (1986): 1141–51.

127 **Juries with authoritarian beliefs:** Robert M. Bray and Audrey M. Noble, "Authoritarianism and Decision in Mock Juries: Evidence of Jury Bias and Group Polarization," *Journal of Personality and Social Psychology* 36 (1978): 1424–30.

127 **Corporate boards are more likely:** Cass R. Sunstein and Reid Hastie, *Wiser: Getting Beyond Groupthink to Make Groups Smarter* (Boston: Harvard Business Review Press, 2014).

127 **Polarization is reinforced:** Liran Goldman and Michael A. Hogg, "Going to Extremes for One's Group: The Role of Prototypicality and Group Acceptance," *Journal of Applied Social Psychology* 46 (2016): 544–53; Michael A. Hogg, John C. Turner, and Barbara Davidson, "Polarized Norms and Social Frames of Reference: A Test of the Self-Categorization Theory of Group Polarization," *Basic and Applied Social Psychology* 11 (1990): 77–100.

128 **when teams try to downplay:** Johannes Berendt and Sebastian Uhrich, "Rivalry and Fan Aggression: Why Acknowledging Conflict Reduces Tension between Rival Fans and Downplaying Makes Things Worse," *European Sport Management Quarterly* 18 (2018): 517–40.

128 **Upon returning from space:** Peter Suedfeld, Katya Legkaia, and Jelena Brcic, "Changes in the Hierarchy of Value References Associated with Flying in Space," *Journal of Personality* 78 (2010): 1411–36.

128 **"From out there on the moon":** "Edgar Mitchell's Strange Voyage," *People*, April 8, 1974, people.com/archive/edgar-mitchells-strange-voyage-vol-1-no-6.

129 **"On Earth, astronauts look to the stars":** Personal interview with Jeff Ashby, January 12, 2018; "How to Trust People You Don't Like," *WorkLife with Adam Grant*, March 28, 2018.

129 **Manchester United soccer fans:** Mark Levine et al., "Identity and Emergency Intervention: How Social Group Membership and Inclusiveness of Group Boundaries Shape Helping Behavior," *Personality and Social Psychology Bulletin* 31 (2005): 443–53.

130 **Kelman set out to challenge:** Herbert C. Kelman, "Group Processes in the Resolution of International Conflicts: Experiences from the Israeli-Palestinian Case," *American Psychologist* 52 (1997): 212–20.

131 **we asked UNC students to help:** Alison R. Fragale, Karren Knowlton, and Adam M. Grant, "Feeling for Your Foes: Empathy Can Reverse the In-Group Helping Preference" (working paper, 2020).

131 **establishes her as different:** Myron Rothbart and Oliver P. John, "Social Categorization and Behavioral Episodes: A Cognitive Analysis of the Effects of Intergroup Contact," *Journal of Social Issues* 41 (1985): 81–104.

132 **"Without sports, this wouldn't be disgusting":** ESPN College Football, www.espn.com /video/clip/_/id/18106107.

133 **"You're actually rooting for the clothes":** *Seinfeld*, season 6, episode 12, "The Label Maker," January 19, 1995, NBC.

133 **A fun but arbitrary ritual:** Tim Kundro and Adam M. Grant, "Bad Blood on the Diamond: Highlighting the Arbitrariness of Acrimony Can Reduce Animosity toward Rivals" (working paper, 2020).

136 **counterfactual thinking involves:** Kai Epstude and Neal J. Roese, "The Functional Theory of Counterfactual Thinking," *Personality and Social Psychology Review* 12 (2008): 168–92.

136 **many stereotypes match up:** Lee Jussim et al., "The Unbearable Accuracy of Stereotypes," in *Handbook of Prejudice, Stereotyping, and Discrimination,* ed. Todd D. Nelson (New York: Psychology Press, 2009).

136 **stereotypes become consistently and increasingly inaccurate:** Lee Jussim, Jarret T. Crawford, and Rachel S. Rubinstein, "Stereotype (In)accuracy in Perceptions of Groups and Individuals," *Current Directions in Psychological Science* 24 (2015): 490–97.

138 **"if you're a Virgo in China":** Jackson G. Lu et al., "Disentangling Stereotypes from Social Reality: Astrological Stereotypes and Discrimination in China," *Journal of Personality and Social Psychology* (2020), psycnet.apa.org/record/2020-19028-001.

138 **our beliefs are cultural truisms:** Gregory R. Maio and James M. Olson, "Values as Truisms: Evidence and Implications," *Journal of Personality and Social Psychology* 74 (1998): 294–311.

139 **there are more similarities:** Paul H. P. Hanel, Gregory R. Maio, and Antony S. R. Manstead, "A New Way to Look at the Data: Similarities between Groups of People Are Large and Important," *Journal of Personality and Social Psychology* 116 (2019): 541–62.

139 **interacting with members of another group:** Thomas F. Pettigrew and Linda R. Tropp, "A Meta-analytic Test of Intergroup Contact Theory," *Journal of Personality and Social Psychology* 90 (2006): 751–83; see also Elizabeth Levy Paluck, Seth A. Green, and Donald P. Green, "The Contact Hypothesis Re-evaluated," *Behavioral Public Policy* 3 (2019): 129–58.

140 **more likely to privilege their own perspectives:** Jennifer R. Overbeck and Vitaliya Droutman, "One for All: Social Power Increases Self-Anchoring of Traits, Attitudes, and Emotions," *Psychological Science* 24 (2013): 1466–76.

141 **their perspectives are more likely to go unquestioned:** Leigh Plunkett Tost, Francesca Gino, and Richard P. Larrick, "When Power Makes Others Speechless," *Academy of Management Journal* 56 (2013): 1465–86.

Chapter 7. Vaccine Whisperers and Mild-Mannered Interrogators

143 **Marie-Hélène Étienne-Rousseau went into labor:** See Eric Boodman, "The Vaccine Whisperers: Counselors Gently Engage New Parents Before Their Doubts Harden into Certainty," STAT, August 5, 2019, www.statnews.com/2019/08/05/the-vaccine-whisperers-counselors -gently-engage-new-parents-before-their-doubts-harden-into-certainty.

144 **its mortality rate:** Nick Paumgarten, "The Message of Measles," *New Yorker,* August 26, 2019, www.newyorker.com/magazine/2019/09/02/the-message-of-measles; Leslie Roberts, "Why Measles Deaths Are Surging—and Coronavirus Could Make It Worse," *Nature,* April 7, 2020, www.nature.com/articles/d41586-020-01011-6.

144 **tried to prosecute the problem:** Helen Branswell, "New York County, Declaring Emergency over Measles, Seeks to Ban Unvaccinated from Public Places," STAT, March 26, 2019, www.statnews.com/2019/03/26/rockland-county-ny-declares-emergency-over-measles; Tyler Pager, "'Monkey, Rat and Pig DNA': How Misinformation Is Driving the Measles Outbreak among Ultra-Orthodox Jews," *New York Times,* April 9, 2019, www.nytimes .com/2019/04/09/nyregion/jews-measles-vaccination.html.

144 **The results were often disappointing:** Matthew J. Hornsey, Emily A. Harris, and Kelly S. Fielding, "The Psychological Roots of Anti-Vaccination Attitudes: A 24-Nation Investigation," *Health Psychology* 37 (2018): 307–15.

144 **introducing people to the research:** Cornelia Betsch and Katharina Sachse, "Debunking Vaccination Myths: Strong Risk Negations Can Increase Perceived Vaccination Risks," *Health Psychology* 32 (2013): 146–55.

144 **their interest in vaccination didn't rise at all:** Brendan Nyhan et al., "Effective Messages in Vaccine Promotion: A Randomized Trial," *Pediatrics* 133 (2014): e835–42.

145 **what doesn't sway us:** Zakary L. Tormala and Richard E. Petty, "What Doesn't Kill Me Makes Me Stronger: The Effects of Resisting Persuasion on Attitude Certainty," *Journal of Personality and Social Psychology* 83 (2002): 1298–313.

145 **the act of resistance fortifies:** William J. McGuire, "Inducing Resistance to Persuasion: Some Contemporary Approaches," *Advances in Experimental Social Psychology* 1 (1964): 191–229.

145 **Refuting a point of view:** John A. Banas and Stephen A. Rains, "A Meta-analysis of Research on Inoculation Theory," *Communication Monographs* 77 (2010): 281–311.

146 **clinical psychologist named Bill Miller:** Personal communications with Bill Miller, September 3 and 6, 2019.

146 **core principles of a practice called motivational interviewing:** William R. Miller and Stephen Rollnick, *Motivational Interviewing: Helping People Change,* 3rd ed. (New York: Guilford, 2012).

147 **a neonatologist and researcher named:** Personal interview with Arnaud Gagneur, October 8, 2019.

148 **In Arnaud's first study:** Arnaud Gagneur et al., "A Postpartum Vaccination Promotion Intervention Using Motivational Interviewing Techniques Improves Short-Term Vaccine Coverage: PromoVac Study," *BMC Public Health* 18 (2018): 811.

148 **In Arnaud's next experiment:** Thomas Lemaître et al., "Impact of a Vaccination Promotion Intervention Using Motivational Interview Techniques on Long-Term Vaccine Coverage: The PromoVac Strategy," *Human Vaccines & Immunotherapeutics* 15 (2019): 732–39.

149 **help people stop smoking:** Carolyn J. Heckman, Brian L. Egleston, and Makary T. Hofmann, "Efficacy of Motivational Interviewing for Smoking Cessation: A Systematic Review and Meta-analysis," *Tobacco Control* 19 (2010): 410–16.

149 **abusing drugs and alcohol:** Brad W. Lundahl et al., "A Meta-analysis of Motivational Interviewing: Twenty-Five Years of Empirical Studies," *Research on Social Work Practice* 20 (2010): 137–60.

149 **improve their diets and exercise habits:** Brian L. Burke, Hal Arkowitz, and Marisa Menchola, "The Efficacy of Motivational Interviewing: A Meta-analysis of Controlled Clinical Trials," *Journal of Consulting and Clinical Psychology* 71 (2003): 843–61.

149 **overcome eating disorders:** Pam Macdonald et al., "The Use of Motivational Interviewing in Eating Disorders: A Systematic Review," *Psychiatry Research* 200 (2012): 1–11.

149 **and lose weight:** Marni J. Armstrong et al., "Motivational Interviewing to Improve Weight Loss in Overweight Patients: A Systematic Review and Meta-analysis of Randomized Controlled Trials," *Obesity Reviews* 12 (2011): 709–23.

149 **build grit in professional soccer players:** Jonathan Rhodes et al., "Enhancing Grit through Functional Imagery Training in Professional Soccer," *Sport Psychologist* 32 (2018): 220–25.

149 **teachers to nudge students:** Neralie Cain, Michael Gradisar, and Lynette Moseley, "A Motivational School-Based Intervention for Adolescent Sleep Problems," *Sleep Medicine* 12 (2011): 246–51.

149 **consultants to prepare teams:** Conrado J. Grimolizzi-Jensen, "Organizational Change: Effect of Motivational Interviewing on Readiness to Change," *Journal of Change Management* 18 (2018): 54–69.

149 **public health workers:** Angelica K. Thevos, Robert E. Quick, and Violet Yanduli, "Motivational Interviewing Enhances the Adoption of Water Disinfection Practices in Zambia," *Health Promotion International* 15 (2000): 207–14.

149 **and environmental activists:** Florian E. Klonek et al., "Using Motivational Interviewing to Reduce Threats in Conversations about Environmental Behavior," *Frontiers in Psychology* 6 (2015): 1015; Sofia Tagkaloglou and Tim Kasser, "Increasing Collaborative, Pro-Environmental Activism: The Roles of Motivational Interviewing, Self-Determined Motivation, and Self-Efficacy," *Journal of Environmental Psychology* 58 (2018): 86–92.

149 **opened the minds of prejudiced voters:** Joshua L. Kalla and David E. Broockman, "Reducing Exclusionary Attitudes through Interpersonal Conversation: Evidence from Three Field Experiments," *American Political Science Review* 114 (2020): 410–25.

149 **help separated parents resolve disputes:** Megan Morris, W. Kim Halford, and Jemima Petch, "A Randomized Controlled Trial Comparing Family Mediation with and without Motivational Interviewing," *Journal of Family Psychology* 32 (2018): 269–75.

149 **a body of evidence this robust:** Sune Rubak et al., "Motivational Interviewing: A Systematic Review and Meta-analysis," *British Journal of General Practice* 55 (2005): 305–12.

150 **When people ignore advice:** Anna Goldfarb, "How to Give People Advice They'll Be De-lighted to Take," *New York Times*, October 21, 2019, www.nytimes.com/2019/10/21/smarter-living/how-to-give-better-advice.html.

152 **sustain talk and change talk:** Molly Magill et al., "A Meta-analysis of Motivational Inter-viewing Process: Technical, Relational, and Conditional Process Models of Change," *Journal of Consulting and Clinical Psychology* 86 (2018): 140–57; Timothy R. Apodaca et al., "Which Individual Therapist Behaviors Elicit Client Change Talk and Sustain Talk in Motivational Interviewing?," *Journal of Substance Abuse Treatment* 61 (2016): 60–65; Molly Magill et al., "The Technical Hypothesis of Motivational Interviewing: A Meta-analysis of MI's Key Causal Model," *Journal of Consulting and Clinical Psychology* 82 (2014): 973–83.

152 **"Change talk is a golden thread":** Theresa Moyers, "Change Talk," *Talking to Change with Glenn Hinds & Sebastian Kaplan.*

155 **when people detect an attempt at influence:** Marian Friestad and Peter Wright, "The Per-suasion Knowledge Model: How People Cope with Persuasion Attempts," *Journal of Con-sumer Research* 21 (1994): 1–31.

155 **Betty Bigombe had already hiked:** Personal interviews with Betty Bigombe, March 19 and May 8, 2020; see also "Betty Bigombe: The Woman Who Befriended a Warlord," BBC, August 8, 2019, www.bbc.com/news/world-africa-49269136.

155 **Joseph Kony was the leader:** David Smith, "Surrender of Senior Aide to Joseph Kony Is Major Blow to Lord's Resistance Army," *Guardian*, January 7, 2015, www.theguardian.com/global-development/2015/jan/07/surrender-aide-joseph-kony-blow-lords-resistance-army.

156 **"truly curious questions":** Kate Murphy, "Talk Less. Listen More. Here's How," *New York Times*, January 9, 2010, www.nytimes.com/2020/01/09/opinion/listening-tips.html.

157 **an empathetic, nonjudgmental, attentive listener:** Guy Itzchakov et al., "The Listener Sets the Tone: High-Quality Listening Increases Attitude Clarity and Behavior-Intention Con-sequences," *Personality and Social Psychology Bulletin* 44 (2018): 762–78; Guy Itzchakov, Avraham N. Kluger, and Dotan R. Castro, "I Am Aware of My Inconsistencies but Can Tolerate Them: The Effect of High Quality Listening on Speakers' Attitude Ambivalence," *Personality and Social Psychology Bulletin* 43 (2017): 105–20.

158 **people's attitudes became more complex:** Guy Itzchakov and Avraham N. Kluger, "Can Holding a Stick Improve Listening at Work? The Effect of Listening Circles on Employees' Emotions and Cognitions," *European Journal of Work and Organizational Psychology* 26 (2017): 663–76.

158 **working on being better listeners:** Guy Itzchakov and Avraham N. Kluger, "The Power of Listening in Helping People Change," *Harvard Business Review*, May 17, 2018, hbr.org/2018/05/the-power-of-listening-in-helping-people-change.

158 **"How can I tell what I think":** E. M. Forster, *Aspects of the Novel* (New York: Houghton Mifflin, 1927/1956); see also Graham Wallas, *The Art of Thought* (Kent, England: Solis Press, 1926/2014).

158 **"an inverse charisma":** Wendy Moffat, *E. M. Forster: A New Life* (London: Bloomsbury, 2011).

158 **managers rated as the worst listeners:** Judi Brownell, "Perceptions of Effective Listeners: A Management Study," *International Journal of Business Communication* 27 (1973): 401–15.

158 **their pets were better listeners:** "Poll: 1 in 3 Women Say Pets Listen Better Than Hus-bands," *USA Today*, April 30, 2010, usatoday30.usatoday.com/life/lifestyle/pets/2010-04-30-pets-vs-spouses_N.htm.

158 **doctors to interrupt their patients:** Naykky Singh Ospina et al., "Eliciting the Patient's Agenda: Secondary Analysis of Recorded Clinical Encounters," *Journal of General Internal Medicine* 34 (2019): 36–40.

158 **29 seconds to describe their symptoms:** M. Kim Marvel et al., "Soliciting the Patient's Agenda: Have We Improved?," *Journal of the American Medical Association* 281 (1999): 283–87.

Chapter 8. Charged Conversations

163 **"When conflict is cliché"**: Amanda Ripley, "Complicating the Narratives," *Solutions Journalism*, June 27, 2018, thewholestory.solutionsjournalism.org/complicating-the-narratives-b91ea06ddf63.

163 **Difficult Conversations Lab:** Peter T. Coleman, *The Five Percent: Finding Solutions to Seemingly Impossible Conflicts* (New York: PublicAffairs, 2011).

164 **the article framed the debate:** Katharina Kugler and Peter T. Coleman, "Get Complicated: The Effects of Complexity on Conversations over Potentially Intractable Moral Conflicts," *Negotiation and Conflict Management Research* (2020), onlinelibrary.wiley.com/doi/full/10.1111/ncmr.12192.

165 **simplifying a complex continuum:** Matthew Fisher and Frank C. Keil, "The Binary Bias: A Systematic Distortion in the Integration of Information," *Psychological Science* 29 (2018): 1846–58.

165 **the humorist Robert Benchley:** "The Most Popular Book of the Month," *Vanity Fair*, February 1920, babel.hathitrust.org/cgi/pt?id=mdp.39015032024203&view=1up&seq=203&q1=divide%20the%20world.

165 **a phrase from Walt Whitman:** Walt Whitman, *Leaves of Grass*, in *Walt Whitman: The Complete Poems*, ed. Francis Murphy (London: Penguin Classics, 1855/2005).

165 **"read less like a lawyer's opening statement":** Ripley, "Complicating the Narratives."

166 **Yet polls show bipartisan consensus:** Mike DeBonis and Emily Guskin, "Americans of Both Parties Overwhelmingly Support 'Red Flag' Laws, Expanded Background Checks for Gun Buyers, Washington Post–ABC News Poll Finds," *Washington Post*, September 9, 2019, www.washingtonpost.com/politics/americans-of-both-parties-overwhelmingly-support-red-flag-laws-expanded-gun-background-checks-washington-post-abc-news-poll-finds/2019/09/08/97208916-ca75-11e9-a4f3-c081a126de70_story.html; Domenico Montanaro, "Poll: Most Americans Want to See Congress Pass Gun Restrictions," NPR, September 10, 2019, www.npr.org/2019/09/10/759193047/poll-most-americans-want-to-see-congress-pass-gun-restrictions.

166 **"Purple maps":** Abraham M. Rutchick, Joshua M. Smyth, and Sara Konrath, "Seeing Red (and Blue): Effects of Electoral College Depictions on Political Group Perception," *Analyses of Social Issues and Public Policy* 9 (2009): 269–82.

167 **only 59 percent of Americans:** Moira Fagan and Christine Huang, "A Look at How People around the World View Climate Change," Pew Research Center, April 18, 2019, www.pewresearch.org/fact-tank/2019/04/18/a-look-at-how-people-around-the-world-view-climate-change.

167 **In the past decade in the United States:** "Environment," Gallup, news.gallup.com/poll/1615/environment.aspx; "About Six in Ten Americans Think Global Warming Is Mostly Human-Caused," Yale Program on Climate Change, December 2018, climatecommunication.yale.edu/wp-content/uploads/2019/01/climate_change_american_mind_december_2018_1-3.png.

168 **What we believe depends:** Ben Tappin, Leslie Van Der Leer, and Ryan Mckay, "You're Not Going to Change Your Mind," *New York Times*, May 27, 2017, www.nytimes.com/2017/05/27/opinion/sunday/youre-not-going-to-change-your-mind.html.

168 **higher levels of education predict:** Lawrence C. Hamilton, "Education, Politics and Opinions about Climate Change: Evidence for Interaction Effects," *Climatic Change* 104 (2011): 231–42.

168 **"Some still doubt":** Al Gore, "The Case for Optimism on Climate Change," TED, February 2016, www.ted.com/talks/al_gore_the_case_for_optimism_on_climate_change.

168 **he was called the Elvis:** Steven Levy, "We Are Now at Peak TED," *Wired*, February 19, 2016, www.wired.com/2016/02/we-are-now-at-peak-ted.

169 **contrasted scientists with "climate deniers":** Al Gore, "We Can't Wish Away Climate Change," *New York Times*, February 27, 2010, www.nytimes.com/2010/02/28/opinion/28gore.html.

169 **six camps of thought:** "Global Warming's Six Americas," Yale Program on Climate Change Communication, climatecommunication.yale.edu/about/projects/global-warmings -six-americas.

170 **climate contrarians received disproportionate coverage:** Alexander Michael Petersen, Emmanuel M. Vincent, and Anthony LeRoy Westerling, "Discrepancy in Scientific Authority and Media Visibility of Climate Change Scientists and Contrarians," *Nature Communications* 10 (2019): 3502.

170 **overestimating how common denial is:** Matto Mildenberger and Dustin Tingley, "Beliefs about Climate Beliefs: The Importance of Second-Order Opinions for Climate Politics," *British Journal of Political Science* 49 (2019): 1279–307.

170 **within denial there are at least six different categories:** Philipp Schmid and Cornelia Betsch, "Effective Strategies for Rebutting Science Denialism in Public Discussions," *Nature Human Behavior* 3 (2019): 931–39.

171 **when journalists acknowledge the uncertainties:** Anne Marthe van der Bles et al., "The Effects of Communicating Uncertainty on Public Trust in Facts and Numbers," *PNAS* 117 (2020): 7672–83.

171 **when experts express doubt:** Uma R. Karmarkar and Zakary L. Tormala, "Believe Me, I Have No Idea What I'm Talking About: The Effects of Source Certainty on Consumer Involvement and Persuasion," *Journal of Consumer Research* 36 (2010): 1033–49.

172 **media reported on a study:** Tania Lombrozo, "In Science Headlines, Should Nuance Trump Sensation?," NPR, August 3, 2015, www.npr.org/sections/13.7/2015/08/03/428984912/in -science-headlines-should-nuance-trump-sensation.

172 **The actual study showed:** Vincenzo Solfrizzi et al., "Coffee Consumption Habits and the Risk of Mild Cognitive Impairment: The Italian Longitudinal Study on Aging," *Journal of Alzheimer's Disease* 47 (2015): 889–99.

172 **jolt of instant complexity:** Ariana Eunjung Cha, "Yesterday's Coffee Science: It's Good for the Brain. Today: Not So Fast . . .*" *Washington Post*, August 28, 2015, www.washington post.com/news/to-your-health/wp/2015/07/30/yesterdays-coffee-science-its-good-for -the-brain-today-not-so-fast.

172 **Scientists overwhelmingly agree:** "Do Scientists Agree on Climate Change?," NASA, https://climate.nasa.gov/faq/17/do-scientists-agree-on-climate-change; John Cook et al., "Consensus on Consensus: A Synthesis of Consensus Estimates on Human-Caused Global Warming," *Environmental Research Letters* 11 (2016): 048002; David Herring, "Isn't There a Lot of Disagreement among Climate Scientists about Global Warming?," *Climate-Watch Magazine*, February 3, 2020, www.climate.gov/news-features/climate-qa/isnt-there -lot-disagreement-among-climate-scientists-about-global-warming.

172 **a range of views on the actual effects:** Carolyn Gramling, "Climate Models Agree Things Will Get Bad. Capturing Just How Bad Is Tricky," *ScienceNews*, January 7, 2020, www.science news.org/article/why-climate-change-models-disagree-earth-worst-case-scenarios.

172 **people are more motivated to act:** Paul G. Bain et al., "Co-Benefits of Addressing Climate Change Can Motivate Action around the World," *Nature Climate Change* 6 (2016): 154–57.

172 **preserving the purity of nature:** Matthew Feinberg and Robb Willer, "The Moral Roots of Environmental Attitudes," *Psychological Science* 24 (2013): 56–62.

172 **protecting the planet as an act of patriotism:** Christopher Wolsko, Hector Ariceaga, and Jesse Seiden, "Red, White, and Blue Enough to Be Green: Effects of Moral Framing on Climate Change Attitudes and Conservation Behaviors," *Journal of Experimental Social Psychology* 65 (2016): 7–19.

173 **people will ignore or even deny:** Troy H. Campbell and Aaron C. Kay, "Solution Aversion: On the Relation between Ideology and Motivated Disbelief," *Journal of Personality and Social Psychology* 107 (2014): 809–24.

173 **examples of headlines:** Mary Annaise Heglar, "I Work in the Environmental Movement. I Don't Care If You Recycle," *Vox*, May 28, 2019, www.vox.com/the-highlight/2019/5/28 /18629833/climate-change-2019-green-new-deal; Bob Berwyn, "Can Planting a Trillion

Trees Stop Climate Change? Scientists Say It's a Lot More Complicated," *Inside Climate News*, May 27, 2020, insideclimatenews.org/news/26052020/trillion-trees-climate-change ?gclid=EAIaIQobChMIrb6n1qHF6gIVFInICh2kggWNEAAYAiAAEgI-sPD_BwE.

174 **when news reports about science included caveats:** Lewis Bott et al., "Caveats in Science-Based News Stories Communicate Caution without Lowering Interest," *Journal of Experimental Psychology: Applied* 25 (2019): 517–42.

174 **diversity of background and thought:** See, for example, Ute Hülsheger, Neil R. Anderson, and Jesus F. Salgado, "Team-Level Predictors of Innovation at Work: A Comprehensive Meta-analysis Spanning Three Decades of Research," *Journal of Applied Psychology* 94 (2009): 1128–45; Cristian L. Dezsö and David Gaddis Ross, "Does Female Representation in Top Management Improve Firm Performance? A Panel Data Investigation," *Strategic Management Journal* 33 (2012): 1072–89; Samuel R. Sommers, "On Racial Diversity and Group Decision Making: Identifying Multiple Effects of Racial Composition on Jury Deliberations," *Journal of Personality and Social Psychology* 90 (2006): 597–612; Denise Lewin Loyd et al., "Social Category Diversity Promotes Premeeting Elaboration: The Role of Relationship Focus," *Organization Science* 24 (2013): 757–72.

174 **potential is realized in some situations:** Elizabeth Mannix and Margaret A. Neale, "What Differences Make a Difference? The Promise and Reality of Diverse Teams in Organizations," *Psychological Science in the Public Interest* 6 (2005): 31–55.

174 **(and more accurate): "Diversity is good, but it isn't easy":** Lisa Leslie, "What Makes a Workplace Diversity Program Successful?," *Center for Positive Organizations*, January 22, 2020, positiveorgs.bus.umich.edu/news/what-makes-a-workplace-diversity-program-successful.

174 **"The Mixed Effects":** Edward H. Chang et al., "The Mixed Effects of Online Diversity Training," *PNAS* 116 (2019): 7778–83.

175 **"maintain a consistent narrative":** Julian Matthews, "A Cognitive Scientist Explains Why Humans Are So Susceptible to Fake News and Misinformation," NiemanLab, April 17, 2019, www.niemanlab.org/2019/04/a-cognitive-scientist-explains-why-humans-are-so -susceptible-to-fake-news-and-misinformation.

175 **divide around emotional intelligence:** Daniel Goleman, *Emotional Intelligence: Why It Can Matter More Than IQ* (New York: Bantam Books, 1995) and "What Makes a Leader?," *Harvard Business Review*, January 2004; Jordan B. Peterson, "There Is No Such Thing as EQ," Quora, August 22, 2019, www.quora.com/What-is-more-beneficial-in-all-aspects -of-life-a-high-EQ-or-IQ-This-question-is-based-on-the-assumption-that-only -your-EQ-or-IQ-is-high-with-the-other-being-average-or-below-this-average.

175 **the comprehensive meta-analyses:** Dana L. Joseph and Daniel A. Newman, "Emotional Intelligence: An Integrative Meta-analysis and Cascading Model," *Journal of Applied Psychology* 95 (2010): 54–78; Dana L. Joseph et al., "Why Does Self-Reported EI Predict Job Performance? A Meta-analytic Investigation of Mixed EI," *Journal of Applied Psychology* 100 (2015): 298–342.

175 **when people embrace paradoxes:** Ella Miron-Spektor, Francesca Gino, and Linda Argote, "Paradoxical Frames and Creative Sparks: Enhancing Individual Creativity through Conflict and Integration," *Organizational Behavior and Human Decision Processes* 116 (2011): 229–40; Dustin J. Sleesman, "Pushing Through the Tension While Stuck in the Mud: Paradox Mindset and Escalation of Commitment," *Organizational Behavior and Human Decision Processes* 155 (2019): 83–96.

176 **beneficial in jobs that involve dealing with emotions:** Joseph and Newman, "Emotional Intelligence."

176 **a thousand comments poured in:** Adam Grant, "Emotional Intelligence Is Overrated," LinkedIn, September 30, 2014, www.linkedin.com/pulse/20140930125543-69244073 -emotional-intelligence-is-overrated.

177 **Some teachers are determined:** Olga Khazan, "The Myth of 'Learning Styles,'" *The Atlantic*, April 11, 2018, www.theatlantic.com/science/archive/2018/04/the-myth-of-learning -styles/557687.

177 **they don't actually learn better that way:** Harold Pashler et al., "Learning Styles: Concepts and Evidence," *Psychological Science in the Public Interest* 9 (2008): 105–19.

177 **meditation isn't the only way:** Adam Grant, "Can We End the Meditation Madness?," *New York Times*, October 9, 2015, www.nytimes.com/2015/10/10/opinion/can-we-end-the-meditation-madness.html.

177 **the Myers-Briggs personality tool:** Adam Grant, "MBTI, If You Want Me Back, You Need to Change Too," Medium, November 17, 2015, medium.com/@AdamMGrant/mbti-if-you-want-me-back-you-need-to-change-too-c7f1a7b6970; Adam Grant, "Say Goodbye to MBTI, the Fad That Won't Die," LinkedIn, September 17, 2013, www.linkedin.com/pulse/20130917155206-69244073-say-goodbye-to-mbti-the-fad-that-won-t-die.

177 **being more authentic:** Adam Grant, "The Fine Line between Helpful and Harmful Authenticity," *New York Times*, April 10, 2020, www.nytimes.com/2020/04/10/smarter-living/the-fine-line-between-helpful-and-harmful-authenticity.html; Adam Grant, "Unless You're Oprah, 'Be Yourself' Is Terrible Advice," *New York Times*, June 4, 2016, www.nytimes.com/2016/06/05/opinion/sunday/unless-youre-oprah-be-yourself-is-terrible-advice.html.

178 **the veil of ignorance:** John Rawls, *A Theory of Justice* (Cambridge, MA: Belknap Press, 1971).

178 **randomly assigning people to reflect:** Rhia Catapano, Zakary L. Tormala, and Derek D. Rucker, "Perspective Taking and Self-Persuasion: Why 'Putting Yourself in Their Shoes' Reduces Openness to Attitude Change," *Psychological Science* 30 (2019): 424–35.

178 **imagining other people's perspectives:** Tal Eyal, Mary Steffel, and Nicholas Epley, "Perspective Mistaking: Accurately Understanding the Mind of Another Requires Getting Perspective, Not Taking Perspective," *Journal of Personality and Social Psychology* 114 (2018): 547–71.

178 **Polls show that Democrats:** Yascha Mounk, "Republicans Don't Understand Democrats—and Democrats Don't Understand Republicans," *The Atlantic*, June 23, 2019, www.theatlantic.com/ideas/archive/2019/06/republicans-and-democrats-dont-understand-each-other/592324.

179 **even if we disagree strongly:** Julian J. Zlatev, "I May Not Agree with You, but I Trust You: Caring about Social Issues Signals Integrity," *Psychological Science* 30 (2019): 880–92.

179 **"I have a lot of respect":** Corinne Bendersky, "Resolving Ideological Conflicts by Affirming Opponents' Status: The Tea Party, Obamacare and the 2013 Government Shutdown," *Organizational Behavior and Human Decision Processes* 53 (2014): 163–68.

179 **People get trapped in emotional simplicity:** Patti Williams and Jennifer L. Aaker, "Can Mixed Emotions Peacefully Coexist?," *Journal of Consumer Research* 28 (2002): 636–49.

181 **Japanese gives us** *koi no yokan*: Beca Grimm, "11 Feelings There Are No Words for in English," *Bustle*, July 15, 2015, www.bustle.com/articles/97413-11-feelings-there-are-no-words-for-in-english-for-all-you-emotional-word-nerds-out.

181 **The Inuit have** *iktsuarpok*: Bill Demain et al., "51 Wonderful Words with No English Equivalent," *Mental Floss*, December 14, 2015, www.mentalfloss.com/article/50698/38-wonderful-foreign-words-we-could-use-english.

181 *kummerspeck*, **the extra weight:** Kate Bratskeir, "'Kummerspeck,' or Grief Bacon, Is the German Word for What Happens When You Eat When You're Sad," *Mic*, December 19, 2017, www.mic.com/articles/186933/kummerspeck-or-grief-bacon-is-the-german-word-for-eating-when-sad.

182 **"Racist and antiracist are not fixed identities":** Ibram X. Kendi, *How to Be an Antiracist* (New York: One World, 2019).

182 **Christian Cooper refused:** Don Lemon, "She Called Police on Him in Central Park. Hear His Response," CNN, May 27, 2020, www.cnn.com/videos/us/2020/05/27/christian-cooper-central-park-video-lemon-ctn-sot-intv-vpx.cnn.

Chapter 9. Rewriting the Textbook

185 **"No schooling was allowed to interfere":** Grant Allen [pseud. Olive Pratt Rayner], *Rosalba: The Story of Her Development* (London: G. P. Putnam's Sons, 1899).

185 **Wisconsin's Teacher of the Year:** Personal interview with Erin McCarthy, January 14, 2020; Scott Anderson, "Wisconsin National Teacher of the Year Nominee Is from Greendale," *Patch*, August 20, 2019, patch.com/wisconsin/greendale/greendale-national-teacher -year-nominee-greendale.

188 **It's "a task that":** Deborah Kelemen, "The Magic of Mechanism: Explanation-Based Instruction on Counterintuitive Concepts in Early Childhood," *Perspectives on Psychological Science* 14 (2019): 510–22.

189 **don't have a single right answer:** Sam Wineburg, Daisy Martin, and Chauncey Monte-Sano, *Reading Like a Historian* (New York: Teachers College Press, 2013).

189 **curriculum developed at Stanford:** "Teacher Materials and Resources," Historical Thinking Matters, http://historicalthinkingmatters.org/teachers.

189 **even send students out to interview:** Elizabeth Emery, "Have Students Interview Someone They Disagree With," Heterodox Academy, February 11, 2020, heterodoxacademy.org /viewpoint-diversity-students-interview-someone.

190 **think like fact-checkers:** Annabelle Timsit, "In the Age of Fake News, Here's How Schools Are Teaching Kids to Think Like Fact-Checkers," *Quartz*, February 12, 2019, qz.com/1533747 /in-the-age-of-fake-news-heres-how-schools-are-teaching-kids-to-think-like-fact-checkers.

190 **King Tut:** Rose Troup Buchanan, "King Tutankhamun Did Not Die in Chariot Crash, Virtual Autopsy Reveals," *Independent*, October 20, 2014, www.independent.co.uk/news/ science/king-tutankhamun-did-not-die-in-chariot-crash-virtual-autopsy-reveals -9806586.html.

190 **when sloths do their version:** Brian Resnick, "Farts: Which Animals Do, Which Don't, and Why," *Vox*, October 19, 2018, www.vox.com/science-and-health/2018/4/3/17188186 /does-it-fart-book-animal-farts-dinosaur-farts.

191 **delivered by lecture:** Louis Deslauriers et al., "Measuring Actual Learning versus Feeling of Learning in Response to Being Actively Engaged in the Classroom," *PNAS* 116 (2019): 19251–57.

192 **students scored half a letter grade worse under traditional lecturing:** Scott Freeman et al., "Active Learning Increases Student Performance in Science, Engineering, and Mathematics," *PNAS* 111 (2014): 8410–15.

192 **the awestruck effect:** Jochen I. Menges et al., "The Awestruck Effect: Followers Suppress Emotion Expression in Response to Charismatic but Not Individually Considerate Leadership," *Leadership Quarterly* 26 (2015): 626–40.

192 **the dumbstruck effect:** Adam Grant, "The Dark Side of Emotional Intelligence," *The Atlantic*, January 2, 2014, www.theatlantic.com/health/archive/2014/01/the-dark-side-of -emotional-intelligence/282720.

193 **In North American universities:** M. Stains et al., "Anatomy of STEM Teaching in North American Universities," *Science* 359 (2018): 1468–70.

193 **half of teachers lecture:** Grant Wiggins, "Why Do So Many HS History Teachers Lecture So Much?," April 24, 2015, grantwiggins.wordpress.com/2015/04/24/why-do-so-many-hs -history-teachers-lecture-so-much.

193 **middle schoolers score higher:** Guido Schwerdt and Amelie C. Wupperman, "Is Traditional Teaching Really All That Bad? A Within-Student Between-Subject Approach," *Economics of Education Review* 30 (2011): 365–79.

194 **enter an "experience machine":** Robert Nozick, *Anarchy, State, and Utopia* (New York: Basic Books, 1974).

194 **"I do my thinking through the courses I give":** Asahina Robert, "The Inquisitive Robert Nozick," *New York Times*, September 20, 1981, www.nytimes.com/1981/09/20/books/the -inquisitive-robert-nozick.html.

194 **"Presenting a completely polished":** Ken Gewertz, "Philosopher Nozick Dies at 63," *Harvard Gazette*, January 17, 2002, news.harvard.edu/gazette/story/2002/01/philosopher -nozick-dies-at-63; see also Hilary Putnam et al., "Robert Nozick: Memorial Minute," *Harvard Gazette*, May 6, 2004, news.harvard.edu/gazette/story/2004/05/robert-nozick.

194 **most of us would ditch the machine:** Felipe De Brigard, "If You Like It, Does It Matter If It's Real?," *Philosophical Psychology* 23 (2010): 43–57.

195 **perfectionists are more likely:** Joachim Stoeber and Kathleen Otto, "Positive Conceptions of Perfectionism: Approaches, Evidence, Challenges," *Personality and Social Psychology Review* 10 (2006): 295–319.

195 **they don't perform any better:** Dana Harari et al., "Is Perfect Good? A Meta-analysis of Perfectionism in the Workplace," *Journal of Applied Psychology* 103 (2018): 1121–44.

195 **grades are not a strong predictor:** Philip L. Roth et al., "Meta-analyzing the Relationship between Grades and Job Performance," *Journal of Applied Psychology* 81 (1996): 548–56.

195 **Achieving excellence in school:** Adam Grant, "What Straight-A Students Get Wrong," *New York Times*, December 8, 2018, www.nytimes.com/2018/12/08/opinion/college-gpa-career-success.html.

195 **the most creative ones graduated:** Donald W. Mackinnon, "The Nature and Nurture of Creative Talent," *American Psychologist* 17 (1962): 484–95.

195 **"Valedictorians aren't likely":** Karen Arnold, *Lives of Promise: What Becomes of High School Valedictorians* (San Francisco: Jossey-Bass, 1995).

197 **Dear Penn Freshmen:** Mike Kaiser, "This Wharton Senior's Letter Writing Project Gets Global Attention," Wharton School, February 17, 2016, www.wharton.upenn.edu/story/wharton-seniors-letter-writing-project-gets-global-attention.

197 **one of the best ways to learn is to teach:** Aloysius Wei Lun Koh, Sze Chi Lee, and Stephen Wee Hun Lim, "The Learning Benefits of Teaching: A Retrieval Practice Hypothesis," *Applied Cognitive Psychology* 32 (2018): 401–10; Logan Fiorella and Richard E. Mayer, "The Relative Benefits of Learning by Teaching and Teaching Expectancy," *Contemporary Educational Psychology* 38 (2013): 281–88; Robert B. Zajonc and Patricia R. Mullally, "Birth Order: Reconciling Conflicting Effects," *American Psychologist* 52 (1997): 685–99; Peter A. Cohen, James A. Kulik, and Chen-Lin C. Kulik, "Educational Outcomes of Tutoring: A Meta-analysis of Findings," *American Educational Research Journal* 19 (1982): 237–48.

198 **an ethic of excellence:** Personal interview with Ron Berger, October 29, 2019; Ron Berger, *An Ethic of Excellence: Building a Culture of Craftsmanship with Students* (Portsmouth, NH: Heinemann, 2003); Ron Berger, Leah Rugen, and Libby Woodfin, *Leaders of Their Own Learning: Transforming Schools through Student-Engaged Assessment* (San Francisco: Jossey-Bass, 2014).

199 **hallmarks of an open mind:** Kirill Fayn et al., "Confused or Curious? Openness/Intellect Predicts More Positive Interest-Confusion Relations," *Journal of Personality and Social Psychology* 117 (2019): 1016–33.

199 **"I need time for my confusion":** Eleanor Duckworth, *The Having of Wonderful Ideas* (New York: Teachers College Press, 2006).

199 **Confusion can be a cue:** Elisabeth Vogl et al., "Surprised-Curious-Confused: Epistemic Emotions and Knowledge Exploration," *Emotion* 20 (2020): 625–41.

202 **scientifically accurate drawing of a butterfly:** Ron Berger, "Critique and Feedback—The Story of Austin's Butterfly," December 8, 2012, www.youtube.com/watch?v=hqh1MRWZjms.

Chapter 10. That's Not the Way We've Always Done It

205 **"If only it weren't for the people":** Kurt Vonnegut, *Player Piano* (New York: Dial Press, 1952/2006).

206 **"scariest wardrobe malfunction in NASA history":** Tony Reichhardt, "The Spacewalk That Almost Killed Him," *Air & Space Magazine*, May 2014, www.airspacemag.com/space/spacewalk-almost-killed-him-180950135/?all.

208 **in learning cultures, organizations innovate more:** Matej Černe et al., "What Goes Around Comes Around: Knowledge Hiding, Perceived Motivational Climate, and Creativity," *Academy of Management Journal* 57 (2014): 172–92; Markus Baer and Michael Frese,

"Innovation Is Not Enough: Climates for Initiative and Psychological Safety, Process Innovations, and Firm Performance," *Journal of Organizational Behavior* 24 (2003): 45–68.

208 **make fewer mistakes:** Anita L. Tucker and Amy C. Edmondson, "Why Hospitals Don't Learn from Failures: Organizational and Psychological Dynamics That Inhibit System Change," *California Management Review* 45 (2003): 55–72; Amy C. Edmondson, "Learning from Mistakes Is Easier Said Than Done: Group and Organizational Influences on the Detection and Correction of Human Error," *Journal of Applied Behavioral Science* 40 (1996): 5–28.

208 **the more psychological safety:** William A. Kahn, "Psychological Conditions of Personal Engagement and Disengagement at Work," *Academy of Management Journal* 33 (1990): 692–724.

209 **What mattered most was psychological safety:** Julia Rozovsky, "The Five Keys to a Successful Google Team," re:Work, November 17, 2015, rework.withgoogle.com/blog/five-keys-to-a-successful-google-team.

209 **psychological safety is not:** Amy C. Edmondson, "How Fearless Organizations Succeed," strategy+business, November 14, 2018, www.strategy-business.com/article/How-Fearless-Organizations-Succeed.

209 **foundation of a learning culture:** Amy Edmondson, "Psychological Safety and Learning Behavior in Work Teams," *Administrative Science Quarterly* 44 (1999): 350–83.

209 **engage in self-limiting behavior:** Paul W. Mulvey, John F. Veiga, and Priscilla M. Elsass, "When Teammates Raise a White Flag," *Academy of Management Perspectives* 10 (1996): 40–49.

210 **some engineers did raise red flags:** Howard Berkes, "30 Years after Explosion, *Challenger* Engineer Still Blames Himself," NPR, January 28, 2016, www.npr.org/sections/thetwo-way/2016/01/28/464744781/30-years-after-disaster-challenger-engineer-still-blames-himself.

210 **an engineer asked for clearer photographs:** Joel Bach, "Engineer Sounded Warnings for *Columbia*," ABC News, January 7, 2006, abcnews.go.com/Technology/story?id=97600&page=1.

210 **prevent this kind of disaster from ever happening again:** Personal interview with Ellen Ochoa, December 12, 2019.

211 *How do you know?*: Personal interview with Chris Hansen, November 12, 2019.

213 **gains in psychological safety a full year later:** Constantinos G. V. Coutifaris and Adam M. Grant, "Taking Your Team Behind the Curtain: The Effects of Leader Feedback-Sharing and Feedback-Seeking on Team Psychological Safety," *Organization Science* (2021).

214 **harsh comments from student course evaluations:** Wharton Follies, "Mean Reviews: Professor Edition," March 22, 2015, www.youtube.com/watch?v=COOaEVSu6ms&t=3s.

215 **Sharing our imperfections:** Celia Moore et al., "The Advantage of Being Oneself: The Role of Applicant Self-Verification in Organizational Hiring Decisions," *Journal of Applied Psychology* 102 (2017): 1493–513.

215 **people who haven't yet proven their competence:** Kerry Roberts Gibson, Dana Harari, and Jennifer Carson Marr, "When Sharing Hurts: How and Why Self-Disclosing Weakness Undermines the Task-Oriented Relationships of Higher-Status Disclosers," *Organizational Behavior and Human Decision Processes* 144 (2018): 25–43.

217 **Focusing on results:** Itamar Simonson and Barry M. Staw, "Deescalation Strategies: A Comparison of Techniques for Reducing Commitment to Losing Courses of Action," *Journal of Applied Psychology* 77 (1992): 419–26; Jennifer S. Lerner and Philip E. Tetlock, "Accounting for the Effects of Accountability," *Psychological Bulletin* 125 (1999): 255–75.

218 **we create a learning zone:** Amy C. Edmondson, "The Competitive Imperative of Learning," *Harvard Business Review*, July-August 2008, hbr.org/2008/07/the-competitive-imperative-of-learning.

219 **"will you gamble with me on it?":** Jeff Bezos, "2016 Letter to Shareholders," www.sec.gov/Archives/edgar/data/1018724/000119312517120198/d373368dex991.htm.

219 **a study of California banks:** Barry M. Staw, Sigal G. Barsade, and Kenneth W. Koput, "Escalation at the Credit Window: A Longitudinal Study of Bank Executives' Recognition and Write-Off of Problem Loans," *Journal of Applied Psychology* 82 (1997): 130–42.

Chapter 11. Escaping Tunnel Vision

225 **"A malaise set in":** Jack Handey, "My First Day in Hell," *New Yorker*, October 23, 2006, www.newyorker.com/magazine/2006/10/30/my-first-day-in-hell.

226 *that's an actual research concept:* William B. Swann Jr. and Peter J. Rentfrow, "Blirtatiousness: Cognitive, Behavioral, and Physiological Consequences of Rapid Responding," *Journal of Personality and Social Psychology* 81 (2001): 1160–75.

228 **inspire us to set bolder goals:** Locke and Latham, "Building a Practically Useful Theory."

228 **guide us toward a path:** Peter M. Gollwitzer, "Implementation Intentions: Strong Effects of Simple Plans," *American Psychologist* 54 (1999): 493–503.

228 **they can give us tunnel vision:** James Y. Shah and Arie W. Kruglanski, "Forgetting All Else: On the Antecedents and Consequences of Goal Shielding," *Journal of Personality and Social Psychology* 83 (2002): 1261–80.

229 **escalation of commitment:** Barry M. Staw and Jerry Ross, "Understanding Behavior in Escalation Situations," *Science* 246 (1989): 216–20.

229 **entrepreneurs persist with failing strategies:** Dustin J. Sleesman et al., "Putting Escalation of Commitment in Context: A Multilevel Review and Analysis," *Academy of Management Annals* 12 (2018): 178–207.

229 **NBA general managers:** Colin F. Camerer and Roberto A. Weber, "The Econometrics and Behavioral Economics of Escalation of Commitment: A Re-examination of Staw and Hoang's NBA Data," *Journal of Economic Behavior & Organization* 39 (1999): 59–82.

229 **politicians continue sending soldiers to wars:** Glen Whyte, "Escalating Commitment in Individual and Group Decision Making: A Prospect Theory Approach," *Organizational Behavior and Human Decision Processes* 54 (1993): 430–55.

229 **searching for self-justifications for our prior beliefs:** Joel Brockner, "The Escalation of Commitment to a Failing Course of Action: Toward Theoretical Progress," *Academy of Management Review* 17 (1992): 39–61.

229 **soothe our egos:** Dustin J. Sleesman et al., "Cleaning Up the Big Muddy: A Meta-analytic Review of the Determinants of Escalation of Commitment," *Academy of Management Journal* 55 (2012): 541–62.

229 **Grit is the combination:** Jon M. Jachimowicz et al., "Why Grit Requires Perseverance and Passion to Positively Predict Performance," *PNAS* 115 (2018): 9980–85; Angela Duckworth and James J. Gross, "Self-Control and Grit: Related but Separable Determinants of Success," *Current Directions in Psychological Science* 23 (2014): 319–25.

229 **beyond their planned limits in roulette:** Larbi Alaoui and Christian Fons-Rosen, "Know When to Fold 'Em: The Grit Factor," *Universitat Pompeu Fabra: Barcela GSE Working Paper Series* (2018).

229 **more willing to stay the course:** Gale M. Lucas et al., "When the Going Gets Tough: Grit Predicts Costly Perseverance," *Journal of Research in Personality* 59 (2015): 15–22; see also Henry Moon, "The Two Faces of Conscientiousness: Duty and Achievement Striving in Escalation of Commitment Dilemmas," *Journal of Applied Psychology* 86 (2001): 533–40.

229 **gritty mountaineers are more likely to die:** Lee Crust, Christian Swann, and Jacquelyn Allen-Collinson, "The Thin Line: A Phenomenological Study of Mental Toughness and Decision Making in Elite High-Altitude Mountaineers," *Journal of Sport and Exercise Psychology* 38 (2016): 598–611.

230 **what psychologists call identity foreclosure:** Wim Meeus et al., "Patterns of Adolescent Identity Development: Review of Literature and Longitudinal Analysis," *Developmental Review* 19 (1999): 419–61.

230 **settle prematurely on a sense of self:** Otilia Obodaru, "The Self Not Taken: How Alternative Selves Develop and How They Influence Our Professional Lives," *Academy of Management Review* 37 (2017): 523–53.

230 **"one of the most useless questions":** Michelle Obama, *Becoming* (New York: Crown, 2018).

230 **lack the talent to pursue our callings:** Shoshana R. Dobrow, "Dynamics of Callings: A Longitudinal Study of Musicians," *Journal of Organizational Behavior* 34 (2013): 431–52.

230 **leaving them unanswered:** Justin M. Berg, Adam M. Grant, and Victoria Johnson, "When Callings Are Calling: Crafting Work and Leisure in Pursuit of Unanswered Occupational Callings," *Organization Science* 21 (2010): 973–94.

230 **"Tell the kids":** Chris Rock, *Tamborine*, directed by Bo Burnham, Netflix, 2018.

231 **introducing them to science differently:** Ryan F. Lei et al., "Children Lose Confidence in Their Potential to 'Be Scientists,' but Not in Their Capacity to 'Do Science,'" *Developmental Science* 22 (2019): e12837.

232 **prekindergarten students express more interest:** Marjorie Rhodes, Amanda Cardarelli, and Sarah-Jane Leslie, "Asking Young Children to 'Do Science' Instead of 'Be Scientists' Increases Science Engagement in a Randomized Field Experiment," *PNAS* 117 (2020): 9808–14.

232 **holding a dozen different jobs:** Alison Doyle, "How Often Do People Change Jobs during a Lifetime?," The Balance Careers, June 15, 2020, www.thebalancecareers.com/how-often-do-people-change-jobs-2060467.

233 **tuned out their mentors:** Shoshana R. Dobrow and Jennifer Tosti-Kharas, "Listen to Your Heart? Calling and Receptivity to Career Advice," *Journal of Career Assessment* 20 (2012): 264–80.

233 **we develop compensatory conviction:** Ian McGregor et al., "Compensatory Conviction in the Face of Personal Uncertainty: Going to Extremes and Being Oneself," *Journal of Personality and Social Psychology* 80 (2001): 472–88.

233 **graduates of universities in England and Wales:** Ofer Malamud, "Breadth Versus Depth: The Timing of Specialization in Higher Education," *Labour* 24 (2010): 359–90.

235 **as people consider career choices and transitions:** Herminia Ibarra, *Working Identity: Unconventional Strategies for Reinventing Your Career* (Boston: Harvard Business School Press, 2003).

235 **entertain possible selves:** Herminia Ibarra, "Provisional Selves: Experimenting with Image and Identity in Professional Adaptation," *Administrative Science Quarterly* 44 (1999): 764–91.

236 **relationship health checkup:** James V. Cordova et al., "The Marriage Checkup: A Randomized Controlled Trial of Annual Relationship Health Checkups," *Journal of Consulting and Clinical Psychology* 82 (2014): 592–604.

237 **the more people value happiness:** Iris B. Mauss et al., "Can Seeking Happiness Make People Unhappy? Paradoxical Effects of Valuing Happiness," *Emotion* 11 (2011): 807–15.

238 **a risk factor for depression:** Brett Q. Ford et al., "Desperately Seeking Happiness: Valuing Happiness Is Associated with Symptoms and Diagnosis of Depression," *Journal of Social and Clinical Psychology* 33 (2014): 890–905.

238 **ruminate about why our lives aren't *more* joyful:** Lucy McGuirk et al., "Does a Culture of Happiness Increase Rumination Over Failure?," *Emotion* 18 (2018): 755–64.

238 **happiness depends more on the frequency:** Ed Diener, Ed Sandvik, and William Pavot, "Happiness Is the Frequency, Not the Intensity, of Positive versus Negative Affect," in *Subjective Well-Being: An Interdisciplinary Perspective*, ed. Fritz Strack, Michael Argyle, and Norbert Schwartz (New York: Pergamon, 1991).

238 **meaning is healthier than happiness:** Barbara L. Fredrickson et al., "A Functional Genomic Perspective on Human Well-Being," *PNAS* 110 (2013): 13684–89; Emily Esfahani Smith, "Meaning Is Healthier Than Happiness," *The Atlantic*, August 1, 2013, www.theatlantic.com/health/archive/2013/08/meaning-is-healthier-than-happiness/278250.

238 **meaning tends to last:** Jon M. Jachimowicz et al., "Igniting Passion from Within: How Lay Beliefs Guide the Pursuit of Work Passion and Influence Turnover," PsyArXiv 10.31234 /osf.io/qj6y9, last revised July 2, 2018, https://psyarxiv.com/qj6y9/.

238 **people prioritize social engagement:** Brett Q. Ford et al., "Culture Shapes Whether the Pursuit of Happiness Predicts Higher or Lower Well-Being," *Journal of Experimental Psychology: General* 144 (2015): 1053–62.

239 **"you're still gonna be you on vacation":** *Saturday Night Live*, season 44, episode 19, "Adam Sandler," May 4, 2019, NBC.

239 **joy that those choices bring about is typically temporary:** Elizabeth W. Dunn, Timothy D. Wilson, and Daniel T. Gilbert, "Location, Location, Location: The Misprediction of Satisfaction in Housing Lotteries," *Personality and Social Psychology Bulletin* 29 (2003): 1421–32; Kent C. H. Lam et al., "Cultural Differences in Affective Forecasting: The Role of Focalism," *Personality and Social Psychology Bulletin* 31 (2005): 1296–309.

239 **"You can't get away from yourself":** Ernest Hemingway, *The Sun Also Rises* (New York: Scribner, 1926/2014).

239 **students who changed their actions:** Kennon M. Sheldon and Sonja Lyubomirsky, "Achieving Sustainable Gains in Happiness: Change Your Actions, Not Your Circumstances," *Journal of Happiness Studies* 7 (2006): 55–86; Kennon M. Sheldon and Sonja Lyubomirsky, "Change Your Actions, Not Your Circumstances: An Experimental Test of the Sustainable Happiness Model," in *Happiness, Economics, and Politics: Towards a Multi-disciplinary Approach*, ed. Amitava Krishna Dutt and Benjamin Radcliff (Cheltenham, UK: Edward Elgar, 2009).

240 **built their own microcommunity:** Jane E. Dutton and Belle Rose Ragins, *Exploring Positive Relationships at Work: Building a Theoretical and Research Foundation* (Mahwah, NJ: Erlbaum, 2007).

240 **passions are often developed, not discovered:** Paul A. O'Keefe, Carol S. Dweck, and Gregory M. Walton, "Implicit Theories of Interest: Finding Your Passion or Developing It?," *Psychological Science* 29 (2018): 1653–64.

240 **Their passion grew as they gained momentum:** Michael M. Gielnik et al., "'I Put in Effort, Therefore I Am Passionate': Investigating the Path from Effort to Passion in Entrepreneurship," *Academy of Management Journal* 58 (2015): 1012–31.

240 **actions that benefit others:** Adam M. Grant, "The Significance of Task Significance: Job Performance Effects, Relational Mechanisms, and Boundary Conditions," *Journal of Applied Psychology* 93 (2008): 108–24; Stephen E. Humphrey, Jennifer D. Nahrgang, and Frederick P. Morgeson, "Integrating Motivational, Social, and Contextual Work Design Features: A Meta-analytic Summary and Theoretical Extension of the Work Design Literature," *Journal of Applied Psychology* 92 (2007): 1332–56; Brent D. Rosso, Kathryn H. Dekas, and Amy Wrzesniewski, "On the Meaning of Work: A Theoretical Integration and Review," *Research in Organizational Behavior* 30 (2010): 91–127.

241 **we feel we have more to give:** Dan P. McAdams, "Generativity in Midlife," *Handbook of Midlife Development*, ed. Margie E. Lachman (New York: Wiley, 2001).

241 **"they find happiness by the way":** John Stuart Mill, *Autobiography* (New York: Penguin Classics, 1883/1990).

241 **what scientists call open systems:** Ludwig von Bertalanffy, *General System Theory: Foundations, Development, Applications* (New York: Braziller, 1969).

241 **open systems are governed:** Arie W. Kruglanski et al., "The Architecture of Goal Systems: Multifinality, Equifinality, and Counterfinality in Means-Ends Relations," *Advances in Motivation Science* 2 (2015): 69–98; Dante Cicchetti and Fred A. Rogosch, "Equifinality and Multifinality in Developmental Psychopathology," *Development and Psychopathology* 8 (1996): 597–600.

242 **"you can make the whole trip that way":** Nancy Groves, "EL Doctorow in Quotes: 15 of His Best," *Guardian*, July 21, 2015, www.theguardian.com/books/2015/jul/22/el-doctorow-in-quotes-15-of-his-best.

242 **rethink their roles through job crafting:** Amy Wrzesniewski and Jane E. Dutton, "Crafting a Job: Revisioning Employees as Active Crafters of Their Work," *Academy of Management Review* 26 (2001): 179–201.

242 **how grateful they were for Candice Walker:** Amy Wrzesniewski and Jane Dutton, "Having a Calling and Crafting a Job: The Case of Candice Billups," William Davidson Institute, University of Michigan, November 12, 2009.

243 **ended up rethinking their roles:** Amy Wrzesniewski, Jane E. Dutton, and Gelaye Debebe, "Interpersonal Sensemaking and the Meaning of Work," *Research in Organizational Behavior* 25 (2003): 93–135.

243 **"No, it's not part of my job":** "A World without Bosses," *WorkLife with Adam Grant*, April 11, 2018.

Epilogue

245 **"'What I believe'":** Candace Falk, Barry Pateman, and Jessica Moran, eds., *Emma Goldman*, vol. 2, *A Documentary History of the American Years* (Champaign: University of Illinois Press, 2008).

245 **"write a book that ended with the word Mayonnaise":** Richard Brautigan, *Trout Fishing in America* (New York: Delta, 1967).

247 **"A new scientific truth":** Max K. Planck, *Scientific Autobiography and Other Papers* (New York: Greenwood, 1950/1968).

247 **generations are replaced:** "Societies Change Their Minds Faster Than People Do," *Economist*, October 31, 2019, www.economist.com/graphic-detail/2019/10/31/societies-change -their-minds-faster-than-people-do.

247 **the word *scientist* is relatively new:** William Whewell, *The Philosophy of the Inductive Sciences* (New York: Johnson, 1840/1967); "William Whewell," *Stanford Encyclopedia of Philosophy*, December 23, 2000, last revised September 22, 2017, plato.stanford.edu/entries /whewell.

249 **"above all, try something":** Franklin D. Roosevelt, "Address at Oglethorpe University," May 22, 1932, www.presidency.ucsb.edu/documents/address-oglethorpe-university-atlanta -georgia.

249 **"something unspecified is no better":** "Hoover and Roosevelt," *New York Times*, May 24, 1932, www.nytimes.com/1932/05/24/archives/hoover-and-roosevelt.html.

250 **act of political stupidity:** Paul Stephen Hudson, "A Call for 'Bold Persistent Experimentation': FDR's Oglethorpe University Commencement Address, 1932," *Georgia Historical Quarterly* (Summer 1994), https://georgiainfo.galileo.usg.edu/topics/history/related_article /progressive-era-world-war-ii-1901-1945/background-to-fdrs-ties-to-georgia/a-call-for -bold-persistent-experimentation-fdrs-oglethorpe-university-comme.

ILLUSTRATION CREDITS

Charts on pages 8, 21, 22, 26, 28, 30, 41, 47, 49, 51, 63, 64, 70, 71, 74, 79, 82, 90, 106, 109, 110, 117, 125, 135, 150, 154, 171, 180, 189, 201, 210, 218, 231, and 234 by Matt Shirley.

Page 37: Jason Adam Katzenstein/The New Yorker Collection/The Cartoon Bank; © Condé Nast.

Page 39: Nicholas Bloom, Renata Lemos, Raffaella Sadun, Daniela Scur, and John Van Reenen. "JEEA-FBBVA Lecture 2013: The New Empirical Economics of Management," *Journal of the European Economic Association* 12, no. 4 (August 1, 2014): 835–76. https://doi.org/10.1111/jeea.12094.

Page 43: Zach Weinersmith/www.smbc-comics.com.

Page 44: C. Sanchez and D. Dunning. "Overconfidence Among Beginners: Is a Little Learning a Dangerous Thing?," *Journal of Personality and Social Psychology* 114, no. 1 (2018), 10–28. https://doi.org/10.1037/pspa0000102.

Pages 46, 58, 85: © Doug Savage, www.savagechickens.com.

Page 68: Ellis Rosen/The New Yorker Collection/The Cartoon Bank; © Condé Nast.

Page 103: David Sipress/The New Yorker Collection/The Cartoon Bank; © Condé Nast.

Page 114: CreateDebate user Loudacris/CC BY 3.0. https://creativecommons.org/licenses/by/3.0.

Page 123: Map by casinoinsider.com.

Pages 127 and 133: wordle.net.

Page 145: Calvin & Hobbes © 1993 Watterson. Reprinted with permission of ANDREWS MCMEEL SYNDICATION. All rights reserved.

Page 167: Non Sequitur © 2016 Wiley Ink, Inc. Dist. by ANDREWS MCMEEL SYNDICATION. Reprinted with permission. All rights reserved.

Page 170: A. Leiserowitz, E. Maibach, S. Rosenthal, J. Kotcher, P. Bergquist, M. Ballew, M. Goldberg, and A. Gustafson. "Climate Change in the American Mind: November 2019." Yale University and George Mason University. New Haven, CT: Yale Program on Climate Change Communication, 2019.

Page 177: xkcd.com.

Page 179: Katharina Kugler.

Page 187: © JimBenton.com.

Page 193: Steve Macone/The New Yorker Collection/The Cartoon Bank; © Condé Nast.

Page 198: www.CartoonCollections.com.

Page 202: © 2020 EL Education.

Page 216: © Chris Madden.

Page 220: Hayley Lewis, Sketchnote summary of *A Spectrum of Reasons for Failure*. © 2020 HALO Psychology Limited. Illustration drawn May 2020. London, United Kingdom. / Edmondson, A. C. (2011, April). From "Strategies for Learning from Failure," *Harvard Business Review*. https://hbr.org/2011/04/strategies-for-learning-from-failure. This illustration is protected by UK and International copyright laws. Reproduction and distribution of the illustration without prior written permission of the artist is prohibited.

Page 228: Cartoon © by Guy Downes. For more information: www.officeguycartoons.com.

Page 237: Photo by Arthur Gebuys Photography/Shutterstock.

Page 239: *Saturday Night Live*/NBC.

INDEX

Page numbers in *italics* refer to charts and illustrations.

abortion, conversations on, 139, 163–64,
    165–66
active learning, 186–88
    lectures vs., 190–93, 196
addiction:
    motivational interviewing as tool for
        combating, 149
    as reinforced by failed arguments
        against, 146
agreeableness, 81–82
    as barrier to rethinking, 83
    social harmony vs. cognitive consensus
        in, 89
    see also disagreeable people
Albert, Robert, 81
Allen, Grant, 185
Amazon, 218, 219
amygdala, and attacks on core
    beliefs, 60
animosity, stereotypes and, 127
Anton, Gabriel, 33–34
Anton's syndrome, 33–35
Apple, iPhone introduced by,
    29–31
approval, desire for, politician mindset and,
    18–19, 21, 22, 28, 80, 233
Arbery, Ahmaud, 10

arguments:
    hierarchy of, 114
    prosecutor mindset and, 18, 19, 26, 233
    see also debates
Aristotle, 247–48
armchair quarterback syndrome, 37
    as barrier to rethinking, 42
    impostor syndrome vs., 51
Arnold, Karen, 195
arrogance, 54
    humility vs., 45
Ashby, Jeff, 129
Asimov, Isaac, 59
assumptions, 8, 9–12
    active questioning of, 25
    learning to rethink, 18
astrological signs, stereotyping and, 137–39
astronauts, overview effect and, 128–29
attachment, to erroneous ideas, 62
Austin (first grader), 201–2
autism, vaccination mistakenly linked to,
    144, 158–59
awestruck effect, 192

Barsade, Sigal, 89
Battier, Shane, 131
Beethoven, Ludwig van, 114–15

beliefs and opinions, 26
  attachment to, 62
  attacks on, as threats to sense of self,
    59–60, 63–64, 127
  biases and, *see* biases
  blind spots in, 75
  calcification of, 4, 10, 17
  challenges to, as opportunities for
    rethinking, 74, 75–76
  convincing others to rethink, 97–160
  core values vs., 64, 66n, 253
  counterfactual thinking and, 137–39
  debates about, *see* debates
  detaching sense of self from, 12, 62–64,
    69–70, 74, 76, 253–54
  erroneous, *see* erroneous thinking
  evidence vs., 24–25, 48, 73
  evolution of, 26, 58
  freedom of choice in, 60, 148, 257
  Murray's experiment on, 55–58, 60, 74–75
  need for rethinking of, 12, 17, 18, 24,
    55–76, 243
  overconfidence and, 44
  politician mindset in, *see* politician
    mindset
  preacher mindset in, *see* preacher
    mindset
  prosecutor mindset in, *see* prosecutor
    mindset
  as reinforced by failed arguments against,
    144–45
  scientist mindset in, *see* scientist mindset
  second opinions and, 18, 52
  staying true to, 16
  weakly held, 59, 116–17
Benchley, Robert, 165
Berger, Ron, 198–203, 246
best practices, process accountability vs.,
  216–19, 258
Beugoms, Jean-Pierre, 65–66
  election forecasting by, 66–67, 69–71, 70,
    71, 72–73
  and joy of being wrong, 70, 71–72
  scientist mindset of, 66–67
Bezos, Jeff, 72, 219
Bhutan, Gross National Happiness index
  of, 237
biases:
  binary, 165–66, 169, 181
  confirmation, 25, 174n, 254
  denial of, 25
  desirability, 25, 168, 173, 174n
  status quo, 194n

Bigombe, Betty, in Uganda peace talks,
  155–57, 159
binary bias, 165–66, 169, 181
Bird, Brad, 83, 87–88, 89
BlackBerry, 16, 23, 29, 31
Blakely, Sara, 47
blindness, patients' denial of, 33–35
blind spots, mental, 60
  as barrier to rethinking, 35
  confidence and, 41, 45
  recognition of, 54
  self-awareness and, 48
blirtatiousness, 226–27
Boodman, Eric, 148
Boston Red Sox, Yankees' rivalry with,
  122–24, 126–27, 127, 128, 133–36
brain, reward centers in, 123
Brautigan, Richard, 245n
Breuhaus, Rachel, 111
Brexit, 66, 69
business, motivational interviewing in,
  151–53

career choices, 225–43
  as actions vs. identities, 230
  author and, 225–26
  escalation of commitment in,
    229–30
  identity foreclosure and, 230, 242
  overthinking and, 235n
  periodic checkups on, 233–35
  rethinking, 228, 230, 242–43
  of Ryan Grant, 226–28, 230, 241
  scientist mindset and, 235
  "what do you want to be" question and,
    225–26, 230, 231, 232
  see also life plans
Cassidy, Chris, 205–7
caveats, 173–74, 176, 257
Cavett, Dick, 143
Central Park bird-watching incident,
  181–83
challenge networks, 83–84, 200,
  218, 255
  author's use of, 86–87, 246
  corporate cultures and, 86
  Pixar's use of, 83–84
  shared values in, 84n
  Wright brothers as, 89–90
Challenger space shuttle disaster, 207
change, continuity and, 31
change talk, in motivational interviewing,
  152–53

charged conversations, 163–83
    binary bias and, 165, 166
    complexification in, 165–66, 167–68, 257
    emotions in, 179–83, 179, 257, 258
    idea cults and, 176–77
    nuance in, 168, 171, 174, 176, 183
    perspective-taking vs. perspective-seeking
        in, 178
    productive vs. unproductive, 179–80,
        179, 180
    scientist mindset in, 183
Chatman, Jennifer, 89
children, see kids
choice, freedom of, 148, 257, 258
climate change, beliefs about:
    binary bias and, 169
    complexity and, 172–73
    desirability bias and, 168
    media and, 170–73
    preacher mindset and, 168
    skepticism vs. denial in, 169
    spectrum of, 169–70, 170
    in U.S., 167, 168
climate deniers, 169
Clinton, Hillary, in 2016 election,
    69, 71
cognitive ability, emotional intelligence vs.,
    175–76
cognitive flexibility, see mental flexibility
cognitive laziness, 7–8
    as barrier to rethinking, 4
Coleman, Peter T., 163–64, 179
collective rethinking, 11, 161–222, 257–59
Columbia space shuttle disaster, 207,
    210–11, 220
Columbia University, 163
commitment, escalation of, 229–30
Committee for Skeptical Inquiry, 169–70
common ground, search for, 104–5, 107,
    108–9, 256
common identity, 129
competence:
    confidence vs., 33–54, 39, 43, 44, 49, 254
    humility and, 215n
complexification, 199
    caveats and contingencies in, 173–74,
        176, 257
    in charged conversations, 165–67, 257
    media and, 171–73
    as signal of credibility, 171, 174
conclusions:
    author's view of, 245–46
    in fiction, 245

confidence, 46–48
    in capacity to learn, 48, 254
    competence vs., 33–54, 39, 43, 44, 49, 254
    humility and, see confident humility
    ignorance and, 33, 40–41, 42–46, 43, 44
    as measure of faith in self, 46–47, 47, 49, 53
    mental blindness and, 41, 45
    see also armchair quarterback syndrome;
        impostor syndrome
confident humility, 46–48, 47, 49, 52–54,
    67, 72n, 112, 116–19, 215, 250
    in motivational interviewing, 147, 157
confirmation bias, 25, 28, 29, 174n, 254
conflict:
    avoidance of, 81–82
    constructive, 77–93, 255
    as energizing for disagreeable people,
        82, 84
    in families, 80–81
    in low-performing vs. high-performing
        groups, 78–80, 79
    see also relationship conflict; task conflict
conformity, group polarization and, 127–28
confusion, in learning process, 199, 257, 258
constructive conflict, 77–93, 255
contingencies, 174, 176, 257
continuity, change and, 31
Cooper, Christian, 181–83
core values, 55–56
    beliefs vs., 64, 66n, 253
coronavirus pandemic, 248, 250
    rethinking assumptions in, 9–10
Costanza, George (char.), 68, 118
counterfactual thinking:
    beliefs and, 137–39
    destabilizing stereotypes with, 134–40
Coutifaris, Constantinos, 213
craft, mastery of, 198
Crane, Frasier (char.), 55
creative tension, 81
crises, reversion to learned responses in, 5–7
criticism, reception to, 87n
Csikszentmihalyi, Mihaly, 27
cult-leader mindset, 32
Cuomo, Andrew, 250
curiosity, 27–28, 59, 67, 92, 102, 105, 106,
    115, 117, 137, 140, 145, 147, 156–59, 165,
    174, 180, 188, 197, 199, 200, 203, 211,
    214, 221, 253, 257
    in motivational interviewing, 147, 157

Dalio, Ray, 63
Darwin, Charles, 33

Davis, Daryl, in encounters with white
    supremacists, 121–22, 140–42, 151
Davis, Murray, 59
Dear Penn Freshmen (website), 197
debates, 97–119
    adversarial approach to, 102–3, 107
    brick walls in, 116
    confident humility in, 116–17
    curiosity in, 117
    disagreements reframed as, 91–92
    focusing on key points in, 109–11, 256
    as negotiations, 104
    nuance in, 117
    politician mindset, 107–8
    preacher mindset, 110
    prosecutor mindset, 110
    question-based approach in, 112–13
    responses to hostility in, 113–16
    scientist mindset in, 102–6, 107, 108–9
    search for common ground in, 107,
        108–9, 256
defend-attack spirals, 105, 109
deniers, skeptics vs., 169
desirability bias, 25, 28, 29, 71, 168,
    173, 174n
detachment:
    of opinions from identity, 62, 69–70, 76
    of past from present sense of self, 62–63,
        69, 76, 253
Difficult Conversations Lab, 163–64, 179
disagreeable people:
    conflict as energizing for, 82, 84
    as good critics, 86–87
    task conflict and, 83, 84
    task conflict encouraged by, 90
    see also pirates
discovery, joy of, 69, 188, 198, 203
Disney, 85
Doctorow, E. L., 242
Dodge, Wagner, 1–2, 5–6, 8, 11
doubt, 4, 28, 30–31, 45, 65, 67, 92, 165, 208,
    211, 221, 234, 243, 251
    benefits of, 47–49, 52, 54, 80, 251
    debilitating effect of, 46–47, 52–53
    in rethinking cycles, 27, 45, 67, 83, 92,
        112–13, 137, 140, 147, 158, 165, 171, 187,
        188, 208, 234, 253
    see also confident humility; self-doubt
drafts and revisions, in learning process,
    199–203, 258
Duke University, UNC rivalry with, 131
dumbstruck effect, 192
Dunning, David, 38, 40, 44, 158

Dunning-Kruger effect, 38–39, 40–41, 42n,
    43, 52, 53, 254
Durant, Kevin, 124n
Dutton, Jane, 242

Earth, as seen from space, 128–29
echo chambers, 61, 164, 254
Edmondson, Amy, 208–9, 217–18
education:
    entrenched beliefs in, 17
    teaching students to question knowledge,
        185–203
    see also learning; teachers, teaching
Einstein, Albert, 22
elections, U.S., of 2016, 66–67, 69–71, 70,
    71, 164
EL Education, 201–2
emotional intelligence:
    cognitive ability vs., 175–76
    overestimating, 42
emotions, 24, 59, 63, 69, 75, 78
    binary bias in, 180
    in charged conversations, 179–83,
        179, 257
    mixed, 180–81
    as works in progress, 180, 257
England, career choices in, 233n
entrepreneurship:
    decisiveness as overvalued in, 21–22
    scientist mindset and, 20–22, 21, 253
erroneous thinking, 55–76
    attachment to, 62
    echo chambers and filter bubbles in, 61,
        164, 254
    joy of acknowledging, 61–62, 65–66, 69,
        70, 71–72, 89, 254
escalation of commitment, 229–30
Étienne-Rousseau, Marie-Hélène, 143, 145,
    147–48, 155, 158–59
Étienne-Rousseau, Tobie, 143, 145,
    147–48, 155
Eversley, Karina, 206
excellence, ethic of, 198, 200
experience, expertise vs., 43–44
experience machine, 194
expertise, experience vs., 43–44
experts, questioning judgment of, 18

Facebook, precursor to, 8
fallibility, acceptance of, 59
feedback, 86, 212–13, 258
Feynman, Richard, 59
fiction, conclusion in, 245

fight-or-flight response, 60
filter bubbles, 61, 164, 254
Floyd, George, 10
forecasting, accuracy of, 65–73
    rethinking and, 67–68, 248
forecasting tournaments, 65, 67, 73
Forster, E. M., 158
Fragale, Alison, 131

Gagneur, Arnaud, 148–49, 155, 158–59
Gates, Bill, 212
Gates, Melinda, 212
    Mean Reviews video and, 214–15
Gates Foundation, 208
    Mean Reviews video at, 214–15
    psychological safety at, 212–13, 214–15
Give and Take (Grant), 62n
givers, success rate of, 61, 62n
Goldman, Emma, 245
Goleman, Daniel, 175
Good Judgment, 65, 67
Goodwin, Doris Kearns, 121
Google, 209
Gore, Al, 167, 168–69
Graf, Steffi, 124n
Graham, Paul, 114
Grant, Adam (author):
    agreeableness trait of, 81–82, 89
    approach to debate, 103–4, 113–15
    career choices and, 225–26
    challenge network of, 86–87
    complexifying conversations, 174–77
    family background of, 226
    and joy of being wrong, 62, 89
    motivational interviewing and, 151–53
    online social network and, 8–9
    questioning stereotypes, 137–38
    as teacher, 195–98
Grant, Ryan, medical career of, 226–28, 230, 241–42
Great Depression, 250
greatness, of composers, 114–15
Great Recession, 10
Greenspan, Stephen, 18, 19
Grindle, Nicole, 88–89
grit, 229–30
group polarization:
    conformity and, 128
    stereotypes and, 127–28
groups:
    contact between, 139
    stereotypes and, 139
gun control, 164

habits, 8, 9
    cognitive laziness and, 7–8
Handey, Jack, 225
Hansen, Chris, 207, 211
Hansen, Michele, 117–18
happiness, pursuit of, 237–38
    environment and, 238–40
    meaning vs., 238, 240–41
harmony, 81
Hemingway, Ernest, 87, 239
Holocaust deniers, 189–90
Holocaust survivors, 130, 132, 189–90
hostility, responses to, 113–16
hot dog sandwich survey, 125, 125
humility, 27, 45–48, 52–54, 106, 112, 117, 119, 137, 147, 157–58, 165, 200, 214–15, 221, 234, 243, 250–51, 258
    competence and, 215n
    as groundedness, 46–48
    intellectual, *see* intellectual humility
    self-doubt vs., 46
    see also confident humility
hypotheses, testing of, 20, 21, 23

Ibarra, Herminia, 235
IBM, Project Debater of, 97–102, 107–10
Iceland, 2008 financial crisis in, 35–36
idea cults, 176–77
identity, *see* self, sense of
identity foreclosure, 230, 232–33, 234, 242
ideology, *see* beliefs
ignorance, confidence and, 33, 40–41, 42–46, 43, 44
Ig™ Nobel Prize, 38
impostor syndrome, 36, 37–38, 49–51
    armchair quarterback syndrome vs., 51
    gender and, 51n
    in high achievers, 50
    possible benefits of, 50–54
Inconvenient Truth, An (film), 167
Incredibles, The (film), 83, 84, 87–88
influencing, defense mechanisms against, 154–55, 154
influencing, listening and, 155–60
information, *see* knowledge
instincts, 8, 9
integrity, passion as sign of, 179
intellectual humility, 27–28, 31, 45–48, 52–54, 62, 102, 106, 112, 117, 119, 137, 147, 157–58, 165, 187, 200, 203, 214–15, 221, 250–51, 255
    arrogance vs., 45
International Space Station, 205–7

internet:
    misinformation on, 164
    simplification and, 171
interpersonal rethinking, 10–11, 95–160,
    255–57
interviewing, motivational, *see* motivational
    interviewing
iPhone, 23
    Jobs's resistance to, 29–31
iPod, 30
IQ scores:
    emotional intelligence and, 175
    mental flexibility vs., 24–27
    stereotyping and, 24–25
Israel-Palestine conflict, 131
    stereotyping in, 130

Jeff (biotech CEO), 151–53, 155
Jehn, Karen "Etty," 78
Jimmy Kimmel Live! (TV show), 214
Jobs, Steve, iPhone resisted by, 29–31
Johnson Space Center, 221
joy of being wrong, 61–62, 65–66, 69, 70,
    71–72, 89, 254
judging, of self vs. work, 201

Kaczynski, Ted, 60, 74–75
Kahneman, Daniel:
    and joy of being wrong, 61–62
    scientist mindset of, 62
Kelemen, Deborah, 188–89
Kelly, George, 127
Kelman, Herb, 130, 131
Kendi, Ibram X., 182
kids:
    encouraging rethinking by, 258, *see also*
        teachers, teaching
    unlearning and, 189–90, 258
    "what do you want to be" question and,
        225–26, 230, 231, 232
knowledge:
    exponential expansion of, 17
    oral transmission of, 247
    overconfidence and, 92–93
    of what we don't know, *see* intellectual
        humility
Knowlton, Karren, 130–31
Kolbert, Elizabeth, 60
Kony, Joseph, 157
    Bigombe's meetings with, 155–56
Kreider, Tim, 97
Kruger, Justin, 38, 158
Krumrei Mancuso, Elizabeth, 52

Ku Klux Klan, 121–22, 140–42, 151
Kundro, Tim, 126, 129–30, 131, 133

Lazaridis, Mike, 31
    in failure to rethink marketplace, 23–24
    as science prodigy, 15–16, 23
    as smartphone pioneer, 16, 23
    as victim of overconfidence cycle, 29
leaders, rethinking by, 248–50
learning:
    capacity for, confidence in, 48, 254
    challenge networks in, 200
    confusion in, 199, 257, 258
    inquiry-based, *see* active learning
    scientist mindset in, 186
    textbooks and, 185–87
    see also lifelong learning
learning cultures:
    "how do you know" questions in, 211–12
    in organizations, 205–22, 258–59
    performance cultures vs., 209
    psychological safety in, 209, 212–13,
        214–15, 258
    rethinking in, 207–8
    rethinking scorecards in, 218–19, *218*, 259
lectures, active learning vs., 190–93, 196
Lewis, Jerry Lee, 121
lifelong learning, 11, 54, 253, 255
    charged conversations in, 163–83
    focus on results as obstacle to, 217
    teachers and, 185–203
    at workplace, 205–22
life plans, 225–43
    identity foreclosure and, 232–33
    periodic checkups on, 235–37, 259
    rethinking, 233, 235–37, 259
    tunnel vision and, 228–29
    see also career choices
listening, 143–59
    as expression of respect and care, 159–60
    influencing and, 155–60
    in motivational interviewing, 153
    persuasive, 255
    reflective, 147
listening circles, 157–58
logic, faulty, prosecutor mindset, 102, 104
Lord's Resistance Army, 155, 156*n*, 157
Lyne, Andrew, 73

McCann, Lauren, 196–97
McCarthy, Erin, 185–87, 189–90, 203
Maclean, Norman, 5
Madoff, Bernie, 18, 19

managers:
feedback and, 213–14
self-rating of, 39–40, *39*
Mann Gulch wildfire, 1–2, 5–7
outmoded assumptions as factor in, 11–12
mastery, 198
Matrix, The (film), 194
meaning, pursuit of, happiness vs., 238,
240–41
Mean Reviews videos, 214–15
"Mean Tweets," 214
measles, 148
mortality rate of, 144
resurgence of, 143–44
media:
climate change and, 170–73
complexification and, 171–73
medical errors, psychological safety and,
208–9
mental flexibility, 2–3, 8, 9–10, 253
IQ scores vs., 24–27
rethinking and, *see* rethinking
scientist mindset and, 27
Mercz, Ursula, 33–34
Michigan, University of, 132
Mill, John Stuart, 241
Miller, Bill, 146, 152, 153, 154, 156
misfits, *see* disagreeable people; pirates
Mitchell, Edgar, 128
Morrell, Kjirste, forecasting skill of,
68–69
motivation:
ineffective approaches in, 150
pay and, 114
motivational interviewing, 146–51
in business, 151–53
confident humility in, 147
curiosity in, 147, 157
in everyday life, 149–51
freedom of choice in, 148, 257
listening in, 153
open-ended questions in, 147, 148, 156
resisting righting reflex in, 156
summarizing in, 153
sustain talk vs. change talk in, 152–53
as tool for changing behavior, 148
Mount Stupid, *43*, 44, 45, 254
Moyers, Theresa, 152
Mozart, Wolfgang Amadeus, 114–15
Murphy, Kate, 156
Murray, Henry:
beliefs experiment of, 55–57, 60, 74–75
spy assessment test of, 56

NASA:
emerging learning culture at, 221
lack of psychological safety at, 210–11
overconfidence cycles at, 208
and Parmitano's spacesuit malfunction,
205–7, 211
performance culture at, 207–8, 210–11,
216–17
rethinking failures at, 207–8, 217, 222
space shuttle disasters of, 207, 210–11, 220
Natarajan, Harish:
debate championships of, 97
question-based approach of, 112
in school subsidy debate, 97–103,
106–10, 112
negotiations, *106*
adversarial approach vs. search for
common ground in, 104–5
asking questions in, 105–6
debates as, 104
focusing on key points in, 105
humility and curiosity in, 105–6
networks, challenge, *see* challenge networks
New York Times, 248–49
New York Yankees, Red Sox rivalry with,
122–24, 126–27, 128, 133–36
Nomad Health, 241
North Carolina, University of, Duke rivalry
with, 131
Nozick, Robert, 194–95
nuance, 117, 168, 171, 174, 176, 183

Obama, Michelle, 230
Ochoa, Ellen, 217, 220–21
and *Columbia* space shuttle disaster,
210–12
Oddsson, Davíð:
in campaign for Iceland's presidency, 37,
41, 54
career of, 41
and 2008 financial crisis, 36–37, 45
Office, The (TV show), 117–18
Office of Strategic Services, 56
Ohio State University, 132–33
open systems, 241
identities as, 243
opinions, *see* beliefs and opinions
Originals (Grant), 116
overconfidence, 92–93
overconfidence cycles, 28–29, *28*, 61, 165,
188, *189*, 208, 233, 254
overthinking, 235n
overview effect, in astronauts, 128–22

Parmitano, Luca, in spacesuit malfunction, 205–7, 211
passion, as sign of integrity, 178
passion talks, 197
pay, motivation and, 114
perfectionists, rethinking as difficult for, 195–96
performance cultures, 207–8, 221
    best practices and, 216–17
    learning cultures vs., 209
persuasion, beliefs as reinforced by failed attempts at, 144–45, 146
persuasive listening, 255
Peterson, Jordan, 175
pirates (misfits), 83, 84–85, 88–89
Pixar, 82–83
    pirates at, 83, 84–85, 88–89
Planck, Max, 247
Plutarch, 132
polarization, political, 164
polarizing issues, conversations on, see charged conversations
police brutality, rethinking assumptions about, 10
politician mindset, 233, 248, 252
    in collective rethinking, 163, 166, 169, 183
    in individual rethinking, 18–19, 21, 22, 25, 27, 28, 29, 32, 53, 62, 67, 80, 85–86, 88
    in interpersonal rethinking, 107, 108, 145, 156
preacher mindset, 233, 248, 253
    in collective rethinking, 165, 167, 169, 175, 177, 183, 192, 200, 216
    in individual rethinking, 18, 19, 20, 21, 22, 22, 25, 27, 28, 29, 32, 39, 60, 62, 67, 76, 80, 91, 92
    in interpersonal rethinking, 102, 104, 107, 108, 110, 111, 117n, 119, 124, 127, 132, 141, 144, 145, 146, 155, 156, 157
Prectet, Debra Jo, see Project Debater
prejudice, 121–41
    conversation as antidote to, 140–42
    see also rivalries; stereotypes
preschool subsidies, debate on, 97–102, 106–10, 112
presidents, U.S., intellectual curiosity and, 27
process accountability, best practices vs., 216–19, 258
Project Debater, in school subsidy debate, 97–102, 107–10, 112
proof, as enemy of progress, 219

prosecutor mindset, 230, 233, 248, 253
    in collective rethinking, 165, 167, 169, 175, 177, 183, 192, 200
    in individual rethinking, 18, 19, 20, 21, 22, 22, 25, 26, 27, 28, 29, 32, 39, 53, 60, 62, 67, 76, 80, 91, 92
    in interpersonal rethinking, 102, 104, 107, 108, 110, 113, 119, 124, 127, 132, 141, 145, 146, 155, 156, 157
psychological safety, 208–9, 210, 258
    author's experiments on, 212–13
    at Gates Foundation, 212–13, 214–15
    "how do you know" question and, 211–12
    as lacking at NASA, 210
    medical errors and, 208–9
    process accountability and, 217–18

Quakers, clearness committees and, 156n
question-based approach:
    in debates, 112–13
    encouraging rethinking through, 255–56
    in scientist mindset, 25–26
questions:
    counterfactual, 137–39, 256
    as encouraged by self-doubt, 53–54
    "how do you know," 211–12
    "how" vs. "why," 256
    open-ended, 147, 148, 156
    skilled negotiators' use of, 105–6
    "what do you want to be," 225–26, 230, 231, 232

racial injustice, rethinking assumptions about, 10
racism, 10, 121–22, 140–42, 181–83
Rackham, Neil, 104, 105
Rawls, John, 178
reasoning, flawed:
    prosecuting, 110, 111
    prosecutor mindset, 21, 22, 60, 76, 80, 91, 92
reflective listening, 147
relationship conflict, 78–80, 79
    as barrier to rethinking, 80
    task conflict and, 90, 91–93
relationships, rethinking in, 236–37
rethinking, 3–4
    dilemmas of, 248–49
    encouraging others to adopt, see interpersonal rethinking
    in individuals, see individual rethinking
    in lifelong learning, see collective rethinking

making time for, 259
as mindset, 16
negative responses to, 30
process of, 246–50
see also unlearning
rethinking cycle, 27, 28, *28*, 45, 67, 83, 92,
112–13, 137, 140, 147, 158, 165, 171, 187,
188, 208, 234, 253
rethinking scorecards, 218–19, *218*, 259
revisions and drafts, in learning process,
199–203, 258
righting reflex, 156
Ripley, Amanda, 163, 165
rituals, sports rivalries as, 133
rivalries:
animosity in, 124–25
in business, 124
group polarization in, 128
humanizing the other side in, 130–31
in sports, *see* sports rivalries
see also prejudice; stereotypes
Rock, Chris, 230
Rollnick, Stephen, 146, 152, 153, 154, 156
Roosevelt, Franklin D., trial-and-error
method of, 248–50

Sandler, Adam, 238–39
Saturday Night Live (TV show), 238–39
school closings, in coronavirus
pandemic, 10
Schulz, Kathryn, 67
science:
peer-review process in, 86
unlearning in, 188–90
scientific method, 20, 199, 247–48
skepticism in, 169–70
"scientist", coining of term, 247
scientist mindset, 23, *32*, 53, 62, 66–67, 74,
76, 92, 93, 116, 145, 186, 250–51
as actively questioning beliefs and assumptions, 25–26
author's adoption of, 26–27
career change and, 235
caveats and contingencies in, 173–74,
176, 257
in charged conversations, 183
and consistent narrative vs. accurate
record, 174–75
in debates, 102–6
entrepreneurs and, 20–22, *21*, 253
humility as characteristic of, 28
rethinking as central to, 19–20,
247–48, 253

Scotland, career choices in, 233*n*
Scott, Michael (char.), 118
second opinions, 18
Seinfeld, Jerry, 133
Seinfeld (TV show), 68, 118
Seles, Monica, 124*n*
self, sense of, 8, 9, 12
commonality in, 129
detaching beliefs and opinions from, 62,
63–64, 69–70, 76, 253–54
identity foreclosure and, 230
as open system, 243
present vs. past, 62–63, 69, 76, 253
rethinking as challenge to, 4, 7, 42
tribes and, 125–26
self-awareness, 39, 48
self-deprecation:
gender and, 72*n*
self-confidence and, 72
self-doubt:
asking questions as encouraged by,
53–54
benefits of, 49–54, 254
humility vs., 46
see also impostor syndrome
self-esteem, evolution of, 241
Seneca, 35
sexism, 10
Shandell, Marissa, 234–35
Shaw, George Bernard, 15
Silver, Nate, 66
simplification:
internet and, 171
media and, 171
resistance to, *see* complexification
skepticism, in scientific method,
169–70
skeptics, deniers vs., 169
smartphone revolution, 16, 22, 23, 31
Smith, Will, 73
social networks, polarizing issues and,
164–65
space, Earth as seen from, 128–29
sports, stock market influence of, 126
sports rivalries, 122–28
author's experiments on, 131–32, 133–36
group polarization in, 128
as rituals, 133
stereotyping in, 127
status quo bias, 194*n*
stereotypes, 121–41
animosity and, 127
as barrier to rethinking, 124

stereotypes, (cont.)
conversation as antidote to, 140–42
group polarization and, 127–28
groups and, 139
of groups vs. individuals, 131
intergroup contact and, 139
in Israel-Palestine conflict, 130
racist, 121–22, 140–42
rethinking timeline for, 135
shaky foundations of, 140
in sports rivalries, 127
tribes and, 136n
see also prejudice; rivalries
stereotypes, arbitrariness of, 133–34
counterfactual thinking as destabilizing,
134–40
stereotyping, IQ scores and, 24–25
stock market, influence of sports matches
on, 126
Storm King Mountain wildfire, 6–7
stress:
learned responses to, 5–7
Murray's experiment on, 55–58, 60, 74
Strohminger, Nina, 40n
summarizing, in motivational
interviewing, 153

task conflict, 78–80, 79
disagreeable people and, 83, 84
as encouraged by disagreeable people, 90
encouragement of, 88
politician mindset and, 85–86
relationship conflict and, 90, 91–93
rethinking as fostered by, 80, 255
Taylor, Breonna, 10
teachers, teaching:
Berger as, 198–203
Grant as, 195–98
lecturing vs. active learning in, 190–93, 196
lifelong learning and, 185–203
McCarthy as, 185–87, 189–90, 203
Nozick as, 194–95
textbooks and, 185–87
unlearning and, 188–90
technology, exponential expansion of, 17
TED talks, 192, 195, 196
teenagers, see kids
test-taking, rethinking and, 3–4
Tetlock, Phil, 18, 67
Tewfik, Basima, 50, 51n
textbooks, 185–87
Theseus paradox, 132–33
Time, 36–37

Tómasdóttir, Halla, 35–36
in campaign for Iceland's presidency, 36,
49, 53–54
impostor syndrome and, 36, 38, 49, 52–54
totalitarian ego, 59–61, 73, 74
Toy Story (film), 82
tradition, pressure, 208
tribes:
identity and, 126
stereotyping and, 136n
Trump, Donald, in 2016 election, 66–67,
69–71, 70, 71
tunnel vision, 235n
life choices and, 228–29
Tussing, Danielle, 52
2008 financial crisis, 35–36, 45

Uganda, civil strife in, 155–57, 159
uncertainty, 53
unlearning, 2, 12, 188–90
kids and, 189–90, 258
in stress situations, 5–7
see also rethinking
Urban, Tim, 45

vaccination:
autism mistakenly linked to, 144, 158–59
unfounded fear of, 143–44
vaccine whisperers, 145–49, 158–59
Voldemort (char.), 146–47
Vonnegut, Kurt, 205

Wales, career choices in, 233n
Walker, Candice, 242–43
Walker, John, 87–88, 89
Weick, Karl, 7
Wharton School, 9
Mean Reviews video at, 214
"what do you want to be" question, 225–26,
230, 231, 232
WhatsApp, 24
white supremacists, Davis's encounters with,
121–22, 140–42, 151
Whitman, Walt, 165
Wilde, Oscar, 77
wildfires, firefighters' behavior in, 1–2, 5–7
workplace:
best practices in, 216–17
grades as poor predictor of performance
in, 195
learning cultures at, 205–22
psychological safety and, see psychological
safety

World War, II, 56
Wright, Katharine, 91
Wright, Wilbur and Orville, 77, 81
   as built-in challenge network, 89–90
   in conflict over propeller, 91–93
Wrzesniewski, Amy, 242

X (company), 86

Young Men and Fire
   (Maclean), 5

Zuckerberg, Mark, 8

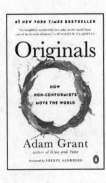